EVIDENCE OF ABSENCE

A GUIDE TO COGNITIVE ASSESSMENT IN AUSTRALIA

SIMON F. CROWE PhD

FOREWORD BY STEPHEN C. BOWDEN PhD

First published in 2010
Australian Academic Press
32 Jeays Street
Bowen Hills Qld 4006
Australia
www.australianacademicpress.com.au

National Library of Australia cataloguing-in-publication entry:

Author:	Crowe, Simon F.
Title:	Evidence of absence : a guide to cognitive assessment in Australia / Simon Crowe.
Edition:	1st ed.
ISBN:	9781921513626 (pbk.)
	9781921513633 (eBook)
Subjects:	Neuropsychological tests.
	Cognition--Testing.
	Cognition disorders.
Dewey No:	612.8233

Cover image: John Brack
Australia 1920–1999
Collins St., 5 p.m. 1955
oil on canvas
114.8 x 162.8 cm
National Gallery of Victoria, Melbourne
Purchased, 1956
© National Gallery of Victoria.

Cover design by Maria Biaggini.

Dedication

To Jan, with thanks for the good days and
apologies for the not-so-good ones.

Nothing matters but the facts. Without them, the science of criminal investigation is nothing more than a guessing game.

Blake Edwards

FOREWORD

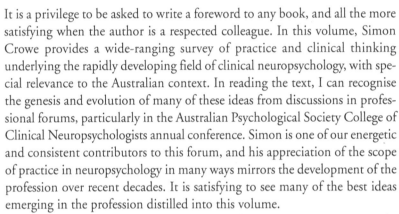

It is a privilege to be asked to write a foreword to any book, and all the more satisfying when the author is a respected colleague. In this volume, Simon Crowe provides a wide-ranging survey of practice and clinical thinking underlying the rapidly developing field of clinical neuropsychology, with special relevance to the Australian context. In reading the text, I can recognise the genesis and evolution of many of these ideas from discussions in professional forums, particularly in the Australian Psychological Society College of Clinical Neuropsychologists annual conference. Simon is one of our energetic and consistent contributors to this forum, and his appreciation of the scope of practice in neuropsychology in many ways mirrors the development of the profession over recent decades. It is satisfying to see many of the best ideas emerging in the profession distilled into this volume.

Simon provides a representative survey of approaches to practice in the opening chapter. He highlights the need for a firm foundation of knowledge in clinical neuroscience, together with critically important aspects of decision science and principles of psychological assessment. Chapter 2 provides a succinct summary of the fundamental principles of clinical decision-making, and in particular the biases to which clinical judgment is subject. Every neuropsychologist should be intimately familiar with these fundamental precepts that provide the stepping stones to improved clinical thinking.

Building on the scientific concepts, Chapter 3 describes typical testing practices, sampling sources on practice habits in the United States and Australia. Here Simon provides a contrasting conceptual model of neuropsychological abilities and an empirically based survey of test use and test validity. More than any other chapter in this volume, Chapter 3 highlights the need for a comprehensive model of cognitive abilities to inform the assessment of patients with neuropsychological disorders. The challenge to provide a theoretically based approach to cognition is clear in Simon's aspirations for an integrated approach to research and clinical practice.

The search for a comprehensive theory of cognitive abilities, provides the springboard for Chapter 4, in which Simon introduces the reader to a theoretically motivated approach to assessment. Against this background, an approach to neuropsychological assessment is described that embodies empirically anchored data collection with patient-centred clinical thinking. It has sometimes been said that there is no such thing as neuropsychological tests, only neuropsychological interpretations. Paradoxically, the field is replete with accounts of cardinal neuropsychological deficits on tests. In a clear attempt to lift the debate to a theoretical level, the approach to assessment outlined in Chapter 4 describes assessment of common cognitive abilities, utilising a sample of the best available techniques. Whether or not one chooses to use the same tests, the need for a theoretical justification of testing practices is paramount and ably illustrated in Simon's recommendations.

The expectation that every neuropsychologist should develop advanced technical skills in clinical data interpretation is also clearly indicated in the approach to assessment described in Chapter 4. To provide accurate ipsative and normative formulations of their client's behaviour, neuropsychologists need to be sophisticated psychological scientists, and here lies one of the great challenges for contemporary training.

The next three chapters provide detailed examples of this principled approach, with illustrative case scenarios. In the context of a theoretically motivated neuropsychology, these case examples are invaluable teaching material. Chapter 7 extends the exposition of assessment techniques with a detailed description of symptom validity evaluations and related case-formulation considerations. The following chapter provides a succinct but lucid description of report writing, with some very useful guidelines for clear structure and communication in reports.

Chapter 9 concludes the exposition of practice style by highlighting six important and current dilemmas in clinical inference. Although brief, description of each dilemma provides focus on the high quality of scholarship required to be a competent clinician. Understanding of each of these clinical dilemmas will undergo continued research and refinement in the near future. Every practitioner can benchmark their own professional development by the extent to which they incorporate recent research developments, regarding these dilemmas, into their clinical practice.

In this book Simon Crowe highlights the challenges for the student of neuropsychology, to be both a scholar of clinical neuroscience and a scholar of the science of psychological assessment in its broadest sense. To meet the often complex needs of our clients, neuropsychologists need an advanced range of skills. Simon is to be commended for providing a practical and wide-ranging introduction to the practice of clinical neuropsychology in Australia. I would recommend this book to any student of neuropsychology in Australia as the best description, to date, of fundamentals of neuropsychological practice published from our shores.

Stephen C. Bowden, PhD

Contents

LIST OF TABLES

LIST OF FIGURES

CHAPTER ONE

BACKGROUND, FOREGROUND AND METHODOLOGICAL CONSIDERATIONS

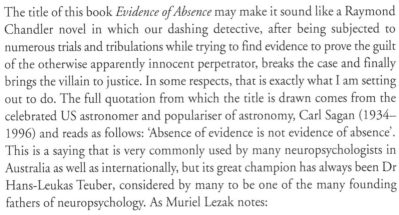

The title of this book *Evidence of Absence* may make it sound like a Raymond Chandler novel in which our dashing detective, after being subjected to numerous trials and tribulations while trying to find evidence to prove the guilt of the otherwise apparently innocent perpetrator, breaks the case and finally brings the villain to justice. In some respects, that is exactly what I am setting out to do. The full quotation from which the title is drawn comes from the celebrated US astronomer and populariser of astronomy, Carl Sagan (1934–1996) and reads as follows: 'Absence of evidence is not evidence of absence'. This is a saying that is very commonly used by many neuropsychologists in Australia as well as internationally, but its great champion has always been Dr Hans-Leukas Teuber, considered by many to be one of the many founding fathers of neuropsychology. As Muriel Lezak notes:

> One must never misconstrue a normal intelligence test results as an indication of normal intellectual status after head trauma, or worse, as indicative of a normal brain; *to do so would be to commit the cardinal sin of confusing absence of evidence with evidence of absence* [italics mdl]. (Teuber, 1969, as cited in Lezak, Howieson, & Loring, 2004, p. 22)

The appeal of this statement for Teuber and for most other neuropsychologists is that, in almost all neuropsychology, the most important part of the examination is focused on identifying what is *not* there, rather than those aspects of the individual's intellectual functioning that are. Comprehensive assessment is based upon identifying those aspects of intellectual functioning which *should be there*, but are impaired or altogether missing in those individuals who have sustained acquired brain impairment. Thus, in all neuropsychological assessment, establishment of the fact that there is *evidence of absence* is at the heart of the neuropsychological enterprise. As a result, clear and specific demonstration of that which should be there but which is not, is at the core of good neuropsychological assessment.

How then do we characterise that which is not there? Hopefully, your attempts to grapple with this crucial question has prompted your purchase of this book in the first place, and through the various arguments justifying the methodology that I will outline in the following pages, I hope that I will provide ample return on your capital investment. As with the journeys described by Sagan in his powerful and thought-provoking television series *Cosmos*, the universe of evidence, and its absence, lies alluringly before us!

Whither Are We Drifting?

This book will provide you with a systematic guide to the clinical interpretation of cognitive assessment undertaken in Australia, with a particular focus on assessments made using the Wechsler Adult Intelligence Scale Fourth Edition (WAIS-IV; Wechsler, 2008c), the Wechsler Memory Scale Fourth Edition (WMS-IV; Wechsler, 2009c) and other associated neuropsychological instruments. The aim of the book is to provide you with sensible, psychometrically sound guidelines for conducting assessments of intelligence and memory in clinical settings and to do so in a way that is both clinically and statistically meaningful.

We live in a world that is ever more complicated by information overload due to the wealth of material provided by the web and the associated unprecedented level of electronic storage of text and data, which means that the response to any question we might ask becomes quickly associated with such a wealth of detail and documentation that we reel from the sheer scope of the material provided. I am sure that we all hope that being provided with yet more information is affording us with better answers to our questions, however I fear that the reverse is ever more the reality.

A single assessment undertaken with the WAIS-IV and the WMS-IV for example, can yield as many as 100 individual scores from the client assessed. The amount of information it is possible for an individual clinician to simultaneously consider in the context of making any clinical decision has been shown to limited (Malhotra, 1982) by the intrinsic constraints of our working memory span. As a result, when an assessment is undertaken using these instruments, some rational means of reducing the cacophony of the information gathered to a sensible set of clinical indicators is essential for us to be able to make best use of it. This book will provide you with a guide to reducing the wealth of detail provided by these instruments to a more manageable scale and then provide a set of decision rules that will allow you to make both sensible and most importantly, defensible, clinical decisions about these findings.

The approach to the reduction of these complex datasets to a more sensible and manageable proportion must take place in a systematic and measured way. The approach that this book will advocate is the one developed and championed by Alan Kaufman and his colleagues (Kaufman, 1979; Kaufman & Lichtenberger, 1999, 2006; Lichtenberger & Kaufman, 2009; Lichtenberger, Kaufman, & Lai, 2002) that analyses the results of the cognitive assessment with the Wechsler scales in a logical and systematic fashion providing, in my view, the most comprehensive summation of the outcomes of the assessment and doing so in systematic and careful way.

The Australian flavour to the presentation of the material will come in the interpretation of the case material that we will consider, as well as the background clinical and legal issues unique to cognitive assessment in Australia. This reaches into areas such as the consideration of the appropriate normative basis to be used in interpretation of intellectual assessments conducted in Australia, the further development of the scales, taking into consideration conditions particular to Australia, as well as in the sociocultural and legal context of the uses to which intellectual assessment is put in the Australian context.

The heart of this discussion, however, is the clinical case material that will constitute Chapters 5 to 7 of the book. In these chapters we will survey a number of the most likely clinical presentations that you will encounter in your practice, whether you are undertaking intellectual assessment on a regular or on a somewhat less regular basis. The case material will focus upon assessment in the area of intellectual disability and the use of clinical assessment in acquired brain injury, focusing on traumatic brain injury. We will also address the issue of less than genuine effort and how this might be identified in the context of the clinical assessment. In Chapter 8, I will present some guidelines for report writing, taking into consideration the specific referral questions that have prompted the request for assessment, and in Chapter 9 we will consider six vexing clinical dilemmas that commonly emerge in the context of intellectual assessment.

Why Assess?

Adult assessment is most often conducted to measure cognitive potential and to obtain clinically relevant information, with more than 85% of the 277 psychologists surveyed in a study conducted by Harrison and colleagues (Harrison, Kaufman, Hickman, & Kaufman, 1988) indicating that they assess adults for the purposes of measuring potential or capacity. A similar number did so to obtain clinically relevant information and 78% used the tests to obtain information about the functional integrity of the brain. Less than 50% of test usage was for making educational or vocational placements or interventions. It is thus clear that psychological assessment increasingly focuses on the implication of test performance to functional localisation within the brain, with its associated implication for behaviour in terms of diagnosis and prognosis.

What is Assessment?

Assessment is 'the systematic collection, organisation, and interpretation of information about a person and his (or her) situation' (Sundberg & Tyler, 1962, p. 8). Different assessment procedures are indicated for different clinical purposes and the determination of which form of assessment to use in each circumstance is prompted by the reason that the person has been referred in the first place, as well as the scope of practice of the practitioner. Some of the many purposes of referral could include: cognitive assessment, intellectual assessment, behavioural assessment or for the determination of eligibility. The range of assessment undertaken and, as a consequence, the information gathered will differ as a result of the nature of the referral purpose.

In conducting intellectual assessment, various sources of information can inform the final assessment. The sources of information commonly provided to practitioners often include: the background documentation, including the referral letter, which will invariably describe the intended purpose that the referrer hopes to achieve by the assessment; a comprehensive medical and psychosocial history including an analysis of previous drug and alcohol issues as well as issues of a forensic nature; a comprehensive evaluation and reconstruction of the nature of the injury, and its consequent neural impact; direct behavioural observations of the client in the assessment situation; elicitation of the client's view as to the nature of the impact of the injury to them; evidence gathered from someone who has known the individual before the 'injury', as well as both the quantitative test scores from the various instruments administered, and the qualitative aspects of the test performance. Clearly, the most comprehensive and definitive answers to the questions posed by the referrer, involve an integration of *all* of this information.

What is Neuropsychology?

The consortium of representatives of various professional neuropsychological organisations and associations, who came together at the 1997 Houston Conference on Specialty Training in Neuropsychology, concur that clinical neuropsychology can be defined as 'the application of assessment and intervention principles based on the scientific study of human behaviour across the lifespan as it relates to the normal and abnormal functioning of the central nervous system' (Hannay et al., 1998, p. 161).

The National Academy of Neuropsychology (NAN, 2001) defines a clinical neuropsychologist as:

> … a professional within the field of psychology with special expertise in the applied science of brain–behavior relationships. Clinical neuropsychologists use this knowledge in the assessment, diagnosis, treatment, and/or rehabilitation of patients across the lifespan with neurological, medical, neurodevelopmental and psychiatric conditions, as well as other cognitive and learning disorders. The clinical neuropsychologist uses psychological, neurological, cognitive, behavioral, and physiological principles, techniques and tests to evaluate patients' neurocognitive, behavioral, and emotional strengths and weaknesses and their relationship to normal and abnormal central nervous system functioning. The clinical neuropsychologist uses this information and information provided by other medical/healthcare providers to identify and diagnose neurobehavioral disorders, and plan and implement intervention strategies.

Clinical Versus Statistical Decision-Making

All clinical specialists in the behavioural sciences are called upon to diagnose and predict human behaviour. In the history of psychology a debate has emerged that centres on the two contrasting approaches to the prediction of psychological outcomes. These are the clinical method and the statistical method.

In the clinical method the clinician observes the client, gathers data, formulates hypotheses about a client's problem, processes this information in his or her head and then predicts the outcome. The term 'clinical' in this description should not be equated with the notion of a clinical psychologist or setting, but rather with the judgment method employed in coming to the final opinion.

In the statistical method, the human judge is eliminated in large part and the conclusions rest solely upon the empirically established relationships between data and the condition or event of interest (Meehl, 1954). The term 'statistical' should not be confused with automated (i.e., such as automated programs for test interpretation). In order for a method to be truly statistical, the conclusions drawn must be based on established empirical frequencies or base rates of occurrence of the particular pattern of results in the population of interest (Wedding & Faust, 1989).

In 1954, Paul Meehl's seminal book, *Clinical Versus Statistical Prediction: A Theoretical Analysis and Review of the Evidence,* was published. The major finding of the review of 20 studies comparing the predictive accuracy of clinical versus statistical decision-making was that the statistical models were equal to or superior to the clinical models in 19 of the 20 studies reviewed. The one study that favoured the clinical method was subsequently shown not to support the conclusion because of methodological complications. A subsequent review conducted by Meehl, examined 50 empirical studies and reaffirmed the earlier conclusions (Meehl, 1965). More data on this issue has been collected over the years supporting the original observations and culminating in Meehl's observation that 'I am unaware of any other controversial matter in psychology for which the evidence is now so massive and almost 100% consistent in pointing in the same direction' (Meehl, 1984, p. xii).

It continues to be hard to imagine how, in a discipline such as ours in which incontrovertible facts are so hard to come by, that one of the most replicable and pervasive findings of our science, is one that is so commonly treated with disdain. Meehl's observations provide for psychology one of our most unassailable facts, yet clinicians of various stripe continue to neglect or to outright dismiss the message and the meaning of this core finding of our discipline.

Contemporary Approaches to Cognitive Assessment

Within the range of contemporary neuropsychology there are three principal approaches that have been adopted by most neuropsychologists. These are the fixed battery approach, the process approach and a flexible battery approach.

- In the fixed battery approach a standard battery of tests is routinely administered in a consistent manner to all examinees who are evaluated. The scores obtained from the battery are compared to empirically derived cut-off scores that have been established to distinguish between brain impaired and non-brain impaired individuals. The two most commonly employed fixed batteries are the Halstead Reitan Battery (HRB; Reitan & Wolfson, 1993a) and Luria Nebraska Battery (LNB; Golden, Purisch, & Hammeke, 1985).

- The process approach is an evaluation of the individual often employing standardised tests and using normative data, if these are suitable and available, but which emphasises the manner in which the problem or task is solved rather than with a particular focus on the standardised score of the performance. Intrinsic to the approach is the focus on the type of errors produced and the manner in which the client solves the problems in achieving the final outcome.

- The flexible battery approach is characterised by test selection that varies depending on a number of factors including the referral question, the manner and pattern of the performance of the individual during the testing session and progressive hypothesis generation, but which typically relies upon a core of common, psychometrically well-validated neuropsychological tests that survey function across a range of cognitive areas. The standardised scores arising from the assessment are considered the principal focus of the interpretation, however qualitative aspects of the performance are also viewed as of value (Pieniadz & Kelland, 2001).

Figure 1.1 provides a scheme for considering the various forms of neuropsychological assessment that are commonly practised.

The Fixed Battery Approach

The fixed battery approach endorses the use of a predetermined set of measures that samples behaviour in a wide range of areas of interest. The authors of the battery would generally intend that all examinees be given the full set of tests, regardless of the examinee's presenting problem, suspected aetiology or reason for referral.

The Halstead-Reitan Battery (HRB; Reitan & Wolfson, 1993a) represents perhaps the most widely known example of a fixed test battery still in common clinical use. The HRB eschews specific theoretical assumptions (other than the basic assumptions of lateralisation of function) and focuses on sampling a broad range of behaviour, in order to make inferences about the integrity of cerebral function. The battery consists of tests in five categories: (1) input measures, (2) tests of verbal abilities, (3) measures of spatial, sequential and manipulatory abilities, (4) tests of abstraction, reasoning, logical analysis and concept formation, and (5) output measures. The tests cover a

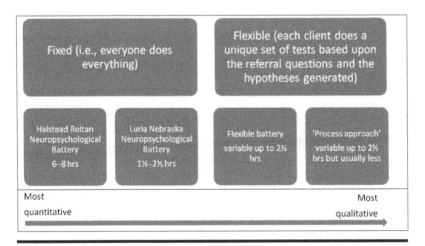

Figure 1.1
A comparison of current approaches to neuropsychological assessment.

broad range of difficulty, ranging from the very simple to the most complex tasks available. Measures of attention, concentration and memory are distributed throughout the battery just as they would occur in the tasks any individual would face in their daily activity. Many of the tests require immediate problem-solving capabilities, others depend upon stored information and some require simple perceptual skills focusing on the sensory modalities of vision, hearing or touch (Reitan & Wolfson, 1986, 1993a).

Most current modifications of the HRB use five of the original seven tests, dropping the Critical Flicker Fusion Test and the Time Sense Test as these do not identify brain-impaired individuals with sufficient accuracy to be diagnostically useful (Boll, 1981). The battery generally includes the following tests: (1) the Category Test, (2) the Tactual Performance Test, (3) the Seashore Rhythm Test, (4) the Speech Sounds Perception Test and (5) the Finger Tapping Test. Other tests recommended by Reitan (Reitan & Wolfson, 1986, 1993a) include: the Trail Making Test; the Aphasia Screening Test; the sensory examination of finger gnosis; graphaesthesia; and sensory extinction in the tactile, auditory and visual modalities; the Wechsler Scales; a measure of grip strength using a hand dynamometer; and the Minnesota Multiphasic Personality Inventory. Examiners who employ this set of tests often also include some memory tests and other tests of specific functions (Reitan & Wolfson, 1986).

The administration time for the HRB commonly runs from between 6 to 8 hours. The results of the five tests yield seven scores, three from the Tactual Performance Test, and the scores from each of the four other tests from the core battery. The final performances are combined into an impairment index. A number of computer-scoring techniques has been developed with a battery with a mixed set of results (Lezak et al., 2004).

The development of the Luria-Nebraska Battery (LNB) represents the attempt by Golden et al. (1985) to standardise and quantify the methods used by Luria in the evaluation of brain-injured patients (Golden & Maruish, 1986). Many of the test items used by Luria, and particularly those contained in Christensen's kit, were incorporated into a standardised, qualitatively oriented fixed-test battery. Although many of Luria's items were used, they were employed in a manner quite differently from Luria's original approach. For instance, unlike Luria's method whereby neuropsychological investigation proceeds on an individualised model and tests are given on the basis of the presenting complaints the LNB, like the HRB, involves the administration of some version of the entire test procedure to all examinees over a sustained period of time.

The LNB is drawn from Christensen's formalisation of Luria's test procedure. The actual test consists of 269 items, representing approximately 700 test procedures, which culminate in 28 factor scales reflecting more specific sensory and cognitive functions. The battery features 12 clinical scales (Motor Functions, Rhythm, Tactile Functions, Visual Functions, Receptive Speech, Expressive Speech, Writing, Reading, Arithmetic, Memory, Intellectual Processes and Intermediate Memory [Form II only]), as well as two optional scales — spelling, and motor writing. In addition, the battery features eight localisation scales (Left Frontal, Left Sensorimotor, Left Parietal–Occipital, Left Temporal, Right Frontal, Right Sensorimotor, Right Parietal–Occipital and Right Temporal); and five summary scales (Pathognomonic, Left Hemisphere, Right Hemisphere, Profile Elevation and Impairment). The LNB can be administered in only 1.5 to 2.5 hours. Test results are interpreted by analysis of the patterns on all aspects of the scales, including performance on the individual items and on the obtained qualitative data (Golden, Freshwater, & Vayalakkara, 2000; Golden & Maruish, 1986; Golden et al., 1985).

The 'Process' Approach

The most widely known example of the 'process'/behavioural neurology (these terms are used interchangeably to describe this method) originally arose from the writings of Alexander Luria (Luria, 1966, 1973, 1990), and were later standardised by his colleague Anna-Lise Christensen (Christensen, 1975) into a kit of stimulus materials. Luria's method of examination proceeded with the evaluation of the presenting complaint, reason for the assessment and initial clinical impression as the basis for the initial selection of tasks. Luria did not employ statistics or externally generated normative standards and many of his prominent theoretical positions were based upon single case studies. There is little doubt of the value of such studies in correlating brain behaviour relationships, as reflected by a the pivotal role of such celebrated cases as Henry Gustav Molaison — known worldwide within the neuropsychological literature as HM (who died on December 4, 2008), and Phineas Gage, who have defined investigation in the areas of memory and executive functions respectively. However, many of the cases used by Luria had very large lesions and the atypical nature of these patients raises many questions about the specificity of the tasks and their interpretation, as well as their generalisability to other less seriously impaired individuals.

Other criticisms of Luria's approach have been directed at the individualised and, some have argued idiosyncratic, techniques of task selection that have made the technique difficult to emulate by examiners other than Luria himself. Partly in response to these criticisms, Christensen (Christensen, 1975) attempted to impose some structure and organisation on Luria's method while trying to preserve the inherent flavour of his approach. Christensen (Christensen, 1975) provided specific, discrete items organised into sections, as well as appropriate stimulus material. Christensen's view of the cognitive assessment is very similar to the one propounded by Luria in that she believes that: 'the neuropsychologist should be a skilled observer of the patient's reactions in all situations, be able to invent small experimental situations and formulate hypotheses that can be verified or rejected by more specific examinations'. Luria has compared the work of the neuropsychologist with that of a detective; it is more complex and less logical than a scientific experiment' (Christensen, 1984, p. 10). As noted above, Christensen's kit has been formalised and standardised into a fixed battery format by Golden and his colleagues (Golden et al., 2000; Golden & Maruish, 1986; Golden et al., 1985).

No discussion of the 'process' approach is complete without consideration of the foundational work of Edith Kaplan, who notes:

> Most standardized tests, designed to assess cognitive functioning are predicated on the notion that the final solution to a problem is an objective measure of some underlying unitary mechanism. In a paper entitled 'Process and Achievement: A Basic Problem of Education and Developmental Psychology', Heinz Werner (1937) demonstrated that a given final solution may be arrived at via diverse processes which themselves may reflect the activity of distinctly different structures in the central nervous system. Further, Werner's assumption that any cognitive act involves 'microgenesis', i.e. an 'unfolding process over time' (1956), warrants close observation of behaviour en route to a solution. (Kaplan, 1988a, p. 309)

Thus, the process approach is primarily focused upon how the client solves the problem, rather than necessarily upon whether they achieve the correct answer or not. In line with the suggestions of Luria and in keeping with the behavioural neurology tradition, the emphasis upon how the answer is achieved rather than the content of the answer, is the principal focus of the clinical assessment.

A valuable insight into the suggestions raised by Kaplan (1988b) is provided by her clinical observations regarding the performance of the Block Design subtest:

> Incorrect responses that all receive a score of zero may run the gamut from eating the blocks (in a confusional state) all the way to a flawless, systematic but slow construction (completed in 65s, or 5s over the time limit) of a non-demented patient with Parkinson's disease. (p. 134)

Clearly the two performances although yielding the same score, are quite distinct.

Kaplan's massive contribution to the field has included the development of many of the neuropsychological weapons in the contemporary armamentarium including the Wechsler Adult Intelligence Scale — Revised (WAIS-R; Wechsler, 1981) as a Neuropsychological Instrument (WAIS-R NI), which was developed to augment and expand the WAIS-R as a means of tapping into the cognitive processes underlying examinees' final problem solutions (Kaplan, Fein, Morris, & Delis, 1991); the two revisions of the California Verbal Learning Test (CVLT; Delis, Kramer, Kaplan, & Ober, 1999; Delis, Kramer, Kaplan, & Ober, 1987); the Delis–Kaplan Executive Function System (DKEFS), a battery of tests designed to measure the various facets of the executive functions (Delis, Kaplan, & Kramer, 2001) as well at various other approaches and procedures that have changed the face of neuropsychology, particularly those associated with language processing including the Boston Naming Test (Kaplan, Goodglass, & Weintraub, 1976) and the Boston Diagnostic Aphasia Examination (BDAE — 3rd edition; Goodglass, Kaplan, & Barresi, 2001). In keeping with her stated philosophy, each instrument was developed with the principal aim of focusing upon the explanation of the symptom rather than its psychometric manifestation, although not ruling this issue out in the test construction and test administration procedures.

A crucial issue then in evaluating the quality of cognitive assessment is dependent upon which approach is employed as the preferred assessment strategy. The approach that clinicians adopt in practice depends upon a number of factors, including the problem posed, the clinician's knowledge, their experience and familiarity with the published tests and procedures available, the original tradition in which the clinician was trained, as well as their knowledge of the merits and limitations of the two contrasting approaches.

The major advantage of a fixed battery approach is its comprehensiveness, the suitability for technician administration and the feasibility of combining research with clinical objectives. The disadvantages pertain to the redundancy of obtained information, its inappropriateness for particular types of problems, its poor ability to account for the mechanism of failure and the fact that some areas of functioning (e.g., the HRB battery contains no formal assessment of memory functioning) may remain poorly examined (Incagnoli, Goldstein, & Golden, 1986). Also, once the clinician is familiar with and committed to a certain approach or battery, there tends to be an intrinsic reluctance to try new (and potentially more effective and reliable) test procedures, because to do so would compromise the objectives and value of a fixed battery. As a result, a fixed battery may unwittingly contribute and sustain its own obsolescence (Tarter & Edwards, 1986).

The advantages of adopting a process approach is that the battery maximises the efficiency and speed of the collection of information for clinical diagnosis, because only those tests or even some component or subpart of a particular test that should, in the clinician's opinion, be administered, is administered. The approach also takes into account the client's situation in the broadest sense of the term, including social history, present life circumstances, medical history and circumstances surrounding the examination (Darby & Walsh, 2005). Although there are obviously advantages of this method in clinical work (particularly in the context of a busy neurology department in a large metropolitan hospital), this approach does not afford the opportunity to develop a systematic or unified database, as each assessment is virtually unique. This limitation inherently prevents clinicians from assessing their own clinical activities in the context of program evaluation, and also fails to capitalise on the unique opportunity to acquire systematic data on individuals with rarely occurring disorders (Tarter & Edwards, 1986).

The initial selection of tests using a flexible approach is dependent upon the clinician's clinical judgment. For instance, the client's presenting complaint, reason for referral, social and medical history along with the clinical impression formed on the basis of the initial interview, dictates the selection of tests. As we will see in Chapter 2, error or bias in clinical judgment may result in incorrect selection of tests, or worse yet, an incorrect diagnosis. Furthermore, the use of the process approach does not allow clinicians to retrospectively analyse data that could serve as pilot data for undertaking prospective research, or for monitoring the impact of the assessment process itself.

It seems that there is no simple resolution to the debate as to which it is the 'correct' assessment strategy. The selection of either a fixed or a flexible battery depends upon the relative emphasis given to clinical or statistical aims.

The Best of Both Worlds: The Flexible Battery/Hypothesis Testing Approach

Despite the somewhat pessimistic tone of the last sentence it is certainly the case that an integration between the qualitative and quantitative assessment techniques is both attractive and preferable. Not only does integration recognise the importance of combining contrasting forms of information — including data obtained from clinical observation, client history, client interview, information garnered from the client's significant others, the background information, test-taking behaviour and test scores — in the interpretation of the condition, but more importantly it offers a compromise between the clinical versus statistical controversy extensively discussed by Meehl (Meehl, 1986) as adverted to above. No longer is the concern centred around which method is best, to the exclusion of the other, but rather has moved to the issue of how might the available methods be combined to produce the most accurate, efficient and reliable answers to the posed cognitive questions?

The assumption underlying the integration of the qualitative and quantitative datasets is that each method of itself is incomplete without the other — test scores interpreted without reference to the context and processes of the examination may well be objective but meaningless in their individual application. As a maxim often associated with Albert Einstein states: 'Not everything that can be counted counts, and not everything that counts can be counted'. Similarly, clinical observations unsupported by standardised and quantifiable testing may be masked by clinical bias or error. Thus 'to do justice to the complexity, variability and subtleties of a patient's behaviour, the neuropsychologist needs to consider qualitative and quantitative data together' (Lezak, 1983, p. 131). The 'hypothesis testing'/flexible battery approach best represents the middle ground in the qualitative–quantitative continuum, using psychometrically sound instruments but within the context of an economical clinical approach.

The focus of the hypothesis testing is centred on efficiency in assessment and in answering the clinical problem at hand (S.C. Bowden, 1995). As Stephen Bowden (1995, p. 37) notes:

> Fortunately, there may be a compromise position, where we can invoke the best available standards of objectivity in behavioural assessment, while retaining a reasonably economic clinical style. In place of the requirement for an individually tailored control group for every patient, we can substitute the provision of a standardized and well-normed test of the relevant ability. In this way, we retain a high standard of objectivity in the process of testing relevant clinical hypotheses.

Bowden goes on to note that after the data has been obtained in the most rigorous fashion possible, integration of that data with the clinical and background variables can then take place. Kaufman (1990) compares assessment to the conduct of a research study in which, after the data is gathered, the results are integrated and interpreted in the context of the pertinent background research and theory. Similarly, after the data including history, test data, clinical observations and qualitative aspects of performance is gathered, integration and interpretation of the performance can then take place (Bowden, 1995).

The hypothesis testing technique begs the question: what has brought the client to clinical attention? The direct observation of psychological dysfunction, changes in habitual behaviour and experience of disordered cognition and emotion (Saling, 1995) presented in the form of the client's history and the referral question are indeed the focus upon which the request for assessment has arisen. Qualitative data then, prompts the need for examination.

The hypothesis testing assessment follows successive elimination of alternative diagnostic possibilities. It begins with the clinician formulating the first set of hypotheses based upon the qualitative data presented by the examinee. Hypotheses formulated at this stage of the assessment, derived from the direct observations of the psychological dysfunction, often determine the shape of the quantitative assessment. Thus, rather than applying a routine battery of cognitive tests, many of which may be irrelevant to the purposes of the assessment, the tests are selected on the basis of the clinical problem. As Shapiro (1970, p. 659) has noted: 'which test one gives, if any, depends upon one's assessment of the validity of one's tools for answering a particular question, and then upon the initial hypotheses suggested by the patient's state and history'.

For instance, the clinician may decide that more medical or social information about the client is needed, or that it would be more appropriate and useful to observe rather than to test the patient, or that he or she needs to interview another person, such as the complaining spouse or an intact sibling to obtain an adequate understanding of the patient's condition (Lezak et al., 2004). Methods that strictly adopt either the quantitative or the qualitative methodology, to the exclusion of the other, are restrictive, preventing clinicians from generating serial hypotheses for identifying subtle or discrete dysfunction or to make fine diagnostic discriminations (Lezak et al., 2004).

As the examination proceeds, the clinician can progressively refine general hypotheses (for example, whether the examinee is suffering from some form of organic brain disorder) to increasingly more specific hypotheses (whether the disorder is most likely to be a focal or a diffuse brain condition) by examining the obtained quantitative and qualitative data. The interest for the neuropsychologist in applying the single case methodology is to determine whether function X is impaired while functions P, Q and R are not. As Benton (1994) has argued, symptoms must be viewed as expressions of the disturbance in a system, not as direct expressions of focal loss of neuronal tissue. The final stage of the examination concludes with the hypotheses being supported or rejected, leading on to the development and evaluation of further, more detailed, hypotheses.

In Table 1.1, I provide a survey of the relative advantages and disadvantages of each of the methods that we have touched upon in the discussion so far.

Table 1.1

The Advantages and Disadvantages of the Principal Approaches
to Neuropsychological Assessment

Approach	Advantages	Disadvantages
Fixed battery: Halstead Reitan Battery	• empirically designed to characterise neuropsychological deficits • huge body of validating data • good reliability • good data on various different patient groups • can be administered by a technician	• very lengthy, commonly taking as much as 8 hours to complete • due to the complexity of the derived measures, it is difficult to know specifically which functions are being measured by the indices • does not include some important functions such as memory functioning as a part of the index scores
Fixed battery: Luria-Nebraska Battery	• an empirically defined and derived battery arising from the elegant theoretical model proposed by Alexander Luria • single scales presented for most cognitive domains, reasonably quick to administer • some published support, but tends to be relatively patchy and published in books more commonly than journals	• purists sometimes contend that it is not an accurate interpretation of Luria's method as it is battery based, rather than presented as a series of hypothesis-led clinical experiments • far less uptake than the HRB, with far less published empirical support • the single scales do not well reflect Luria's views about individual variation
The 'process' approach	• maximal flexibility in matching the testing and data gathering to the referral question • good descriptive power • allows extended use of available, psychometrically validated, instruments by the 'testing the limits' approach	• has a relatively weak published basis because each assessment is unique making the development of the database of particular conditions and presentations almost impossible • very reliant upon the skill and experience of the clinician, particularly with regard to - observational skills focusing upon 'process'-related issues • requires intensive apprenticeship-based training
The flexible battery approach	• economical in terms of the number of tests employed as only those necessary to respond to the hypothesis generated • sound psychometric properties of the instruments employed • lends itself well to the consideration of both clinical and statistical significance of the observed results	• reliant upon the skill of the clinician in terms of knowledge and familiarity with the published literature • so far little psychometric validation of the measures as a group rather than the individual components of the battery, but the data base is growing • places less emphasis upon the means by which the right answer was obtained, but does not eschew this information completely

Further Up and Further In

Before we move to the business of testing hypotheses with the Wechsler scales that we will begin in Chapter 5, it is important that we sensibly establish the ground rules under which we need to operate in conducting cognitive assessment. In the next chapter, we will examine the issue of bias in the context of cognitive assessment with a view to ensuring that our clients are assessed in as fair and thorough a manner as possible and sensitising ourselves to the issue of defensive and defensible cognitive assessment.

CHAPTER TWO

THE VULNERABILITIES OF COGNITIVE EVIDENCE

It is my view that the basic standard by which every cognitive assessment must be evaluated is the degree to which it will stand up to scrutiny in a court of law. You may wonder why I place such a strong emphasis upon medico–legal disputation as the standard to which all clinicians must aspire in their day-to-day practice of cognitive assessment. After all, how many of the clients that you see will ultimately end up in a court of law? While the answer to this question is probably more than you might hope, my caution applies because the fundamental standard by which cognitive assessment is ultimately judged and the place in which clinicians are truly held accountable for the opinions that they give, is when they come into contact with the legal system. As a result, every assessment that you conduct is one that you would be happy to be the subject of a subpoena and that you would gladly defend before the triers of fact.

Support for the idea that we are seeing an increasing presence of neuropsychological evidence in our courts, is provided by the fact that between November 14, 1983 and February 26, 2010 the word 'neuropsychology' (or 'neuro-psychology') was noted to occur no less than 912 times in the legal judgments of Australian courts. This clearly indicates the importance of the speciality, but also underlines the point that neuropsychological and other forms of cognitive assessment are on the legal radar and the increasing likelihood that evidence surrounding the assessment of cognition by the courts is becoming a workaday reality.

Sydney Burwell, Former Dean of Harvard Medical School has noted that: 'half of what you are taught as ... students will in 10 years have been shown to be wrong. And the trouble is, none of your teachers knows which half' (quoted in Sackett, Straus, Richardson, Rosenberg, & Haynes, 2000, p. 29). Equally as well, you are never going to know which of the cognitive assessments you have conducted may end up disputed in a court of law. Thus, the only sensible way to ensure that you are never caught short is to make certain that *every* assessment you conduct is one you would be happy to have disputed. Thus, I fear I am going to add to your paranoia and insist that you think of every assessment that you undertake as being one that you will ultimately need to defend in a court of law. This form of 'defensive and defensible cognitive assessment' should be the benchmark to which you aspire in all of the assessments that you conduct.

A second component of this argument is the legitimate question as to why you would be prepared to adopt a lesser standard of proof and conviction about your clinical case formulation if it was not to be disputed in a court of law. Surely, every client has the fundamental right that the fullest extent of effort will be expended on their behalf at a level equivalent to those who will see the inside of a court room. This is a question about your own professionalism, personal standards and quality assurance. Why indeed, should your nondisputed cases receive anything less than your highest standards of clinical assessment and care? Are they any less deserving of your best efforts?

The Vulnerabilities of Neuropsychological Assessment

The eminent Louisiana neuropsychologist, John Mendoza (2001) has noted:

> Clinical assessment and report writing involve multiple levels of subjective judgements on the part of the neuropsychologist. These include the following decisions: (a) what data to collect and report, (b) how the data should be interpreted, and (c) how the data should be organised and reported. Any time there is subjective judgement involved, there is always the possibility of error. Some errors may simply be due to carelessness, or may be relatively inconsequential (e.g., spelling and grammatical errors), whereas others may be much more egregious, potentially reflecting examiner bias, conceptual misunderstanding, or even basic incompetence. The latter usually have far more serious implications for the consumer as well as for the integrity of the profession. Because of this, both consumers (e.g., patients, referral sources, etc) and practising neuropsychologists should be aware of potential sources of error. (Mendoza, 2001, p. 114)

In line with these cautions, there are five substantive issues that make cognitive assessments vulnerable in courts of law (Guilmette & Giuliano, 1991). These are:

1. the lack of uniformity in cognitive assessment
2. the tenuous nature of the relationship between training, experience, and judgement accuracy

3. the modest capacity of cognitive test results to predict everyday and work functioning
4. their relatively poor ability to detect malingering, and
5. the problems that clinicians have with integrating complex data.

To this list we could also sensibly add:

6. the effects of bias in the referral, in the assessment itself, and in the further information gathering.

At this stage we will not address issues 3 and 4, as each of these issues will be dealt with more extensively in a separate chapter in association with an illustrative case report later on in our discussion (i.e., in Chapter 7 in the case of less than genuine effort and in Chapter 9 in the case of the ecological validity of assessment respectively). While many of these problems apply to all experts in the study of behavioural phenomena, this discussion will be limited to only those aspects of vulnerability that impinge upon cognitive assessment and reporting.

The Lack of Uniformity in Cognitive Assessment

As we noted in Chapter 1, there is no absolute standard with regard to what constitutes the definitive cognitive assessment and a number of possible approaches to this issue can be taken and justified. The issue at the heart of this chapter, however, is the degree to which the same examinee, if examined by different practitioners using different techniques, would demonstrate the same diagnosis and level of impairment.

In both Australia and in the U.S. jurisdictions, rules specific to the admissibility of scientific evidence in courts of law arise from the case of *Frye v. U.S.* (1923). The Frye case established a general acceptance test requiring that the scientific evidence introduced in a disputed matter must be established and recognised in a particular field of expertise in order to be admitted into evidence. Thus, as based upon a national surveys of cognitive assessment (e.g., Guilmette & Faust, 1991; Guilmette, Faust, Hart, & Arkes, 1990; Lees-Haley, Smith, Williams, & Dunn, 1996; Seretny, Dean, Gray, & Hartlage, 1986; Sullivan & Bowden, 1997), 'the Halstead-Reitan Battery, the Luria-Nebraska Battery and Kaplan's (Kaplan, 1988a) 'process/qualitative' approach are generally accepted methods, and hence clearly satisfy the Frye test' (Martell, 1992, p. 329).

In a much-discussed case in the United States (*Chapple v. Granger,* 1994) the Daubert standard was applied for the first time to the use of fixed (standardised) versus flexible (nonstandardised) cognitive test batteries in the Federal Court. The Daubert standard arose as a result of the case of *Daubert v. Merrell Dow Pharmaceuticals* (1993) in which the US Supreme Court instituted the

Daubert standard and eliminated the use of Frye in the Federal Court in an effort to establish a standard for the admissibility of scientific evidence that could be implemented with greater uniformity and consistency.

> The court firmly grounded the Daubert standard in orthodox scientific principles, with the focus primarily upon legal relevance and scientific validity, reliability, method, and procedure ... While not intending to produce a definitive list, the Supreme Court suggested four general factors to aid the lower courts in the review of scientific evidence: first whether the theory or technique in question can be (and has been) empirically tested using scientific methodology to determine possible falsifiability; second, whether evidence was adequately subjected to peer review including publication; third, consideration of the known or potential rate of error of the particular technique used including consideration of the existence and maintenance of controls and standards used in the technique's operations; and fourth, whether the theory or technique employed has engendered widespread general acceptance of a relevant scientific community. (Reed, 1996, pp. 316–317)

In contrast to Frye, the Daubert standard relies far less heavily upon the acceptance of the relevant scientific community and, uniquely, puts the tribunal at the centre of the determination of whether the evidence presented to it by its experts is 'scientific'. Whereas, under the Frye standard, the general acceptance by a body of experts was sufficient in and of itself to justify the acceptance of the method employed; the Daubert standard fundamentally shifts this determination to the court itself as the trier, not just of the scientific facts themselves, but also of the methods and techniques that have produced these facts as well as their intrinsic vulnerabilities. These determinations with regard to method must also be made in the context of the continuing deliberation regarding the matters that constitute the substance of the case in the first place. It should be noted that the Frye standard still applies in all Australian jurisdictions (Freckelton & Selby, 1989), however, the self-examination and soul-searching, which has been caused by this shift in the quality of expert opinion (neuropsychological as well as every other forensic specialist), continues to be felt not only in the United States but also in our own courts of law.

The case of *Chapple v. Granger* involved three cognitive assessments that were administered to determine the effects of a closed head injury sustained by a 10-year-old boy in a motor-car accident (Reed, 1996).

Plaintiff's[1] counsel used a clinical neuropsychologist and a clinical psychologist, who each administered a flexible battery of tests. The first battery administered by the clinical psychologist included: the Aphasia Screening Test, the Benton Visual Retention Test, Draw a Bicycle, Draw a Clock, the Category Test, the Rey Complex Figure Test, the Lateral Dominance Test, the Manual Finger Tapping Test, the Sensory Perceptual Test, the Tactual Performance Test, the Verbal Fluency Test, the Wide Range Achievement Test — Revised (WRAT-R), Woodcock-Johnson Selected Subtests, Draw a Family, Draw a Person, the Grooved Pegboard, the Incomplete Sentences test, the Knox Cubes, the Peabody Picture Vocabulary Test, the Ruff Figural Fluency, the Stroop–Color Word Test, the Symbol-Digit Modalities Test, the Wechsler Intelligence Scale for Children — Revised (WISC-R), the Wisconsin Card Sorting Test, the Trail Making Test, the Speech Sounds Perception Test and the Seashore Rhythm Test (details regarding a number of these tests will be provided in Chapter 4). Based upon the history and results obtained, the examiner concluded that the child had sustained a mild traumatic brain injury that had resulted in mild cognitive problems and moderate behavioural disturbance (Reed, 1996).

One year after the accident, a second flexible cognitive test battery was administered. The neuropsychologist reported that the patient obtained normal scores on the Kaufman Brief Intelligence Test, the Trail Making Test, the Sentence Imitation Test, the Word Sequence and Oral Direction subtests of the Detroit Test, the Taylor Complex Figure, the Individual Achievement Test, the Wechsler Reading Comprehension and Listening Comprehension Test, and the Hooper Visual Organization Test. The neuropsychologist noted significant impairment in the Attention Capacity subtest of the Auditory Verbal Learning Test, the Sound and Visual Symbol Recall Test, the paragraph copy test, and the child's reading speed level. The clinical neuropsychologist diagnosed the patient with a moderate-to-severe traumatic brain injury with frontal lobe involvement, secondary to the automobile accident. The examiner went on to conclude that the child was likely to be left with permanent residual problems with attention, memory and executive functions (Reed, 1996).

The defendants'[1] counsel then initiated a third cognitive examination employing Dr Reitan, one of the authors of the HRB, as their expert. Dr Reitan administered most of the HRNB for older children and reported that nine of the 18 obtained test scores were higher than the scores of normal controls, four were within the normal range and only the grip strength and the localisation score on the Tactual Performance Test were clearly below the normative scores of the normal control group. He further noted that the latter test was invalidated due to an error made in the test's administration. Dr Reitan reviewed the patient's history, the results and the reports of the previous assessments, the patient's school records and qualified his conclusions with the clinical opinion that very mild left-sided cerebral deficits compatible with the injury might possibly be present. He noted that while most of the obtained scores fell in the normal range, some mild deviations could be attributed to minor brain dysfunction, but overall the scores were representative of the non-brain-damaged child population (Reed, 1996).

Under the Daubert standard, the District Judge noted the lack of medical and scientific evidence to support the conclusions made by the Plaintiff's two expert witnesses, even though each had administered a comprehensive and flexible cognitive test battery and had based their conclusions on the obtained results. The judge accepted as scientific evidence the test results obtained from the fixed HRB administered by Dr Reitan, and also accepted his scientific expert medical testimony that was derived from this data.

> Applying the Daubert standard to the cognitive test results and opinions of the expert witnesses, the District Judge held that the entire reasoning process, and not simply part of the reasoning process upon which the expert witness derives a conclusion must reflect scientific methodology. (Reed, 1996, p. 315)

Greiffenstein and Cohen (2005), in their comprehensive review of the judgment made in the case, disagreed with Reed's interpretation, noting that:

> … even cursory study of the judge's written decisions revealed *all* neuropsychological testimony was admitted. The judge only put greater weight on testimony from a fixed battery advocate for a reason that had nothing to do with battery composition. There was no *Daubert* challenge to a flexible battery at all. There was only a *Daubert* challenge to a vocational counsellor offering intuitive testimony. (p. 70)

Greiffenstein and Cohen (2005) went on to note that the Daubert challenge does not require or oblige the use of only a commercially available fixed battery. In their view, test selection should be based on a 'sound assessment doctrine' including the cautions that each assessment should:

- feature a standardised approach
- never rely on a single test of a function
- use tests in common use that have a sound scientific basis
- always test effort and symptom validity
- use tests with a sound normative basis
- use logical and relevant test selection
- avoid 'homemade' and novel approaches.

Who could but agree with such a simple, practical and sensible set of guidelines?

As I have already indicated, while the Frye standard still applies within Australia, there had been one notable legal discussion in our tribunals regarding what is an acceptable standard for the use of psychological tests and psychological assessment practices that is worthy of note. Associate Professor Arthur Shores (2006a) discusses this issue within the context of the guidelines for the New

South Wales Compulsory Third-Party Scheme under the Motor Accidents Authority of New South Wales regarding the Chelmsford Royal Commission into Deep Sleep Therapy conducted in New South Wales in the 1980s.

> With these criteria in mind, the enquiry into deep sleep therapy revealed a number of inappropriate testing practices by the psychologist at Chelmsford Hospital, including:
> * the tests used were of low validity or reliability;
> * the tests were used in a shortened form and/or combined with other shortened tests which exaggerated problems with unreliable tests or undermined the reliability of otherwise valid test;
> * using clinical judgements on relationships or profiles from combinations of test in the absence of adequate objective material to support this approach;
> * idiosyncratic use of component traits in the case; and
>
> making use of clinical and subjective historical or other material without proper explanation of the source of the material when providing conclusions. These were presented as percentile scores when they were based on other material' (Volume 9, Commissioners Report, cited in New South Wales Health, 1996, p. 49).
>
> As a result, Acting Justice Slattery concluded that the results reached by the psychologist had been 'infected by an inappropriate subjective approach' [New South Wales Health, 1996, p. 50]. Furthermore, he said that the testing results contributed to the justification of Deep Sleep Therapy at Chelmsford Hospital. The psychologist's defence was that he used the test as he did because it was impractical to do otherwise given the length of the tests, the time available and the fatigue of the patient. It was also argued that this was a routine way of using the tests at the time. However, Acting Justice Slattery did not accept the practical and historical justification. He said the historical justification was to his mind an unappealing argument, did not justify what the psychologist did, and if true rather condemned his contemporaries[2]. (p. 4)

It is clear that Acting Justice Slattery's cautions (1990) continue to be relevant to clinical practice in Australia today, and that the use of the so-called Nuremberg defence[3] (i.e., I only administered or interpreted the tests in this way because my instructor, colleague or supervisor told me to), will not absolve assessors from the requirement to employ appropriately justified, and justifiable clinical standards of practice. In short, just because Suzy, Bill, Fred and Tony do it that way, it does not mean that you can too!

This point is particularly disconcerting in the context of the recent review of neuropsychological practice concerning the evaluation of decision-making capacity by Australian neuropsychologists undertaken by Elizabeth Mullaly and her colleagues (Mullaly et al., 2007). These investigators note that: 'the Wechsler scales are frequently used, albeit with preference given to selected sub-tests' and further that 'when questioned about the relative importance of different types of tests, 56% rated standardised tests equally to non-standardised tests, and 42% rated standardised test tests above non-standardised tests. One participant rated non-standardised tests above standardised tests' (p. 182). Perhaps most disconcerting of all was the statement that: 'very few stated that they would resolve borderline determinations by consciously erring on the side of patient's rights or consciously erring on the side of protecting the patient from harm' (p. 184). So much for the presumption of innocence!!

In responding to the Daubert challenges, the recourse to the defence of the cognitive assessment approach taken as reliant on the 'process' approach similarly may not of itself be sufficient to establish the legitimacy of the data obtained. As Guilmette and Guiliano (1991) have noted:

> For instance, an attorney could easily challenge a very cogent and esoteric description of the process/qualitative approach with the question, 'So what you're basically telling this court, Doctor, is that you make it up as you go along?' The attorney also may demand that expert witnesses provide evidence that their approach to cognitive assessment has been scientifically demonstrated to be superior to all other methods. (p. 200)

As I have indicated, the repercussions of the Daubert standard, even in jurisdictions that are still operating under the Frye rules, have created increased scrutiny on the nature of expert decision-making, necessitating a positive defence of the practices and standards employed as being of the highest scientific quality and rigour.

'It should be stated at the outset that there is no psychological (or other) test available that is 100% sensitive and specific' (McGuire, 1999, p. 165). As such, the requirement for the administration of a variety of tests assessing a variety of functions is essential to identify brain impairment. As noted in Chapter 1, there continues to be a lack of consensus about which approach to neuropsychological assessment is the correct one and, as Lees-Haley and colleagues (P.R. Lees-Haley et al., 1996) have noted, with regard to perhaps the most reliably and consistently administered test battery in the neuropsychological domain (remember *Chapple v. Granger*) ' ... the definition of HRB as represented in forensic reports varies. Batteries characterized by examiners as the HRB vary from five to eight or more of the procedures described by Reitan and Wolfson.' (p. 48). Lees-Haley and colleagues further noted that 'in the examination of 100 forensic reports not one neuropsychologist used precisely the same battery as any other neuropsychologist except a few experts who only used one to four tests in their evaluations' (p. 48). At something of a stretch of the imagination, perhaps it could be said that, just as noted above, only Luria can reliably administer the Luria battery, perhaps only Dr Reitan himself can now reliably administer the HRB. For the remainder of us, procedures based upon sound, scientifically based, clinical practice, as recommended Greiffenstein and Cohen (2005), seem the only defensible resort.

All cognitive techniques, including the HRB, are subject to the challenge that the examiner is selectively applying the assessment instruments. Until such time as the definitive test or set of tests of brain impairment has proven itself to the field (something that still looks like it will be a long time coming) the examiner is left with his or her own approach to the task, based upon the available data obtained from the contemporary literature. The most prudent step for the examiner to take is not to embark on procedures that are out of the mainstream in assessment approaches.

The Tenuous Nature of the Relationship Between Training, Experience and Judgment Accuracy

The standard of conviction of the expert regarding the evidence that they will present differs relative to the tribunal. In civil jurisdictions the expert's opinions must be made on 'balance of probability', a level of conviction concerning the evidence that is somewhere between likely and probably. Quantitatively this would represent a conviction regarding the evidence of at last 51% or greater. In criminal matters the belief of guilt must be made 'beyond reasonable doubt', somewhere between absolutely and probably. Weinstein and Dewsbury (2006, p. 173) contend that for a lay juror, this level of conviction should be based upon 'a nonquantitative formulation plus a numerical formulation such as 'in the high 90s' seems to make the most sense'.

To achieve these requirements, the expert must present their testimony as based upon objective, scientific evidence. Courts refuse to accept expert evidence on matters that are considered to be within their own knowledge (i.e., 'something of which an intelligent unskilled person would be aware'). As a result of this rule of evidence, there are a number of topics on which experts may not present expert opinion, including: the voluntariness of admissions, the credit of witnesses, susceptibility of ordinary persons to stress, the capacity to form an intent to do a criminal act, the behaviour of 'normal' children, the operation of memory and the process of identification (i.e., the issues associated with eyewitness testimony) (Freckleton & Selby, 1998). With regard particularly to this issue, even though it may well be the case that the knowledge of the common man may not be sufficiently comprehensive to reliably characterise the available scientific evidence on these matters, it is still the case that these are not the preserve of expert opinion.

To demonstrate that an expert opinion is required in the disputation, it is necessary for the party calling the expert to: (1) establish that an opinion needs to be tendered in an area of specialist knowledge in a recognised and organised body of knowledge and/or experience that is beyond the experience of ordinary members of the lay community and (2) that the witness possesses sufficient expertise within that field to qualify as an expert. The evaluation of this latter point must be made on the basis of qualifications and training; years of experience; places of employment; the relevance of clinical experience, particularly with regard to special populations (e.g., paediatric or geriatric populations); particular types of disorders (e.g., individuals with psychiatric or degenerative conditions) or clinical presentations; and demonstration of relevant professional education, specialist training and relevant research experience.

The base level qualification of the examiner from 1 July, 2010 is that he or she is a registered psychologist as recognised by the Psychology Board of Australia (PBA). The PBA endorses seven specialities in psychology (clinical psychology, clinical neuropsychology, counselling psychology, educational end developmental psychology, forensic psychology, organisational psychology and sport and exercise psychology). As well as this means of assessment of professional competence, the Australian Psychological Society has a specialist College of Clinical Neuropsychologists which requires a demonstration of relevant training, specialist supervision, and continuing education in the specialty for membership.

The basic specialist degree to practice in clinical neuropsychology is offered by a number of Australian universities, including La Trobe University, Macquarie University, Monash University, the University of Melbourne, the University of Queensland, the University of Sydney, the University of Western Australia and Victoria University. Most practitioners have obtained a Master's degree or much less commonly, a PhD, but the advent of Doctor of Psychology degrees has now been implemented in almost all of the universities offering specialist training, and this degree is now becoming more common. Completion of specialist training in clinical neuropsychology at the Masters level allows the candidate to register as an associate member of the College of Clinical Neuropsychologists of the Australian Psychological Society, but the candidate must complete further specialist training (i.e. an additional 80 hours of stipulated professional development of which at least 40 hours must be by direct supervision by a senior colleague) before they can become a full member of the College. At this point in time, candidates who complete the Doctor of Psychology degrees in the speciality are granted direct entry to the College upon the completion of the qualification. These arrangements, however, are likely to be subject to change with the full implementation of a National Registration and Accreditation Scheme (NRAS). At this stage the PBA will require a further two years of supervised experience following a Masters degree and a further one year of supervision following a doctoral degree for endorsement in its recognised specialities. The PBA website (i.e. www.psychologyboard.gov.au) should be accessed for more up to date information.

A distinction should be made between professional associations that require a demonstration of competence for membership, with those that do not. In Australia, membership of the College of Clinical Neuropsychologists of the Australian Psychological Society implies a rigorous evaluation process and examination of previous study and referee reports. This type of examination should be distinguished from the interest group-based membership or other organisations such as the Australian Society for the Study of Brain Impairment (ASSBI), the International Neuropsychological Society (INS), or the National Academy of Neuropsychologists of the United States (NAN), which denote interest in the area, but do not necessarily imply competence in the practice of clinical neuropsychology.

Walsh and Darby (1999) also raise another concern with a view to identifying experts in the area of neuropsychological assessment:

> A neuropsychologist with excellent academic qualifications who has published numerous research papers may have very little experience of the specific matters under debate in court, which are the province of those with the extensive *clinical* experience even though the latter may be less qualified academically. (p. 452, emphasis added in the original)

Both the quality and the relevance of the previous experience of the expert are crucial in determining their authority.

It should be stressed that the practice of clinical neuropsychology does not overlap with specialist knowledge of the other clinical domains involved in the disputation process, including psychiatry, neurology, neurosurgery, clinical psychology or forensic psychology. The nature of the neuropsychological opinion must be developed in the context of the intersection of contemporary neuroscience; the psychiatric, neurological, neurosurgical and psychological evidence presented by other experts in the case; contemporary measurement theory; as well as in the context of extensive clinical experience with the populations of interest. The disciplines of medicine and of psychology, particularly neuropsychology, are vastly different in terms of their scope, methodology and database, and each conveys a unique perspective about the effects of the brain impairment on the individual.

One of the techniques used to undermine clinical neuropsychological evidence in courts of law is to suggest that it is in some way inferior to material gathered by a specialist medical practitioner, indicating that the discipline does not have a well-developed, and most importantly a discrete, knowledge base. An appropriate response to this sort of suggestion might be to indicate to the lawyer that if he could have obtained a similar opinion from a medical practitioner, then why did he/she not use one. Obviously, this is because the neuropsychological opinion can contribute unique evidence that is not contained in an equivalent medical opinion.

There are areas of overlap between the various clinical specialties that practice in the area of civil litigation, particularly with regard to personal injury matters, and it can be difficult to determine which specialist is appropriate to tender evidence in a particular case. In a review in the *Australian Forensic Psychiatry Bulletin* R.J. Stanley, QC (Stanley, 1989) noted glowingly that:

> Perhaps this is because of the advent of well-qualified and experienced neuropsychologists whose evidence is of particular assistance in cases involving brain damaged patients. In such cases, issues such as the capacity of the plaintiff to undertake employment or to marry and live an independent existence are the subject of neuropsychological evidence, whilst for the diagnosis and prognosis the neurologist is called. In most such cases in my experience lawyers see little place for the psychiatrist witness. (p 5)

While my head swells with such praise (and I fear for the livelihood of my psychiatrist colleagues), the clinical neuropsychologist must be cautious about creating an unduly unrealistic expectation of the discipline. With regard to whom the examinee should marry, I only wish one of my colleagues had wisely stepped in before my imprudent action that culminated in the requirement for a specialist in the area of family law.

Of late there has been an increasing tendency for expert witnesses to become associated with particular types of litigation and the tendency to become seen as 'wearing the guernsey' of one particular party. There have thus been increasing numbers of attacks mounted against the professional integrity and objectivity of expert witnesses. It is commonplace for experts to be cross-examined in the civil jurisdiction at length and with vigour as to the nature of their practice (e.g., how much work is clinical as opposed to medico-legal work, how much work was done for insurance companies as against plaintiffs, whether they see their role as investigative? [Stanley, 1989]), and it is only prudent on the part of the advocate to ensure that any unpleasant surprises regarding the expert do not emerge on the witness stand. Increasingly, it is also the case that the respective experts from the defence and the prosecution may be required to 'hot tub' a joint statement regarding the matters under consideration to elucidate the matters on which the respective experts agree and those matters on which they disagree.

In the discussion above with regard to who should be viewed as an expert in the forensic setting, considerable emphasis was placed upon experience, training and membership of professional societies. The theoretical position underlying this suggestion is that experts as determined by these means would perform significantly better in their clinical judgments than would non-experts. Evidence to support this proposition, however, has not been plentiful and in fact may indicate that this may not be the case. Faust, Hart and Guilmette (1988) have noted that more experienced practitioners were slightly more likely to overdiagnose abnormality but, other than this, they found no relationship between training, experience and accuracy (See Wedding & Faust, 1989, for a review of this evidence).

Despite these data, it is important to note that this same literature did not indicate that lack of experience increased judgment accuracy (Guilmette & Giuliano, 1991). Overall, the trained clinicians were capable of achieving a hit rate of 80% in identifying cases with evidence of brain impairment. Accuracy decreased, however, in making the determinations of the more specific details regarding the nature of the brain impairment, including whether it was progressive or not or in specifying its location.

Another issue at work here is that this data has largely been gathered from qualified practitioners, thus the correlational relationship is relatively lower as all the practitioners are at a similar level of experience. The most appropriate test would be to compare qualified versus nonqualified individuals to ascertain the relationship between training, experience and judgment accuracy (Guilmette & Giuliano, 1991). Nonetheless the prudent clinician cannot dismiss the published evidence on this topic out of hand and a reasoned interpretation of the issue that variables such as training, experience or confidence do not of themselves contribute to judgment accuracy must be conceded. In short, if you intended to assert that this is the state of the individual in your 'clinical opinion', recognise that this assertion of itself will not be sufficient justification for your opinion and a sensible second suit in hard, scientifically justified, clinical data would be a useful adjunct to your personal view when you are on the witness stand.

The Problems That Clinicians Have With Integrating Complex Data

Many investigators in the area of clinical cognitive assessment, including me, have stressed the importance of gathering information from a variety of sources including background information, interviews with the client and his or her relatives, assessment of previous educational and employment records, as well as the huge collection of data associated with the assessment itself.

Despite the appeal of such statements, the literature clearly suggests that clinicians have a limited ability to integrate multiple units of information in their assessment processes (Wedding & Faust, 1989).

The exercise of clinical judgment involves the clinician in numerous information-processing activities including collecting, storing, retrieving, interpreting and integrating the various information gathered in the clinical assessment. Dealing with such huge loads of information constrains the clinician to resort to various forms of heuristics and rules of thumb to overcome the intrinsic limitations of their information-processing capabilities, including an intrinsically limited working memory capacity.

Despite the fact that confidence increases in proportion to increasing information, the relationship between the level of information and judgment accuracy is neither simple nor necessarily positive. Once a limited amount of information has been assimilated, additional information does not appear to produce a substantial improvement in judgment accuracy (Faust, 1986, 1991; Oskamp, 1965; Wedding, 1983). Worse still is the observation of Wedding (1983) of the inverse relationship between confidence and accuracy in judges evaluating protocols from the HRB. Wedding (1991) has noted that many neuropsychologists were totally confident about decisions that were totally wrong in a study designed to test the ability of neuropsychologists to detect paediatric malingering.

One line of research in this area has examined the ability of clinicians to improve their judgmental accuracy when provided with various amounts of information. The research indicates that once clinicians are provided with a limited amount of valid information, additional information does not appear to lead to significant gain in judgmental accuracy (Faust, Ziskin, & Hiers, 1991). In fact, the literature seems to support the notion that diagnostic errors are more common if the decision is based on more rather than less data (Wedding, 1983). Overall, the conclusions arising from this area of study indicate that a clinician's decisions, even those that they believe depend upon configural analysis, can be largely duplicated by procedures that do not rely on this assumption.

The Effect of Bias in the Assessment and Information Gathering

There are clearly many sources of bias in the cognitive assessment. These may apply in the original approach to the clinician by the advocate, in the process of the assessment itself or in the gathering of the history and background information.

Van Gorp and McMullen (1997) have noted a number of possible sources of bias in the initial contact between the advocate and the expert. These include:

1. the financial relationship between the retaining party and the expert

2. the initial contact between the advocate and the expert in which a particular interpretation of the facts may be pressed home

3. failing to provide all available evidence at the time that the assessment is conducted, which may colour the interpretation of the evidence gathered

4. the appropriate selection of a comprehensive, sensitive and specific battery of tests to ensure that sufficient assessment of all cognitive sequelae of the injury is made

5. appropriate selection of the normative standard of the individual relevant to the demographics of that individual

6. caution in applying the blind yet biased belief that a single test can be a pathognomonic indicator of brain impairment.

All of these cautions must be exercised in a comprehensive collection of data are regarding the examinee.

Within the assessment process itself Wedding and Faust (1989) have identified a number of common information-processing strategies used by clinicians that contribute to errors in judgment in their clinical assessments. These include:

1. hindsight bias

2. confirmatory bias

3. overreliance on salient data

4. underutilisation of base rates

5. a failure to analyse co-variation.

Hindsight bias is the tendency to believe that, once the outcome of an event is known, the outcome could have been predicted more easily than is actually the case. As a result of this, information about the outcome can exert considerable and often unrecognised biasing of judgment. This problem can be of particular concern to neuropsychologists, who typically obtain outcome information (i.e., that the examinee has had a head injury) prior to test interpretation, which often culminates in a tendency on the part of the clinician to overdiagnose pathology (Guilmette & Giuliano, 1991). Reitan (Reitan & Wolfson, 1993b) has even gone so far as to suggest that it may be prudent to gather the history after the testing, rather than the more conventional practice of history gathering before testing, to ensure that the information gathered in history taking does not contaminate the independence of the data gathering.

Confirmatory bias involves the practice on the part of the clinician to seek and value supporting evidence at the expense of contrary evidence. In the data collection this might involve the selective search for information that supports one's original hypothesis, rather than searching for facts and evidence that may adjust initial impressions. This may result in the outcome that the original hypotheses are preserved often even in the face of contradictory evidence (Ross, Lepper, & Hubbard, 1975; Ross, Lepper, Strach, & Steinmetz, 1977).

Overreliance on salient data involves the practice in which clinicians tend to overemphasise concrete and salient date in comparison to data that is more informative but bland. A somewhat dull history of unbroken normal employment may be overshadowed by a single but dramatic elicitation of a pathognomonic sign.[4]

Base rates refer to the frequency with which something occurs within a given population. For example, if a disorder occurs in one in 100 individuals then the base rate is 1%. The frequency with which particular events or differences occur is crucially important in diagnosis and prediction. In order to determine whether a relationship exists between a given diagnostic sign and a disorder, it is not sufficient to know how frequently the two co-occur.

> One must also know how often a sign occurs among individuals without the disorder. Unless the sign is more common among those with the disorder than those without it, the sign does not bear a valid relationship to the disorder. (Faust, 1991, p. 212)

To be assured that the sign is truly useful in identifying the disorder or in predicting the outcome one must also know the frequency of the disorder or outcome (Guilmette & Faust, 1991). The diagnostic value of any sign or symptom depends on the proportion of correct to incorrect identifications they produce and the frequency of the condition or event to be identified.

Failure to analyse covariation occurs because clinicians have a great deal of difficulty in correctly determining the relationship that exists between the variables that they would seek to measure and the diagnoses they would hope to make. A clinician's diagnostic decisions must be based upon the frequency with which the sign is observed, both in the absence and in the presence of the condition. Due to the failure of a direct and perfect relationship between the sign and the diagnosis occurring, this inevitably influences decisions due to the failure of examiner to apprehend the imperfect relationship between the sign and the diagnosis.

Another source of bias may arise from the manner in which the clinician elicits the background history and symptoms from the examinee. Some clients provide misleading information because they are generally unaware of their own behaviour; others, however, may be less genuine. A striking example of the former issue was provided by Lilienfeld and Graham (1958) who noted that 35% of a sample of 192 men answered the question 'Are you circumcised?' incorrectly. How clients interpret clinician's questions, their background, education and their attitudes towards their problems can each affect the quality of the clinical data obtained.

An interesting example of this phenomenon is the presentation of response bias in gathering the examinee's history (Lees-Haley, 1992; Lees-Haley et al., 1997). Lees-Haley and colleagues (1997) gathered data on a total of 446 subjects (comprising 131 litigating and 315 nonlitigating adults from five locations across the United States) and noted that the litigating clients consistently reported themselves to be hyper-normal before their injury. These differences applied to areas as diverse as life in general, concentration, memory, level of depression, level of anxiety, level of alcohol abuse, work or school performance, level of irritability, level of headache, level of confusion, level of self-esteem, fatigue, level of sexual functioning, quality of their marriage and the relationship to their children. Only level of drug abuse did not differ between the forensic group and the controls.

Overall, the individuals in litigation perceived their functioning before the injury to be more satisfactory and trouble-free than the level observed in equivalent noninjured individuals. This effect, now referred to as the 'good old days' effect, may occur as these individuals evaluate their present performance as a benchmark for the previous performance and this results in an overestimate of the level of premorbid function.

This sort of evidence must sensitise the examiner to the possible inflation of the presently reported symptoms and concerns of the examinee to ensure that examinee bias in the presentation of the history and symptomatology is not reinforced by the reporting.

Conclusion

With regard to how clinicians may defend themselves against charges of bias on the witness stand, a number of corrective strategies should be taken (Wedding & Faust, 1989). These include:

- Clinicians need to be aware of the literature which documents their errors in judgment.
- Clinicians should not depend on insight alone and should adopt an active reasoning processes in order to counter flawed judgment practices.
- Clinicians should avoid premature abandonment of useful decision rules in the absence of systematic data collection or evidence that indicates that they are not working.
- Clinicians should regress extreme estimates and confidence in relation to the level of uncertainty of the tests that they use by employing techniques such as confidence intervals.

- Clinicians must separate statistical fact from statistical artefact and beware of the imperfect psychometric properties of the instruments that they use.

- Clinicians must be aware of their tendency to become overly focused on the esoteric and must maintain a balance between those features based upon unique features and those upon common features.

- Clinicians should avoid reliance on highly correlated measures.

- Clinicians should start with the most valid information first in the assessment, thus relying on the information that has the most predictive validity.

- Clinicians should list alternative diagnoses and options and seek evidence for each before moving to premature closure.

- Clinicians should systematically list disconfirmatory information.

- Clinicians should 'think Bayesian', and systematically apply base rate information in decision-making. They should familiarise themselves with the base rate data of symptoms and diagnoses in their own clinical settings and the normative populations and use this information to inform their clinical decision-making.

- Clinicians should use and apply appropriate age, sex and education adjusted norms.

- Clinicians should make a deliberate effort to obtain feedback to ascertain how accurate their judgments have been and to modify their decision-making criteria in the context of this.

Endnotes

1 In civil legal matters, the plaintiff is the person who initiates the case, while the defendant is the party who must defend against the charges made by the complainant (i.e., the plaintiff). So, for example, a plaintiff in a personal injury case would be the injured person themselves, while the defendant might be an insurer such as the Victorian WorkCover Authority or the Transport Accident Commission in the Victorian context.

2 Emphasis added

3 The Nuremberg defence is the justification provided by the Nazis who were tried before the war crimes tribunal conducted in Nuremberg, Germany following World War II, which contends that the acts undertaken by these individuals were done so under instructions from a superior officer, and therefore the person following the lawful order should not be subject to prosecution for doing so.

4 A pathognomonic sign is a clinical sign that is characteristic of the given condition and of no other. Unfortunately, these are very rare and more commonly many conditions present with quite similar features (see the more extensive discussion of this matter in Chapter 9).

CHAPTER THREE

HOW MANY NEUROPSYCHOLOGICAL FUNCTIONS ARE THERE?

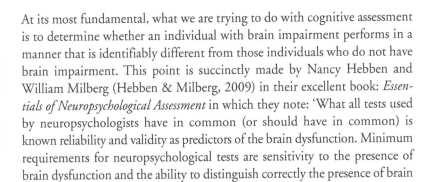

At its most fundamental, what we are trying to do with cognitive assessment is to determine whether an individual with brain impairment performs in a manner that is identifiably different from those individuals who do not have brain impairment. This point is succinctly made by Nancy Hebben and William Milberg (Hebben & Milberg, 2009) in their excellent book: *Essentials of Neuropsychological Assessment* in which they note: 'What all tests used by neuropsychologists have in common (or should have in common) is known reliability and validity as predictors of the brain dysfunction. Minimum requirements for neuropsychological tests are sensitivity to the presence of brain dysfunction and the ability to distinguish correctly the presence of brain damage from normal brain functioning' (p. 4).

Thus, before we launch into any discussion about the clinical syndromes, we must attempt to determine the answer to the sticky question of just how many cognitive functions are there? One answer to this question might be: the number of cognitive functions is equivalent to the number of instruments that have been proposed to test them. Clearly then, if we examine contemporary cognitive test compendia (Lezak et al., 2004; Strauss, Sherman, & Spreen, 2006), then the number of cognitive functions is massive! How then can we pare this massive number down to a more manageable set?

One approach that I think has some value is to break the functions into more discernible and hopefully dissociable cognitive domains. This might be represented by the cognitive pyramid presented in Figure 3.1.

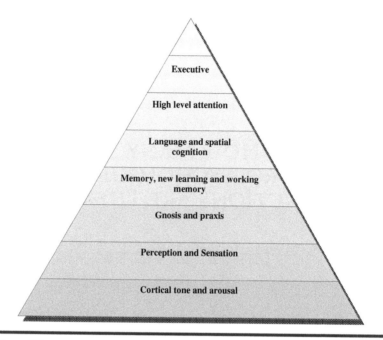

Figure 3.1
The pyramid of cognitive skills.

The use of the pyramid is not merely because of my fascination with things Egyptological, but also because there is a hierarchy of these cognitive functions such that if there is a breakdown at the lower levels, then this has significant implications for the performance of the tasks that operate at the higher levels in the hierarchy. This is not to suggest that there is a direct one-to-one association between the breakdown at one level of the hierarchy to higher levels, but merely to indicate that the higher levels of the pyramid cannot be successfully negotiated if the lower ones are not intact and functioning appropriately.

A good example of this approach can be observed if we consider the Wisconsin Card Sorting Test (WCST; Grant & Berg, 1948). The WCST is a task that requires the client to sort a series of cards having from one to four shapes: circle, cross, triangle or star presented in each of four colours: red, blue, green or yellow. The client's task is to sort the cards into categories under each of the four example cards, with the only available feedback being the correctness or incorrectness of the response, as indicated by the examiner after each card has been sorted. After the client correctly sorts for a sequence of ten correct placements, the category changes in the order colour, form and then number. The client is not informed when the category changes.

Deficits at lower orders of performance can equally impair performance at the highest levels of the pyramid. For example, an individual with hemineglect,[1] may fail to attend to the left side of space thus producing aberrant responding on the task, because targets in the neglected field have not been 'seen'. Equally, an individual with Alzheimer's disease may have difficulty recalling the previously sorted card, the category and possibly, the name for triangles, which also makes it difficult to perform the task. An individual with damage to the frontal lobe however, may have difficulty in discerning the rules of the sort, persevere with the category after it has ceased to be rewarded, may have difficulty with the recall of the previously sorted card sequence, or may sort in an impulsive and random fashion. Thus, although each client may do poorly at the task, each may do so for quite a different reason.[2]

Cognitive tasks are, by necessity and by design, multifactorial in nature (Brown, 1989) and even the most apparently simple task calls on many, if not all, of the levels of the cognitive hierarchy proposed in Figure 3.1. How then is it possible for us to say anything about a cognitive deficit in a way that does not classify it all as generalised or global? One possible solution to this problem is to examine performances at the lower level of the hierarchy and to determine that these are intact, ruling these functions out as contributing to the observed cognitive deficit. Thus, if our patient with the hemineglect is assessed on a visual tracking task in our examination of gnosis[3] or spatial cognition and is found to be impaired, then it is fair to say that the poor performance on the WCST is due to a lower-order deficit and, as a consequence, the deficit cannot be considered to be one exclusively attributable to frontal/executive impairment. How then can we conclude that a particular deficit is attributable to compromise in the frontal executive system? If we have excluded deficits at all other levels of the hierarchy then it is likely that the poor performance is due to an executive problem.

On Test Selection

Over the years, a number of studies have been undertaken with clinical neuropsychologists in the attempt to determine which neuropsychological instruments are in most common use (e.g., Guilmette et al., 1990; Lees-Haley et al., 1996; Sullivan & Bowden, 1997).

Lees-Haley et al. (1996) reviewed 100 forensic neuropsychological reports in the United States. Cases were selected on the basis that the author had been named as a forensic neuropsychological expert for a case in litigation. The sample included data from 20 states within the United States and the province of Ontario in Canada. Of the tests used by these examiners the authors compiled a list of 44 tests commonly used in forensic neuropsychological reports (the numbers in brackets represent the frequency with which the tests were used in the reports).

These were:

1. Wechsler Adult Intelligence Scale (WAIS) and WAIS — Revised (76%)
2. Minnesota Multiphasic Personality Inventory (MMPI and MMPI-2: 68%)
3. Wechsler Memory Scale (WMS) and WMS — Revised (51%)
4. Trails A (48%)
5. Trails B (47%)
6. Finger Oscillation Test/Finger Tapping Test (38%)
7. Bender Gestalt (34%)
8. Category Test (all forms) (32%)
9. Wisconsin Card Sorting Test (29%)
10. Sentence Completion Test (28%)
11. Tactual Performance Test (26%)
12. Wide Range Achievement Test (WRAT and WRAT — Revised: 25%)
13. Beck Depression inventory (25%)
14. Reitan-Kløve Sensory Perceptual Examination (23%)
15. Grooved Pegboard (23%)
16. Seashore Rhythm Test (23%)
17. Speech Sounds Perception Test (21%)
18. Boston Naming Test/Boston Naming Test — Revised (21%)
19. Hooper Visual Organization Test (20%)
20. Grip strength (17%)
21. Rey-Osterreith Complex Figure Design Test (16%)
22. Stroop Neuropsychological Screening Test, Stroop–Colour Word Test (15%)
23. Rorschach (14%)
24. Lateral Dominance Examination (13%)
25. Symbol Digit Modalities Test (13%)
26. Human Figure Drawing Test, House, Tree, Person; Draw a Person (12%)
27. Aphasia Screening Test (Reitan) (12%)
28. Paced Auditory Serial Additions Test (12%)
29. California Verbal Learning Test (CVLT) and CVLT — Revised (11%)
30. Neuropsychological Symptom Check Lists (11%)

31. Controlled Oral Word Association Test (10%)
32. Rey Auditory Verbal Learning Test (10%)
33. Luria-Nebraska Battery or Partial Luria (10%)
34. Millon Clinical Multiaxial Inventory (MCMI and MCMI-II) (9%)
35. Rey 15 Item Test (8%)
36. Wahler Physical Symptoms Inventory (8%)
37. Raven's Standard Progressive Matrices (7%)
38. Verbal Fluency (7%)
39. Thematic Apperception Test (6%)
40. IPAT Anxiety Scale (6%)
41. Tactile Form Recognition Test (5%)
42. Benton Visual Retention Test (BVRT) (5%)
43. IPAT Depression Scale (5%)
44. Symptom Check List–90 (SCL-90) and SCL-90-R (5%)

Lees-Haley et al. (1996) noted that consistently across their own studies undertaken in 1980, 1990 and in 1994 the Wechsler Intelligence and Memory scales were in the first ranks.

A similar survey was undertaken by Karen Sullivan and Stephen Bowden (1997) in Australia. All of the members of the Australian Psychological Society College of Clinical Neuropsychologists listed in the 1994 membership directory were mailed an anonymous questionnaire. Two hundred and fourteen people from all states in Australia were contacted, including seven members, 20 associates, 81 affiliates, and 106 full members. One hundred and two useable replies were analysed. The results revealed a similar pattern of test usage in this sample.

1. Wechsler Intelligence Scales (98%)[1]
2. Complex Figure Test (Rey) (88%) [21]
3. Wechsler Memory Scale (83%) [3]
4. Verbal Fluency/Controlled Oral Word Association Test (81%) [31]
5. Trail Making Test (81%) [4 & 5]
6. Rey Auditory Verbal Learning Test (77%) [32]
7. Austin Maze (54%) [not listed]
8. National Adult Reading Test (51%) [not listed]
9. Wisconsin Card Sorting Test (49%) [9]
10. Goldstein Scheerer Colour Form Sorting Test (38%) [not listed]
11. Benton Visual Retention Test (32%) [42]

12. The Beck Depression Inventory (31%) [13]
13. Schonell Graded Word Reading Test (27%) [not listed]
14. Wide Range Achievement Test (23%) [12]
15. Self-reported complaints checklist or questionnaires (19%) [30/44]
16. Porteus Mazes (17%) [not listed]
17. Ravens Progressive Matrices Test (15%) [37]
18. MMPI or MMPI-II (14%) [2]
19. California Verbal Learning Test (14%) [29]
20. Stroop Colour and Word Test (11%) [22].

Numbers in brackets denote the comparable ranking in the 44 tests compiled by Lees-Haley et al. (1996).

Of the clinicians surveyed (Sullivan & Bowden, 1997), 86% had multiple reasons for testing, including assessments to investigate the degree of organic involvement, describing the current functioning, assisting with rehabilitation programs, or providing information in medico-legal cases. Clearly, some of the differences identified between the frequencies noted by Lees-Haley et al. (1996) who investigated forensic assessments and those of Sullivan and Bowden (1997), which investigated a more broadly based sample of clinical practice, were attributable to differences in the reasons for referral.

Nonetheless, the overwhelming similarity in the instruments employed and the frequency with which they were used seems to indicate that these are the instruments that are most commonly employed in most neuropsychological assessment and, as a result, we will use this combined list as the basis on which our brief review of clinical instrumentation is based in the sections below.

There were, however, a number of conspicuous differences between the two lists with the most noticeable difference being the infrequency with which Australian neuropsychologists use the MMPI, as well as the relative absence of tasks that tap into visuomotor and visuoperceptual functions — including the Finger Tapping Test, the Bender Gestalt, various pegboard tests and the sensory and perceptual tests arising from the Halstead Reitan Battery (HRB) (e.g., the Seashore Rhythm Test, the Speech Sounds Perception Test, grip strength). It is difficult to specify why such a marked difference exists, but the tendency for Australian neuropsychologists to favour a 'process' approach— and the fact that in the United States there is a strong tendency for clinical neuropsychologists to also be trained as clinical psychologists (which occurs much less commonly in the Australian context) culminating in a higher emphasis on psychopathological explanations of behaviour — may provide some explanation.

How Many Neuropsychological Functions are There?

As this chapter is intended for the use of the reader who has some knowledge of neuropsychological techniques and theory, it seems unnecessary to detail too many neuropsychological tests. We will thus focus on a select set of instruments, which will be the ones commonly used in forensic and other forms of neuropsychological reports tendered to the courts as outlined in our discussion of the work of Lees-Haley et al. (1996) and Sullivan and Bowden (1997) above. For more detail the reader is directed to recent neuropsychological test compendia (Lezak et al., 2004; Strauss et al., 2006) for an exhaustive listing of neuropsychological instruments.

Using a variety of instruments the clinical neuropsychologist examines and measures a number of higher cortical functions. These instruments will be divided into categories based upon the breakdown of functions outline above. These include:

1. premorbid intellectual functioning
2. achievement measures
3. general intellectual level
4. attention and concentration
5. sensory and perceptual functioning
6. motor functioning
7. processing speed
8. working memory functions
9. speech and language abilities
10. visual spatial abilities
11. memory and new learning
12. executive functions including drive and control
13. emotional and personality functions
14. symptom listing and symptom validity

As we have already noted, cognitive tasks are multifactorial in nature (Brown, 1989) and even the most apparently simple task calls on many, if not all, of the levels of the cognitive hierarchy presented in Figure 3.1. Nonetheless, the assignment of tests to categories will be attempted in line with the available evidence from the literature and if any instrument can be dually classified it will be addressed within each section.

1. PREMORBID INTELLECTUAL FUNCTIONING

In order to provide an assessment of the examinee's present function in comparison to their level of function before the injury (or premorbid functioning), techniques must be employed that are relatively immune to the effects of cerebral insult. As information regarding the individual's premorbid level of functioning in terms of previous standardised testing is not commonly available; the level of the premorbid function must, in most practical situations, be estimated. This can be undertaken either quantitatively or qualitatively.

The assessment of premorbid functioning involves the gathering of previous educational achievement, level of education, performance in the occupational setting, and other vocational achievements including the highest level of employment capacity previously achieved. Inevitably, these techniques rely heavily upon judgments made by the examiner to determine the premorbid level of achievement. This creates the possibility of bias and inaccuracy and, as a result, employment and educational achievement is often combined with standardised tests of premorbid functioning as measured in the present. As a rule, the methods used to estimate premorbid cognitive functioning are based on: (1) demographic information, (2) combined current test performance with demographics (Green, Rohling, Lees-Haley, & Allen, 2001) and (3) current reading (word recognition) ability. These approaches each have drawbacks including difficulty estimating premorbid abilities of people close to the extremes of intellectual functioning (i.e., estimating the premorbid ability of individuals in the gifted or borderline intellectual ranges) (Baade & Schoenberg, 2004).

The 'present abilities' approach is one technique that has been proposed to deal with the problem of estimating premorbid functioning. The can be practiced in either of two ways, the first relies upon the use of the highest subtest score on an instrument such as the Wechsler scales as a means of estimating the premorbid level of the individual. The score on other aspects of the performance is compared to this level and deviance from this level is inferred to represent the level of impairment.

One of the principal problems associated with this technique is that an individual's performance on a test such as the WAIS for example, is intrinsically subject to intersubtest scatter. As a result, it is impossible to determine whether the highest level of performance accurately represents what the individual was capable of before the injury. For example, in the standardisation of the WAIS-III, as with the standardisation of each of the Wechsler scales, the mean of the test is set at 100 and the average subtest score is 10. Nonetheless, of all of the 2,250 individuals on which the standardisation was conducted, no individual in the standardisation sample proved to have a scaled score of 10 on every subtest of the scale. Scatter is intrinsic to the performance of individuals on a test such as the Wechsler scales. That is why this area of scientific enquiry is referred to as individual differences, rather than individual similarities. As a result, this technique should be treated with the utmost caution (Matarazzo, 1990).

The second technique relies upon the fact that some aspects of cognition are affected to a greater degree than are others as a result of cerebral insult. Thus, some subtests within the test battery are considered to be relatively less liable to change than are others. Within the Wechsler scales it has been proposed that the Vocabulary, Comprehension, Similarities and Picture Completion subtests are relatively immune to the effects of brain impairment (e.g., Walsh, 1991). These are often referred to as the 'hold' tests. Thus performances on the other subtests are compared to these and a level of deviation is inferred. The principal problem with this technique is that brain injury is often diffuse rather than specific and, as a consequence, all subtests including the 'hold' tests are subject to change as a consequence of the injury. Thus the examiner is confronted with two sources of unreliability, the first attributable to the unknown change in the hold tests as a consequence of injury, and the second due to the effects of the trauma on the other subtests. Thus although the 'hold' test approach is somewhat better than the highest score approach, it too is subject to imprecision and bias and is best avoided if at all possible (Guilmette & Faust, 1991).

The more reliable technique is found in standardised tests that have been developed with the specific purpose of determining premorbid level of functioning. The most well-researched of these instruments is the National Adult Reading Test (2nd Edition) (Nelson & Willison, 1991). This instrument relies upon two effects commonly noted as a result of brain injury. The first of these is that vocabulary knowledge or 'semantic memory' is relatively immune to cerebral insult and, as a consequence, in most situations is the best preserved of all skills subsequent to injury.[4] The second is that reading ability, particularly the ability to read phonologically irregular words such as 'thyme' or 'syncope', is not commonly reported to alter as a consequence of injury.

National Adult Reading Test (2nd Edition) (NART-2; Nelson & Willison, 1991)
The NART-2 is a word reading list that requires the examinee to read aloud 50 irregular words. The number of errors is used to determine an estimated WAIS-R IQ (Nelson & Willison, 1991). Improvements in the technique by the addition of demographic data (e.g., Crawford, Stewart, Parker, Besson, & Cochrane, 1989) add to precision of the estimate of function. The measurement of premorbid IQ using the NART is, however, subject to a number of qualifications and concerns.

- The range of scores available with the NART is significantly attenuated with scores only possible between predicted full-scale IQs of 69 and 131.
- The approach often underestimates higher IQs and overestimates lower IQs.
- Despite the fact the NART is thought to be relatively immune to deterioration as a consequence of cerebral insult, a number of cases in which deterioration of performance occurred as a consequence of conditions such as schizophrenia have been noted (Crawford, Besson, Bremner, Ebmeier, Cochrane, & Kirkwood, 1992).
- The NART-2 has only been normed to predict performance on the WAIS-R. Flynn (1984, 1987, 1994, 1999) has observed that the norms on an IQ test become outdated at a rate of 3 points per decade; that is, 1/3 to 1/2 of a point per year (the so-called Flynn effect). Thus, in the context of an assessment conducted with the NART-2 in 2008, the accuracy of the estimate would be in error to the tune of 9 IQ points (i.e., 2008–1981, the dates of publication of the WAIS-R and WAIS-IV respectively, × 1/3 = 8.999), rendering the usefulness of this as a predictor of premorbid functioning virtually worthless. Thus scores generated with the instrument produce estimates of functioning that are not in line with the current normative standards of instruments such as the WAIS-III or the WAIS-IV.

The Wechsler Test of Adult Reading (WTAR; PsychCorp, 2001)

The WTAR is an assessment tool used for estimating premorbid intellectual functioning of adults aged 16–89. It was developed and co-normed with WAIS-III and WMS-III, and normed with both US and UK samples. The instrument allows direct comparison between predicted and observed scores on the WAIS-III and WMS-III, and gives discrepancy analysis based on both statistical and clinical significance. The test corrects for age (i.e., two age bands, 16–19 and 20–89, sex, race and the exclusion criteria are the same as those for WAIS-III and WMS-III. The US standardisation sample was 1,134 normals aged between 16–89 with five educational levels: ≤ 8, 9–11, 12, 13–15, 16+, and four racial categories (Whites, African–American, Hispanics and other). With the UK standardisation sample: 331 normals in four age bands: 16–24, 25–44, 45–64, 65–80, with six educational levels: ≤ 8, GCSE, A-Level, Diploma, and Degree.

The WTAR correlates highly with other measures of reading recognition (e.g., the American version of the Nelson Adult Reading Test [AMNART; Grober & Sliwinski, 1991] 0.9, NART 0.78, WRAT-R 0.73), with measures of verbal intelligence (e.g., ranging from .66–.8 with WAIS-III VIQ, .63–8 with FSIQ and less so with PIQ .45–.66; VCI .61–.8, POI .42–.65, WMI .5–

.73, PSI .19–.6), is quick and easy to administer and is normed to predict WAIS-III and WMS-III scores. It has a good sample size and good internal consistency, including test–retest stability and reliabilities (≥ .9).

It is thus preferable to NART-R, but suffers from the same problems as all similar tasks:

- There is no Australian standardisation sample, although there is a sample drawn from the United Kingdom (if this comparison could still be considered more comparable nowadays).
- The spread of scores can be broad (i.e., 95% CI ± 8.1).
- Inevitably it predicts verbal functions better than performance or memory functions; demographic adjustment does improve the estimates but only to a small extent and it is not impervious to disease but generally does hold up quite well.
- The test should not be used for individuals with reading difficulties, developmental language disorder, paediatric brain insult, aphasia, alexia and individuals from non-English-speaking backgrounds (NESB).
- The best results are achieved with the combined demographic and WTAR performances.
- It should not be used for estimating at the high (i.e., 130+) or low (70–) extremes where the utmost caution must be employed.
- If the difference between the demographic prediction and the WTAR performance are greater than 20 do not use the test.

Some evaluation of the application of the WTAR has taken place in the Australian context (Mathias, Bowden, & Barrett-Woodbridge, 2007) and caution has been urged in the use of the instrument due to the fact that while all IQ estimates were related to ability levels, both the WTAR and the NART-2 tended to overestimate the IQs of persons who were below average in ability and to underestimate the IQs of those were of high average or above average ability. As always, constant vigilance in the use of such an instrument is necessary.

The Test Of Premorbid Functioning (TOPF; PsychCorp, 2009)

The TOPF is the updated revision of the WTAR, which predicts performance on the WAIS-IV. The test is similar in form to the WTAR but with 70 rather than 50 words and is based upon a reading paradigm requiring the client to read and pronounce words that have irregular grapheme-to-phoneme translation (PsychCorp, 2009). As already noted, the issues that apply to these tasks (i.e., the degree to which these tests are impervious to cognitive dysfunction, status with regard to language functioning and the other cautions noted above all still apply to the TOPF), but because it is the most recently normed test, it is to be preferred as the means of predicting premorbid level of functioning.

2. ACHIEVEMENT MEASURES

Achievement measures reflect competence that has arisen from specific instruction or learning experiences. Most commonly, these reflect skills that are acquired in the educational setting and tend to focus on competence in basic literacy and numeracy including reading, writing and arithmetic.

Schonnell Graded Word Reading Test (SGWRT; Shearer & Apps, 1975)

The SGWRT is a graded series of regular words that the examinee must read out aloud. This allows a means of establishing an estimated level of intelligence by ascertaining reading level.

Wide Range Achievement Test-4 (WRAT4; Wilkinson & Robertson, 2006)

The WRAT4 is a quick, simple, and psychometrically sound measure of fundamental academic skills. It is the latest version of this test that was first published in 1946.

This test assesses the ability of an individual to perform standardised tasks of reading, writing, and arithmetic. The score in each of these domains allows an estimate of intellectual performance as a result of academic skill. The performance on the test allows the determination of the examinee's academic achievement in terms of grade level, standard score and percentile rank in comparison to the normative sample. The technique is also useful in ascertaining the examinee's performance with regard to specific learning disabilities.

Wechsler Individual Achievement Test-2nd Ed (WIAT-II; The Psychological Corporation Corporation, 2001)

The Wechsler Individual Achievement Test — Second Edition (WIAT-II) is a revision of the Wechsler Individual Achievement Test (WIAT; The Psychological Corporation, 1992). The areas covered by the test remain the same, but the depth and range of subject matter has been increased, with some new items and updates of content to reflect changes in curriculum standards. The subtests include: pseudoword decoding, reading comprehension, spelling, written expression, numerical operations, math reasoning, listening comprehension and oral expression. One particular benefit of the WIAT-II is that it is standardised to produce scores that are directly comparable to those arising from the standardisation of the WAIS-III. I feel sure that in the not too distant future, the development of the WIAT will correspond to similar performances on the WAIS-IV.

3. GENERAL INTELLECTUAL LEVEL

Intelligence testing has an extensive history within the history of psychology, and numerous debates regarding this matter have often bought the discipline to the focus of the general public. Nonetheless, the measurement of intelligence has become accepted in the wider community and is used for a number of roles in the forensic arena. The testing of intelligence involves the measurement of an omnibus series of skills that come under the umbrella of cognition, and inevitably not all of these are measured equally well by all instruments. At the very least, a test of intelligence should measure the skills of: attention, working memory, processing speed, abstract reasoning, memory, language, perceptual and constructional skill, and executive functions. The gold standard in the area has been set by the five revisions of the Wechsler Scales (Wechsler-Bellevue; Wechsler Adult Intelligence Scale [WAIS]; Wechsler Adult Intelligence Scale — Revised [WAIS-R], the Wechsler Adult Intelligence Scale-III: [WAIS-III] and the Wechsler Adult Intelligence Scale-IV: [WAIS-IV]).

Wechsler is also responsible for considerable speculation about the nature of intelligence and his definition has been widely accepted as the benchmark in intelligence testing. Wechsler originally defined intelligence as: 'the capacity of the individual to act purposefully, to think rationally, and to deal effectively with his environment' (Wechsler, 1945, p. 3).

While a number of instruments have been developed to measure adult intelligence including the Stanford Binet intelligence scale (Thorndike, Hagen, & Sattler, 1986), the Woodcock Johnson Psycho-educational battery (Woodcock, McGrew, & Mather, 2000) and the Kaufman Adolescent and Adult Intelligence Test (KAAIT; Kaufman & Kaufman, 1993) among others, far and away the most commonly employed tests of intelligence are those developed by David Wechsler. As we noted above, both in the United States (Lees-Haley et al., 1996) as well as in Australia (Sullivan & Bowden, 1997), the Wechsler scales represent the most commonly employed neuropsychological instrument. In a similar vein, Camara and colleagues (Camara, Nathan, & Puente, 2000) collected data on tests usage from a large pool of clinical psychologists and clinical neuropsychologists randomly selected from the membership lists of the American Psychological Association and the National Academy of Neuropsychology. The final sample consisted only of those clinicians who were engaged in 5 or more hours per week of assessment-related service delivery. The final sample included 179 clinical psychologists and 447 neuropsychologists. Of these clinicians, the largest share of time spent conducting assessments was in the domains of intellectual or achievement testing (34%) and personality testing (32%). In the study, clinical psychologists ranked the WAIS-R as the number one test administered, and clinical neuropsychologists ranked it number two. A survey of 402 US clinical psychologists indicated that 97% use the WAIS or WAIS-R when administering an adult measure of intelligence (Kaufman, 1990).

In fact, the influence of David Wechsler on this area of enquiry is so pervasive that he is still capable of exerting a powerful influence on the area, even following his own death. Interestingly,

> … although Wechsler's name is still listed as the author of all revisions since his death in 1981, this most likely reflects contractual obligations. The publishers of the Wechsler Scales, as well as the work group organized by the publisher, are more accurately responsible for the slow, incremental changes in the Wechsler Scales. Historical continuity and tradition (have) apparently played a stronger role in the revisions of the Wechsler Scales. (Flanagan, McGrew, & Ortiz, 2000, p. 10)

Wechsler Adult Intelligence Scale-IV (WAIS-IV; Wechsler, 2008c)

The WAIS-IV is a compendium of 10 obligatory and five supplemental subtests. The WAIS-IV provides a measure of general intellectual functioning (Full-Scale IQ, FSIQ) and four index scores. It should be noted that the WAIS-IV no longer observes the tradition noted in previous versions of the scales of making a distinction between Verbal versus Performance IQ. Due to the psychometric properties of the scales from the WAIS-R onwards, the factor scores have proven to be more reliable than the individual subtest scores of which they are composed, and are therefore preferable in the interpretation of the performance (Wechsler, 1997a, 2008c). The four indices are: the Verbal Comprehension Index (Core Subtests: Similarities, Vocabulary, Information; Supplemental Subtests: Comprehension); the Perceptual Reasoning Index (Core Subtests: Block Design, Matrix Reasoning, Visual Puzzles; Supplemental Subtests: Picture Completion, Figure Weights), the Working Memory Index (Core Subtests: Digit Span Arithmetic, Supplemental Subtest: Letter–Number Sequencing) and the Processing Speed Index (Core Subtests: Symbol Search, Coding ; Supplemental Subtest: Cancellation).

The description of the subtests as adapted from the *Administration and Scoring Manual of the WAIS-IV* (Wechsler, 2008b; pp. 12–17) is presented below.

Verbal Comprehension Index

Core Subtests:

- Similarities: a series of orally presented pairs of words for which the examinee explains the similarity of the common objects or concepts that they represent.

- Vocabulary: a series of orally and visually presented words that the examinee orally defines.
- Information: a series of orally presented questions that tap the examinee's knowledge of common events, objects, places and people.

Supplemental Subtests:

- Comprehension: a series or orally presented questions that require the examinee to understand and articulate social rules and concepts or solutions to everyday problems.

Perceptual Reasoning Index

Core Subtests:

- Block Design: a set of modelled or printed two-dimensional geometric patterns that the examinee reproduces using two colour cubes.
- Matrix Reasoning: a series of incomplete gridded patterns that the examinee completes by pointing to or saying the number of the correct response from five possible choices.
- Visual Puzzles: the examinee views a completed puzzle and selects three options which, when combined, reconstruct the original design.

Supplemental Subtests:

- Picture Completion, a set of colour pictures of common objects and settings, each of which is missing an important detail that the examinee must identify.
- Figure Weights: the examinee views a scale with missing weights and is required to select the response option that keeps the scale balanced.

Working Memory Index

Core Subtests:

- Digit Span: a series of orally presented number sequences that the examinee repeats verbatim for Digits Forward, in reverse order for Digits Backwards and in ascending order in the case of Digit Span Sequencing.
- Arithmetic: a series of arithmetic problems that the examinee solves mentally and responds to orally.

Supplemental Subtest:

- Letter–Number Sequencing: a series of orally presented sequences of letters and numbers that the examinee simultaneously tracks and orally repeats, with the numbers in ascending order and the letters in alphabetical order.

Processing Speed Index

Core Subtests:

- Symbol Search: a series of paired groups, each pair consisting of a target group and a search group. The examinee indicates, by marking the appropriate box, whether either target symbol appears in the search group.
- Coding: a series of numbers, each of which is paired with its own corresponding hieroglyphic-like symbol. Using a key, the examinee writes the symbol corresponding to its number.

Supplemental Subtest:

- Cancellation: the examinee scans an arrangement of shapes and marks the designated target shapes.

The WAIS-IV was normed on a stratified random sample of 2,200 individuals ranging in age from 16 to 90 years 11 months and stratified on key demographic variables including age, sex, education, and geographical region according to the U.S. census data. As such, the WAIS-IV has the largest available normative database of a psychological test battery available in use at this time. The database also allows the examiner to determine how a given individual performs relative to the standardisation sample. Thus, comparison of base rate performance for the individual can be compared to those noted for the standardisation sample, and determinations can be made as to whether the scores are statistically different from each other, and if such a difference is common or uncommon as compared to the available base rate data. Observing differences which are uncommon in the standardisation sample would indicate that the difference may also be clinically significant in comparison to the standardisation sample. Another advantage of the WAIS-IV (as with the WAIS-III) is that it was co-normed with the Wechsler Memory Scale Version IV (WMS-IV), which allows direct comparisons between the intelligence scale and the memory scale performances.

4. ATTENTION AND CONCENTRATION

The ability to attend and concentrate is at the core of neuropsychological functioning. It is only by being able to focus attention and to maintain this focus over the duration of the assessment process that the examinee can participate effectively in the assessment process. At the very least, attention includes such processes as orienting towards a stimulus, selection (i.e., attending to one stimulus in comparison to a variety of other competing stimuli) and sustaining the focus of attention (Kinsella, 1998). The definition of attention has become an increasingly thorny issue in neuropsychological theory, and considerable speculation as to what attention is and how it might be measured has transpired (e.g., Kinsella, 1998). There is no denying that the construct of attention is a useful one; however, which skills this involves and how these skills can be dissociated from other cognitive domains such as working memory and executive functions remains to be finally clarified. Nonetheless, a number of measures of attention do exist and in addition to the list presented below we could also usefully add tests of simple and choice reaction time; tests of attention span such as forward span of digits, locations in space, tones or other serially presented sequences; tests of letter or symbol cancellation, as well as tests of attention to the entire visual field with a view to assessing hemineglect, such as line bisection or cancellation tasks.

Paced Auditory Serial Additions Test (PASAT; Gronwall, 1977)

The PASAT requires the examinee to listen to an audio recording of a series of single digits. The examinee is required to add each number to the one immediately preceding it. So the first number is added to the second and the sum is presented by the examinee and then the second to the third and so one. This proceeds for a total of 61 digits. The test can be given at different rates of presentation from the slower rate at one digit every 2.4 seconds to the fastest rate of one digit every 1.2 seconds. The test assesses both attention and vigilance, as the examinee is required to recall the numbers in sequence and to respond to the cumulative addition. Clearly, while the test is assessing attention and concentration, working memory functions are also implicated in the performance (Tombaugh, 2006).

Stroop Colour Word Task (Stroop, 1935)

This is a task that consists of either two (Trennery, Crosson, DeBoe, & Leber, 1989) or three (e.g., Stroop, 1935) trials in which the examinee is required to read the names of colours as quickly as possible and then to identify the colour of a series of coloured dots, and finally and most importantly to name the colour of the ink in which a number of colour names have been printed. The colour name does not match the colour of the ink. The task allows the determination of the examinee's ability to respond rapidly and most importantly their ability to be able to inhibit the reading the colour name as opposed to presenting the colour of the ink. The test is an excellent indicator of the loss of control of attentional functioning in maintaining focus on the rule governing the response (i.e., read out the colour of the ink in which the words are printed). Thus, while the test is most commonly considered to be a test of attentional functioning, it also draws heavily upon the skills of response inhibition and response activation (due to the suppression of the dominant response to read the word instead of present the colour of the script) indicating that it also draws upon executive (frontal lobe) functioning requiring flexibility of responding, inhibition of inappropriate responding and response alternation.

5. SENSORY AND PERCEPTUAL FUNCTIONING

The ability to be able to perceive the stimuli in a neuropsychological assessment is one of the basic requirements for an assessment to take place. Thus, tests of visual, auditory and tactile perception are commonly undertaken to ensure appropriate encoding of the stimulus material to ensure that deficits do not exist in the area of sensory responsivity. If sensory deficits are identified the examiner can amend test procedures to compensate or circumvent the impact of the difficulty in the encoding of information. One of the most difficult issues to address in neuropsychological assessment is how and whether the assessment may take place in the context of the examinee from a non-English-speaking background. Some investigation of this area has taken place (e.g., Carstairs, Myors, Shores, & Fogarty, 2006); however, it still presents a very real problem to ascertain how much of the information presented has been encoded by the examinee, and how much of the response produced is accurately relayed to the examiner. Clearly, in the context of assessment undertaken through interpreters, every caution in interpretation of the results as well as the implications of these to the presenting condition must be exercised. We will discuss this issue more extensively in Chapter 9.

Tactual Performance Test (TPT; Reitan & Wolfson, 1993b)

The TPT assesses tactile form perception, form and spatial learning and recall (Lezak et al., 2004). This task relies upon the use of one of several versions of the Seguin-Goddard form board. The examinee is blindfolded and is required to insert the forms into the board over three trials with the preferred and the nonpreferred hands and then with both hands. The score for each trial is the time taken to locate all 10 shapes. On completion of the trials the examinee is required to draw the board from memory.

Reitan Kløve Sensory Perceptual Examination (Reitan & Wolfson, 1993b)

This test is part of the HRB, in which the examinee is required to complete the two subtests: fingertip number writing and tactile finger recognition. In the first task, the examinee must identify numbers written on to the fingertips without visual guidance. In the second, the examinee must identify which finger has been touched by the examiner without visual guidance.

Seashore Rhythm Test (SRT; Reitan & Wolfson, 1993b)

This test is part of the HRB, in which the examinee listens to a series of rhythms recorded on audio tape and must determine whether the rhythms are the same or different. The test items begin with relatively few beats and progress through to items containing many beats. As the examinee must remember both the example rhythm and the choice foil, the task also probably calls upon immediate memory and attentional functioning.

Speech Sounds Perception Test (SSPT; Reitan & Wolfson, 1993b)

This test is also part of the HRB, in which the examinee listens to 60 nonsense syllables recorded on audio tape and must choose among four options of the printed version of the sound, the sound that was heard. One problem in the administration of this procedure is that individuals with a loss of the high frequency sounds such as occurs in industrial deafness may have difficulty in hearing the stimuli.

Lateral Dominance Examination (Reitan & Wolfson, 1993b)

This includes a number of procedures for measuring hand preference, and foot and eye dominance and grip strength, as well as questions about lateral preferences.

Tactile Form Recognition Test (S. Weinstein, 1978)

This test requires the examinee to recognise geometric forms placed in one hand while hidden from view, and to identify a drawing of the object presented in a multiple-choice format.

6. MOTOR FUNCTIONING

Within the neuropsychological assessment, measurement of motor performance is essential to ascertain whether failure in the performance of the given task is occurring as a consequence of processes associated with higher levels of cognitive functioning or to lower-level motor responses. Comprehensive assessment of motor functioning allows the examiner to make the distinction at which level of the hierarchy of cognitive skills the deficit is occurring.

Finger Tapping Test (also known as the Finger Oscillation Test; Reitan & Wolfson, 1993b)

This is a test of the primary motor speed of the index finger of each hand. Examinees tap a finger as quickly as possible for 10 seconds. The test usually consists of five trials with each hand. Large differences between left and right finger speed may reflect compromise to the opposite cerebral hemisphere

Grooved Pegboard (Kløve, 1963)

This is a complicated pegboard task that consists of a 5 × 5 set of slotted holes angled in different directions. Each peg has a ridge along one side that requires it to be rotated into position for correct insertion. The complexity of the task makes it very sensitive to slowing of motor responses. This score is the time required to locate all of the pegs. Both hands should be tested.

Grip Strength: (Reitan & Wolfson, 1993b)

This test measures grip strength in each hand using a hand-held dynamometer. Examinees are given three trials with each hand, with the first usually considered to be a practice. Large differences between left and right grip strength may reflect compromise to the opposite cerebral hemisphere.

7. PROCESSING SPEED

Processing speed is a relatively new concept in neuropsychological theory and is conceptualised as a measure of the individual's ability to process visual information quickly. Speed of processing is very sensitive to many different neuropsychological conditions, and in subtle conditions such as minor traumatic brain injury (TBI), it may be the only detectable deficit. The Coding and Symbol Search subtests make up the 'Processing Speed' factor in the WAIS-IV and the Symbol Digit Modalities Test is reported to be highly correlated with the Coding subtest (Wechsler, 1997a, 2008c). Both of these instruments represent excellent means of assessing this construct.

Symbol Digit Modalities Test (SDMT; Smith, 1982)

The SDMT is similar to the Digit Symbol-Coding subtest of the WAIS-III, except that the examinee writes the number corresponding to its symbol. The SDMT also has the advantage of both an oral and written response modalities. The task measures complex scanning and visual tracking (Shum, McFarland, & Bain, 1990) as well as having its principal weighting on processing speed (Crowe, Benedict et al., 1999).

Trail Making Test (TMT; Army Individual Test Battery, 1944)

The TMT was originally developed as part of the Army Individual Test Battery (US Army, 1944) and is one of the most commonly used tests in neuropsychological practice due to its high sensitivity in diagnosing brain impairment (Armitage, 1946; Lewinsohn, 1973; Reitan, 1986; Spreen & Benton, 1965). The original and most commonly used form of the task requires the subject to perform a tracking task under two conditions. In the first part of the test (Trails A), the subject must trace a trail through a series of circles numbered from 1 through to 25 variously spread over an A4 page. In the second part of the test (Trails B) the subject must perform an alternation between circles containing numbers and letters. The sequence proceeds from the first number to the first letter alphabetically and then to the second number and the second letter. TMT (B) contains 13 circles numbered 1 to 13, alternating with 12 circles lettered A to L. While the task is an excellent index of the presence of brain impairment, poor performance on the task is relatively nonspecific in so far as it does not indicate why the brain impaired individual is performing poorly and this may be attributable to motor slowing, poor coordination, visual scanning difficulties, poor motivation or conceptual confusion (Lezak et al., 2004) to name only a few possible causes. Performance on Trail A uniquely assesses visual search and motor speed, while performance on Trail B uniquely assesses visual search and ability to be able to alternate between the two sequences (Crowe, 1998b). The performance on TMT(B) can be quite illuminating as it can indicate concreteness in idea generation and disinhibition, useful indicators of impairment of the executive functions.

Different forms of the trail making test and adaptations of it have been used in a number of test batteries, including the DKEFS (Delis et al., 2001) (i.e., trials for: visual scanning, number sequencing, letter sequencing, number–letter switching [set-shifting], and motor speed conditions) and elaborations of the task itself, such as the development of the more culturally fair, Color Trails Test (D'Elia, Satz, Uchiyama, & White, 1996), has added to the usefulness of this important neuropsychological instrument.

8. WORKING MEMORY FUNCTIONS

Working memory is a term that has come in to currency in the contemporary neuropsychological literature and is best thought of as a person's information-processing capacity (Baddeley, 2000; Baddeley & Hitch, 1974). The concept of working memory has replaced the concept of short-term memory in contemporary discussion. As the technical manual of the WAIS-III and WMS-III (Corporation, 1997) notes:

> Short-term memory is viewed as a passive form of memory, whereas working memory is viewed as an active form. Traditional short-term memory refers to the passive storage of information while that information either becomes encoded into long-term memory or is forgotten. Working memory, on the other hand, serves as more than a temporary storage space for incoming information. Rather, it is where calculations and manipulations of information occur … The examinee must first process or transform this information and then retain the end product. (p. 5)

The best measures of working memory include a number of the subtests and indices from the Wechsler scales including the Working Memory Indices

(WMI) of the WAIS-IV and WMS-IV, which are respectively composed of the Arithmetic and Digit Span core subtest and the Letter Number Sequencing supplementary subtest in the case of the WAIS-IV, yielding the auditory working memory index (WMI); and the Spatial Addition and Symbol span subsets of the WMS-IV yielding a visual working memory index (VWMI). Another good test of working memory functions is the Brown Peterson technique (Petersen & Petersen, 1959), which requires the examinee to re-present a string of letters after completing various durations of serial subtraction.

9. SPEECH AND LANGUAGE ABILITIES

Disturbances in language function are one of the most notable deficits associated with brain impairment. They can occur as a consequence of specific brain lesions such as in the case of stroke or tumour, or due to generalised deterioration as a result of degenerative conditions such as Alzheimer's disease. Most assessments of language function include investigation of receptive (i.e., comprehension of speech or written material) as well as expressive functions (i.e., solicitation of spontaneous speech, confrontational naming, repetition of words or phrases and writing). While a comprehensive neuropsychological examination should include assessment of disruption of language functioning, it is not uncommon in the Australian context for the assessment to be conducted in tandem with a well-qualified speech pathologist who would comment on the more explicit deficits in language function. A number of batteries of language function have been developed over the years including the Boston Diagnostic Aphasia Examination (Goodglass et al., 2001), and the Multilingual Aphasia Examination (Benton, Hamsher, & Sivan, 1994) as well as other tests of specific functions such as the Token Test (De Renzi & Vignolo, 1962), which specifically assesses comprehension and the Boston Naming Test (Kaplan et al., 1976).

Aphasia Screening Test (Reitan & Wolfson, 1993b)

This test is part of the HRB and is composed of 32 items that assess reading, articulation, spelling, repetition, naming, calculation and construction. Administration takes approximately 15 to 30 minutes and, as each ability is only assessed by only one or two items, the range of abilities is not great. The instrument is really more of a screening test than one for fine-grained differential diagnosis.

Boston Naming Test (BNT; Kaplan et al., 1976)

The BNT requires the examinee to name 60 objects depicted in line drawings. The items range in difficulty from commonly encountered household items such as a pencil or a pair of scissors through to more rarely encountered items such as an abacus or a protractor. If the examinee is unable to name the object immediately, he or she is given a semantic (i.e., it is used for calculation) or a phonemic cue (i.e., ab. ...). The BNT is an excellent measure of confrontational naming ability, a function often compromised in degenerative disorders most notably Alzheimer's disease (Crowe, Dingjan, & Helme, 1997; Crowe & Hoogenraad, 2000), and also as a result of TBI (Bittner & Crowe, 2006b).

10. VISUO-SPATIAL ABILITIES

Visuo-spatial abilities include a number of functional areas of cognition including localisation in both central and peripheral vision; colour and depth perception; perception of line orientation; perception and recognition of shapes and faces; mental rotation and transformations in space; personal rotation and orientation in space; spatial memory; right–left orientation; visual integration and disintegration; complex visuo-spatial functioning including drawing, copying, and constructional abilities; perceptual closure and gestalt; multifactorial spatial functions including complex information processing and transformation involving a combination of visuo-spatial and visual constructional skills that include a planning component (Waterfall & Crowe, 1995).

Bender-Gestalt Test (Bender, 1938)

This is a drawing test that requires the examinee to copy a set of nine designs on to a sheet of plain paper. The instruction to the examinee is to 'just copy the card as exactly as you can'. The test is generally considered a good indicator of the integrity of the parietal lobes (Lezak et al., 2004).

Hooper Visual Organization Test (HVOT; Hooper, 1958)

The HVOT presents the examinee with 30 easily recognised objects that have been cut into parts, like a jigsaw puzzle, and presented in a random array on a printed page. The examinee is required to identify each object. To successfully perform the task, the examinee must mentally reorganise the decomposed picture into a sensible whole. Thus the performance assesses the ability to be able to integrate parts to make a whole, constructional skills and visual perceptual skills generally.

Rey Osterreith Complex Figure Design Test (RCFT; Osterreith, 1944)

The RCFT is a two-component task that requires the examinee in the first instance to copy the complicated design on to a sheet of paper and then at varying periods of time thereafter to reproduce the design from memory. Some forms of the task also include a recognition trial (Meyers & Meyers, 1995). The task is often considered both a test of visuo-spatial planning and draughtsmanship skills, as well as a test of visuo-spatial memory. The task also has a parallel form, the Taylor figure (Taylor, 1969, 1979), which is useful for reassessment (Strauss & Spreen, 1990).

Human Figure Drawing Tests

These are a variety of drawing tasks (i.e., Draw-a-man, House–tree–person tests) that require the examinee to complete tests of free drawing. These types of tests have a long history in both personality and neuropsychological batteries, as well as being popular techniques for the assessment of children's mental abilities. The tests are simple to administer and are untimed. A number of different scoring techniques are available, as well as allowing scope for qualitative interpretation of constructional skills, draughtsmanship and planning.

Raven's Standard Progressive Matrices (J. Raven, Raven, & Court, 1998; J.C. Raven, Court, & Raven, 1995)

The RPM (including the Colour Progressive Matrices, Standard Progressive Matrices and the Advanced Progressive Matrices) are a series of matrix-solving tasks that measure visual concept formation and problem-solving. The examinee is presented with an array of items that are linked by a common rule. It is the task of the examinee to determine which of a series of six choice foils correctly completes the sequence.

11. MEMORY AND NEW LEARNING

Squire (1987) has provided an excellent definition of the distinction between learning and memory: 'learning is the process of acquiring new information, while memory refers to the persistence of learning in a state that can be revealed at a later time' (p. 3). The assessment of memory and new learning is one of the crucial and the most unique assessments undertaken in neuropsychological testing. Memory is not a unitary function, however, and contemporary speculation regarding memory function (e.g., Squire & Kandel, 1999) has suggested that there may be at least five forms of long-term memory store (episodic, semantic, skill learning, priming and conditioning).

One of the principal dissociations that is drawn in memory research is between memory that is a subject to conscious recall (i.e., declarative memory including episodic and semantic memory) and memory that can occur in the absence of awareness (i.e., nondeclarative, implicit or procedural memory) including skill learning, priming and conditioning. All standard tests of memory focus on the measurement of declarative memory. A further distinction is drawn in the context of declarative memory, which divides the concept into two components: semantic memory; knowledge of words and other aspects of facts and information obtained about the world that are context-free; and episodic memory — the ability to be able to recall particular events and episodes that are defined by the context in which the episode occurred (Squire & Kandel, 1999). While it is possible that these represent a continuum of learning experiences, they can be delineated from each other as most aspects of semantic memory are generally preserved following brain injury, while episodic memory is considerably more subject to change as a consequence of injury.

Austin (Milner) Maze Test

The AMT is a 10 × 10 press-button maze that requires the examinee to find a pathway through the maze contingent upon machine-generated feedback. The task is an excellent test of visual memory and visuo-spatial problem-solving (Crowe, Barclay et al., 1999). The test is commonly used in Australia (Sullivan & Bowden, 1997), where it is also considered to be a measure of executive functions, including high-level planning and response inhibition, but is rarely if ever used in the United States or in other jurisdictions.

Benton Visual Retention Test (BVRT; Benton, 1974)

This test has three forms C, D, and E, each composed of 10 plates that feature three figures, usually two large and one small one. The smaller figure is usually to one side, which makes it particularly sensitive to visual inattention problems. The examinee is required to reproduce the designs on paper after a 10-second exposure. The test is sensitive to deficits in visuo-spatial memory and recall.

California Verbal Learning Test (CVLT/California Verbal Learning Test-Second Edition (CVLT-II; Delis et al., 1999; Delis et al., 1987)

The CVLT is a variant of the Rey Auditory Verbal Learning Test (RAVLT-see below) that increases the number of words in each list to 16 and arranges these into four semantic categories. The testing procedure is very similar to the RAVLT but also includes a cued recall trial with the semantic categories that are provided to aid recall. The test is an excellent index of auditory verbal learning and recall, as well as providing information on cueing and semantic encoding as aids to recall and recognition. In the WMS-IV (Wechsler, 2009c) it is possible to substitute the performance on the CVLT-II for the performance of the Verbal Paired Associates learning test, which allows for economy of testing for those individuals who choose to administer both the WMS-IV as well as a list-learning task

Rey Auditory Verbal Learning Test (RAVLT; Rey, 1964)

The RAVLT is a test of verbal learning and recall that requires the examinee to learn a list of 15 words across five trials. After the list is read out each time, the examinee is asked to recall as many words as possible. Following the fifth repetition of the list, an intervening list is presented, and again the examinee is asked to recall as many items as possible. This trial acts as an interference trial resulting in retroactive interference. After the intervening list, the examinee is again asked to recall as many items as possible from the first list. Following this, a recognition trial is given during which the examinee must identify as many of the words on the first list as possible from either a list of words or a prose passage. The test provides a very rich source of data, including measurement of immediate verbal memory (word span), rate of learning across the trials, the effects of both retroactive and proactive interference and recognition performance.

The Wechsler Memory Scale-IV (WMS-IV; Wechsler, 2009c)

The WMS-IV consists of seven subtests, four of which have both immediate and delayed recall conditions. The scale is divided into four domains: auditory memory, visual memory, visual working memory, immediate memory and delayed memory. There are two batteries included in the WMS-IV, one for clients aged between 16 and 69 and an older adult battery for clients aged between 65 and 90. The WMS-IV also includes a brief cognitive status examination, which is an extension of the information and orientation components from the WMS-III that is included as a part of the cognitive screening component of the examination.

The subtests that constitute the auditory memory index include the logical memory and the verbal paired associates. The subtests that constitute the visual memory factor include the designs and visual reproduction subtests. In each case the subtests that constitute these factors have both an immediate and delayed recall trial. The subtests that constitute the visual working memory domain are composed of the spatial addition and symbol span subtests. The WMS-IV provides five index scores: the auditory memory index, the visual memory index, the visual working memory index, the immediate memory index, and the delayed memory index. The WMS-IV also provides for a number of contrasts between the components of the scale, including the contrast between the auditory and visual memory indices, between the visual working memory and visual memory indices and between the immediate memory index and delayed memory indices. The subtests of the scale include:

The cognitive state examination. This subtest assesses a variety of cognitive functions and the client performs a number of different tasks, including demonstrating orientation in time, mental control, drawing, incidental recall, automatic and inhibitory control and verbal production.

Logical memory. This subtest has been a constant feature of the Wechsler memory scale from its inception in the 1940s (Wechsler, 1945) and involves the recall of narrative memory of two prose passages of information (each containing 25 items of information) under a free recall condition, both immediately and after a 20–30 minute delay. The task also includes a recognition trial.

Verbal paired associates. This is another task that has featured in all of the revisions of the WMS (Wechsler, 1945, 1987, 1997b, 2009c). It requires the client to form an association between a series of word pairs, some more frequently associated and some less so. After the word pairs are read to the client, the first item of each pair is presented and the client is asked to provide the corresponding pair. The list of pairs is presented four times. The task includes immediate and delayed recall trials as well as a recognition trial.

Designs. This subtest assesses spatial memory for unfamiliar visual material. The examinee is shown a picture of a grid with four to eight nonsense designs inserted into it for a duration of 10 seconds and then is provided a set of cards (the correct designs plus and equal number of foils) for each item. The client is required to place the correct design in the correct location on the grid. The task includes immediate and delayed recall trials as well as a recognition trial. The task is very similar to the Visual Spatial learning Test (VSLT) developed by Malec, Ivnik and Hinkeldey (Malec, Ivnik, & Hinkeldey, 1991).

Visual reproduction. This subtest involves the reproduction of five geometric designs, which are exposed for a duration of 10 seconds. The client must reproduce a drawing of the design after the removal of the item. The task includes immediate and delayed recall trials as well as a recognition trial.

Spatial addition. This task assesses visuo-spatial working memory, using a visual addition task, similar in form to the n-back tasks of visuo-spatial attention (Owen, McMillan, Laird, & Bullmore, 2005) that have been used extensively in the primate and neuroimaging literature.

Symbol span. This task assesses visual working memory, using novel visual stimuli. The examinee is shown a series of symbols on a page for a duration of 10 seconds and is then asked to select the previously presented symbols in the same sequence that was presented on the example page from an array of symbols.

The WMS-IV represents a further incremental development of the Wechsler Memory Scale, with theoretical and practical improvements over its predecessors. It represents the most comprehensively and recently normed battery of memory available in the current literature.

12. EXECUTIVE (FRONTAL) FUNCTIONS, INCLUDING PLANNING AND CONTROL

The executive functions involve the ability to generate goals, formulate plans to achieve these, evaluate the efficacy of the plan's ability to achieve the desired goal, and to modify and update these plans contingent upon their success. Executive function can thus be divided into two principal areas of function: drive or the ability to be able to generate goals and ambitions; and control, the ability to be able to restrain behaviour in such a way as to achieve one's desired ambitions within socially acceptable parameters (Crowe, 1992; Tate, 1987). Traditionally, executive functions have been ascribed to the frontal lobes, although most investigators now accept that executive functions can be compromised as a result of injuries to areas of the brain other than the frontal lobes and the notion of a distributed frontal/subcortical network is now considered to more accurately reflect the clinical reality (Lichter & Cummings, 2001).

Category Test (CT; Reitan & Wolfson, 1993b)

This test is part of the HRB and tests visual concept formation. The examinee is shown a set of four transparency slides or a booklet form of the stimuli, which has a unifying concept underlying each example. The examinee must identify the concept presented on each slide. This takes place over six sets of slides, and the examination includes a final set of slides viewed in the previous sets as a test of the examinee's recall of the solutions. The task is thus a measure of nonverbal reasoning and concept formation and is one of the more sensitive measures of the HRB.

Controlled Oral Word Association (i.e., Verbal Fluency) Test (COWAT; Benton et al., 1994)

The COWAT assesses the ability of the examinee to generate words in response to a letter (phonological fluency: FAS test) or to a semantic category (e.g., fruits or occupations). The search is governed by a number of rules including the exclusion of proper nouns, numbers, homophones and different forms of the same word. The technique has been found to be a sensitive indicator of brain dysfunction (Lezak et al., 2004), and has been widely employed in a variety of assessments and has been included in the DKEFS battery of executive functioning (Delis et al., 2001). Frontal lesions, particularly those of the left side, cause depression of fluency (Miceli, Caltagirone, Gainotti, Masullo, & Silveri, 1981; Perret, 1974). Benton (1968) for example, has found that patients with left-sided damage produced one third less words than those with right-sided lesions, while those with bilateral involvement had even greater reductions in performance on the task. The COWAT is thus an excellent test of language functions, as well as a useful index of executive functions including disorders of drive and disorders of control (Bittner & Crowe, 2006a, 2007; Crowe, 1992, 1996a, 1996b, 1997, 1998a; Crowe & Bittner, 2001).

Goldstein Scheerer Colour Form Sorting Test (CFS; Goldstein & Sheerer, 1941)

This test consists of 12 tokens coloured red, blue, yellow or green on top and white underneath, which come in three shapes, round, square or triangular. The examinee is asked to sort the shapes into groups and after this has been successfully undertaken, the examinee then is asked to sort them a different way. This simple test relies on the rigidity associated with executive deficits that makes it difficult for the examinee to shift set once the task has been viewed in a particular way. It is a useful test for individuals with relatively severe compromise of executive functions, but less so for less severely impaired individuals where other tasks such as the WCST may be more responsive.

Porteus Mazes Tests (PMT; Porteus, 1965)

This is a test of planning that requires the examinee to negotiate a pathway through a progressively more complex series of mazes without entering any dead ends. The performance is scored in terms of age-related norms, and the task has proven to be sensitive to frontal lobe lesions.

Wisconsin Card Sorting Test (WCST and the WCST-64 Card Version (WCST-64; R.K. Heaton, 1981; Kongs, Thompson, Iverson, & Heaton, 2000)

As noted above, the WCST is a task that requires the examinee to sort a series of cards into categories under four example cards, with the only available feedback being the correctness or incorrectness of the response. It is a test of visual concept formation as well as adding the requirement for the examinee to be able to flexibly shift strategy on the task once the category has changed. As noted above, it is a test sensitive to executive deficits but can also be affected by lesions in other areas of the brain. With the WCST-64 (Kongs et al., 2000), only 64 cards are employed to reduce the duration of the test, and these are sorted in a specified order: colour, form then number.

13. EMOTIONAL AND PERSONALITY FUNCTIONS

A crucial aspect of the assessment of the examinee is the requirement to ascertain that the compromise in cognition that is occurring is as a result of brain impairment, rather than due to any intercurrent emotional or psychiatric illness. It is thus an important part of the neuropsychological assessment to confirm the differential diagnosis of the disorder, to ensure that the observed deficits are occurring as a direct consequence of the injury, which is the matter of the disputation, rather than as a result of the second effect of the injury on emotional functioning, or due to longstanding emotional or psychological concerns on the part of the examinee (Crowe, 1998b).

Beck Depression Inventory-II (BDI-II; Beck, Steer, & Brown, 1996)

This is a 21-question self-reported inventory that elicits the examinee's response to a series of questions associated with depression including: sadness, pessimism, past failures, loss of pleasure, guilt, feelings of punishment, self-dislike and criticism, suicidal thoughts, crying, agitation, loss of interest, indecisiveness, worthlessness, loss of energy, sleep disturbance, irritability, appetite disturbance, concentration difficulties, fatigue and changes to sexual function. Each area is scored on a scale from zero to three, thus scores range from zero to 63. A cut-off score of 13 or above is indicative of mild depression.

IPAT Anxiety Scale and IPAT Depression Scale: (Catell & Scheier, 1963; Krug & Laughlin, 1976)

These are scales of anxiety and depression similar in form and content to those employed by Beck that involve self-report of current symptoms of anxiety and depression.

Millon Clinical Multiaxial Inventory-III (MCMI-III; Millon, 1994)

The MCMI-III is a standardised, self-report questionnaire that assesses a wide range of information related to the examinee's personality, emotional adjustment and test-taking attitude. It is unique in that it focuses upon personality disorders in association with the symptoms that are frequently associated with these disorders. Over the years since its inception it has become one of the most commonly employed inventories, only out-ranked by the MMPI. The MCMI-III comprises 175 items that produce 28 scales divided into the categories of: modifying indices, clinical personality patterns, severe personality pathology, clinical syndromes and severe syndromes.

Minnesota Multiphasic Personality Inventory-II (MMPI-II; Butcher, Dahlstrom, Graham, Tellegen, & Kaemmer, 1989)

The MMPI-II is a self-reported measure of personality functions, which requires the examinee to respond to 567 true/false questions. The questions were selected empirically to differentiate individuals with psychopathology from unimpaired individuals. The MMPI-II has 10 clinical scales and four validity scales, the latter can be quite important for the purposes of assessing dissimulation. Profiles generated in the analysis of the responses allow the examiner to make diagnostic and prognostic interpretations of the performance (Greene, 2000). The MMPI-2-Restructured Form (MMPI-2-RF; Ben-Porath & Tellegen, 2008) provides an alternative to the MMPI-2 test and is composed of 338 items, with the restructured clinical scales at its core.

Rorschach (Exner, 1993)

The Rorschach is a projective test consisting of a set of 10 bilaterally symmetrical inkblots. The examinee is requested to tell the examiner what the inkblots remind them of. The overall goal of the technique is to assess the structure of personality, with particular emphasis upon how individuals construct their experience. Numerous attacks from both within and from outside the field of clinical psychology, for example those of Howard Garb (Garb, 1999), indicate that more scientifically well-founded techniques at assessing psychopathology are to be preferred.

Thematic Apperception Test (TAT; Murray, 1943)

The TAT is another projective technique in which the examinee is requested to create a story about what he or she believes is occurring in the situations depicted on a series of pictures. As with all projective techniques, huge concerns regarding reliability and validity have been raised that largely invalidate these techniques in objective examination.

14. SYMPTOM LISTING AND SYMPTOM VALIDITY

To ensure a comprehensive range of assessment many clinicians also include self-reported inventories of symptoms, as well as measures to assess symptom validity. The latter issue will be taken up in much more detail in Chapter 7 focusing on the assessment of dissimulation. There are numerous self-reported complaints checklists and questionnaires (e.g., Wahler Physical Symptoms Inventory; Sentence Completion Test) and neuropsychological symptom checklists (e.g., Neuropsychological Status Examination) available and, due to the great diversity and often nonstandardised nature of these instruments, only published and relatively commonly employed techniques will be discussed.

Rey 15 Item Test (Rey, 1964)

This is a technique aimed at assessing the examinee's cooperation with the testing process. The examinee is told that they have 10 seconds to memorise 15 different items. After the 10-second exposure they are asked to draw as many of the items as they can remember in their correct location. Two scores are derived: the number of correct rows in which all items are retained in order, and the number of correct items. The technique has proven somewhat useful in assessing dissimulation, however, numerous concerns about the reliability, validity and discrimination associated with the technique have been raised (Guilmette, Hart, Giuliano, & Leininger, 1994). We will discuss these issues as well as elaborating more appropriate means of determining less than genuine effort in Chapter 7.

Symptom Check List 90/90-R (SCL-90-R; Derogatis, 1983)

This is a checklist of 90 symptoms and complaints, common to medical and psychiatric patients, which contribute to a score on one of nine symptom dimensions focusing on somatisation, obsessive–compulsive, interpersonal sensitivity, depression, anxiety, hostility, phobic anxiety, paranoid ideation and psychoticism.

Conclusion

The clinical enterprise of assessment is a constantly evolving one, and new tests and techniques of assessment are constantly being added to the armamentarium. The brief summary of the instrumentation that I have provided in this chapter is really offered only as an introduction to the topic, rather than as a definitive summary. Once again, the reader is directed to the current neuropsychological test compendia (Lezak et al., 2004; Strauss et al., 2006) for a more comprehensive survey of the current enterprise. A huge variety of other possible instruments exist including the DKEFS (Delis et al., 2001), the Tower of London (Shallice, 1982), the Hayling Sentence Completion test and the Brixton Spatial Anticipation test (Burgess & Shallice, 1997), the Test of Everyday Attention (Robertson, Ward, Ridgeway, & Nimmo-Smith, 1994), and the Repeatable Battery for the Assessment of Neuropsychological Status (RBANS; Randolph, 1998) to name only a few of the many newer assessment instruments. In the next chapter we will move on to the important clinical issue of the generation and testing of hypotheses using the techniques that we have introduced in Chapter 3.

Endnotes

1 Loss of attentional focus to one side of the spatial world (usually the left) that most commonly occurs with posterior right parietal lobe damage.

2 This approach to interpretation draws upon the issues raised in our discussion of the process approach in Chapter 1.

3 Recognition and understanding of meaningful stimuli. Disruption of this function culminates in the clinical state of agnosia of various forms.

4 A notable exception to this rule of thumb are those instances in which aphasic syndromes, long-standing learning disabilities or a language other than English are a part of the clinical picture.

CHAPTER FOUR

TESTING HYPOTHESES WITH THE WAIS-IV AND THE WMS-IV

As can clearly be demonstrated by our discussion in Chapter 2, bias in its many forms is our constant companion in cognitive assessment. Your client, just like any individual charged with an offence in a court of law, has a right to a fair trial. He or she is presumed innocent (that is, that they do not have anything wrong with them) until they are found to be guilty (a *genuine* deficit is found). In law, the manner in which a person can seek relief from unlawful detention of himself or another person is by a writ of habeas corpus, which is the right of the individual to be brought before a jury of his peers to ensure that he or she has not been incarcerated unfairly. In our case, it represents a means of preventing the arbitrariness of inefficient clinical decision-making. Interestingly, the comparison to a jury of one's peers is in fact the most sure-footed way for a clinician to prevent anomalous diagnosis; careful comparison to an appropriate normative control group represents *the* most thorough and equitable way to ensure that an individual is not inappropriately condemned to a life of brain impairment.

One way to ensure that this happens is to guarantee a systematic and dispassionate examination of the 'charges' that have been laid. To control for the concerns that we raised in Chapter 2 regarding your objectivity, and to ensure that the highest standards of dispassionate evaluation are maintained, the most effective protection that you can invoke is to carefully identify specific hypotheses regarding the client's performance and to test these in an objective way using the available normative data. As much as possible, the decision rules that guide your assessment must be clear, defensible and definitive.

The principal reason that we are conducting an assessment is to ascertain the answer to the question: Are the patient's performances normal? What this question is really getting at, however, is to determine whether the performance of the client is within the normal variability of the behaviour or whether it is due to some pathological or other form of process. Before you provide a sensible response to this question, perhaps it is worthwhile to review the principal instruments that will be used as a focus of our discussion in this text. These will include the WAIS-IV, the WMS-IV, and a number of other commonly employed neuropsychological instruments.

What is Intelligence?

You may wonder why I consider it necessary to define this elusive construct in the context of attempting to characterise intellectual assessment; surely I am closing the gate after the horse has bolted. This is not, however, merely an armchair philosophical exercise, and it is important in constraining the way in which we report intellectual assessment, as well as in the way in which we think of this construct for our own purposes. Intellectual assessment or assessing intelligence has as many definitions as researchers. Here is one definition that comes from the *Wall Street Journal*:

> Intelligence is a very general mental capacity that, among other things, involves the ability to reason, plan, solve problems, think abstractly, comprehend complex ideas, learn quickly and learn from experience. It is not merely book learning a narrow academic skill, or test-taking smarts. Rather, it reflects a broader and deeper capability for comprehending our surroundings — 'catching on', 'making sense' of things, or 'figuring out' what to do. (*Wall Street Journal*, December 13, 1994, p. A18)

The point of this quotation is that intelligence is not a static, unchangeable construct, but one that is both dynamic and outgoing: intelligence is our ability to be able to embrace the world, to comprehend it and to effectively bend it to our will. In essence, in the terms of some of our pop psychology colleagues, intelligence is a verb, not a noun.

We can go to no better source for a definition of intelligence than that to David Wechsler himself (as we noted above, a researcher and clinician so powerful that he is still capable of leading the field beyond the grave!), who in 1944 noted that intelligence is: 'the capacity of the individual to act purposefully, to think rationally, and to deal effectively with his (or her) environment' (Wechsler, 1944, p. 3).

In Wechsler's view, cognition is only one aspect of intelligence and the other contributors include planning and goal-directedness, enthusiasm, awareness, impulsiveness, field dependence/independence, anxiety and persistence, to name only a few.

One of my favourite observations that pertains to the issue of intellectual assessment and its relationship to acquired brain impairment is one from Eric Miller (E. Miller, 1983, p. 131) who notes that:

> If damage in structure X is known to produce a decline on test T it is tempting to argue that any new subject, or group of subjects, having a relatively poor performance on T must have a lesion at X. In fact the logical status of this argument is the same as reasoning that because a horse meets the test of being a large animal with four legs then any newly encountered large animal with four legs must be a horse. The newly encountered specimen could of course be a cow or a hippopotamus and still meet the same test. Similarly new subjects who do badly on T may do so for reasons other than having a lesion at X.

Failure on tests of cognitive functioning may occur as a consequence of numerous factors and the clinician must be constantly alert to the various causes of poor performance. Similarly, it is possible for two individuals with quite different skill levels, genetic endowments and levels of motivation to perform in a similar way on cognitive testing, even despite the manifest differences in these predisposing factors. Thus the clinician must be alert to the fact that scores on intellectual assessment represent approximations of the patient's reality, rather than a mirror held up to them.

Once again, this observation is simply put by Wechsler himself, in his observation that:

> What we measure with tests is not what tests measure — not information, not spatial perception, not reasoning ability. These are only a means to an end. What intelligence tests measure is something much more important: the capacity of an individual to understand the world about him, and his resourcefulness to cope with its challenges. (Wechsler, 1975, p. 139)

So, How Many 'Intelligences' Are There?

Wechsler considered intelligence to be both global — characterising the individual's behaviour as a whole — as well as specific, composed of elements or abilities distinct from one another. He thus employed a variety of subtests in his scales that were designed with a view to measuring the various aspects of intelligence that he felt to be important including: verbal comprehension, abstract reasoning, perceptual organisation, quantitative reasoning, memory and processing speed. Current research supports this clustering of specific abilities into higher-order cognitive ability domains.

The dominant theoretical view of intelligence maintained by most investigators is the Cattell-Horn-Carroll (CHC) theory of intelligence, which is a synthesis of Horn's development of the Horn and Cattell Gf-Gc theory (Horn, 1989), combined with the work of John Carroll (1993, 1997). Description of the rationale and evidence underlying the theory is beyond the scope of a clinical guide such as this one (but I strongly recommend Ian Deary's, 2001, brief introduction to this topic as an ideal starting point), so I will not labour the point other than to say that the CHC theory dovetails particularly well with a number of the contemporary instruments that are used to measure intelligence, including the Woodcock Johnson Psycho-educational battery (Woodcock et al., 2000), the Stanford–Binet intelligence scale (Thorndike et al., 1986) and the Wechsler scales (Lichtenberger & Kaufman, 2009).

The original Verbal-Performance dichotomy advocated by Wechsler was seen as a practical means of identifying the broad versus specific aspects of the construct of intelligence. Wechsler notes that '… the subtests are different measures of intelligence, not measures of different kinds of intelligence, and the dichotomy of Verbal and Performance areas is only one of several ways in which the tests could be grouped …' (Wechsler, 1958, p. 64). As we noted in Chapter 3, the direct comparison of verbal and performance intelligence is now considered too gross to be clinically meaningful within the WAIS-IV and the more concise comparison based upon the factors (indices) of the Scale (i.e., the Verbal Comprehension Index [VCI], the Perceptual Reasoning Index [PRI], the Working Memory Index [WMI] and the Processing Speed Index [PSI]) provide a more psychometrically meaningful approach to determining the strengths and weaknesses of the client's cognition and is now to be preferred.

Wechsler also acknowledged that no single measure can adequately assess all domains of cognition, as he believed that measures of related factors such as memory or motor skills should be undertaken using appropriate instruments to achieve this end. I concur with this suggestion and I will present some of the further instrumentation that I commonly use in my practice in Chapter 8. He also acknowledged that performance on measures of cognitive ability reflects only a portion of what comprises intelligence. Cognitive functions are functionally and neurologically interrelated, thus it is impossible to measure pure domains of cognitive skill. As cognitive tasks are rarely performed in isolation, the most ecologically valid way to assess cognition is to include a variety of measures, each of which requires the use of multiple cognitive abilities.

Kaufman's Approach to Interpreting the WAIS-IV

From the outset, it is appropriate to recognise that clinicians make neuropsychological diagnoses, not tests. We saw in Chapter 3 that there are numerous tests available to assess a variety of neuropsychological constructs and, as a result, some caution is necessary in our process of assessment. The intrinsic weakness of tests is that they:

> ... do not think for themselves, nor do they directly communicate with patients. Like a stethoscope, a blood pressure gauge, or an MRI scan, a psychological test is a dumb tool, and the worth of the tool cannot be separated from the sophistication of the clinician who draws inferences from it and then communicates with patients and professionals. (Meyer et al., 2001, p. 128)

A test is simply a structured set of stimuli used for the purposes of eliciting behavioural responses, and there is no reason that these stimuli cannot be employed as the basis on which explanatory hypotheses regarding process ensue. The interpretative problem in the use of tests in this way only emerges if you want to interpret them in the context of the norms and thus to make statements about the performances of this individual relative to the population. If you want to use the norms (and I strongly recommend that you do), then you have to use the test in the way that it was originally normed. If you do not, then any normative statements regarding the performance are meaningless and should be assiduously avoided.

As Lichtenberger and Kaufman have noted:

> Standardised administration and scoring means conducting an experiment with $N = 1$ every time an examiner tests someone on an intelligence test. For the results of this experiment to be meaningful, the experimenter/examiner must adhere precisely to the wording in the Manual, give appropriate probes as defined in the instructions, time each relevant response diligently, and score each item exactly the way comparable responses were scored during the normative procedure. Following these rules prevents examiners from applying a flexible clinical investigatory procedure during the administration (as Piaget always advocated with his méthode clinique), from giving feedback to a person who urgently desires it, or from cleverly dislodging from the crevices of the person's brain his or her maximum response to each test item. (Lichtenberger & Kaufman, 2009, p. 109)

The use of standardised administration does not, of itself, preclude the technique of testing the limits of the client's approach to the task in question. Professor Gina Geffen notes that: 'Testing to limits' refers to the procedure of trying to find out a person's capabilities on the particular tasks in subtests of standardised assessment tests by deviating from the standard administration' (Geffen, 1995, p. 45). This approach to exploring the responses on a particular subtest can often give valuable insight into the reasons for failure or confusion. However, this form of supplemental testing must only occur *after* the score has been recorded under appropriate conditions (Lichtenberger & Kaufman, 2009).

The approach to interpretation of the WAIS-IV profile that I advocate is the one developed and championed by Alan Kaufman and his colleagues (Kaufman, 1979; Kaufman & Lichtenberger, 1999, 2006; Lichtenberger & Kaufman, 2009; Lichtenberger et al., 2002) that analyses the results of the WAIS-IV in a logical and systematic fashion. I strongly recommend that you consult his many publications on this topic for a full account of the 'intelligent' testing system. It is worthwhile to note that the approach advocated by Kaufman is very similar to the one advocated in the *Technical and Interpretive Manual of the WAIS-IV* (Wechsler, 2008b, see pp. 123–136). For our purposes, however, we will use the bare bones of the system as a means of evaluating the hypotheses that it is possible to generate about the client's cognitive functioning.

Kaufman's approach to assessment operates under the following three guidelines:

> We recommend interpreting test data within the context of a well-validated theory ... We recommend using composite or clusters, rather than subtests, in intra-individual analysis ... The clusters that are included in the interpretive analysis should represent basic primary factors in mental organisation (e.g., visual processing, auditory short-term memory) ... If a relative weakness revealed through ipsative analysis falls well within the average range of functioning compared to most people, then its meaningfulness is called into question. (Lichtenberger & Kaufman, 2009, pp. 142–143)

Kaufman's method focuses upon the use of all of the available clinical information.

> Diagnostic decisions should not be based on test scores alone; nor should they be based on clinical judgement alone. Rather ... diagnostic decisions should be based on test data, clinical observations during the testing session, background information, data from other assessments, and referral questions geared specifically to the person being evaluated. No rational clinician would interpret low scores on the Wechsler subtest associated with a working memory index (referred to in days gone by as the Freedom from Distractibility factor) as reflecting a person's distractibility without also having observed the person's behaviour during the test session, in the classroom (or workplace), and perhaps in other environments as well. (Lichtenberger & Kaufman, 2009, p. 136)

His approach to assessment of the performance is also both normative (i.e., compares the individual to the standardisation sample) and ipsative (compares the individual to his or her own performances across the profile of tests):

> Interpretation of fluctuations in the person's Index or Factor profile offers the most reliable and meaningful information about WAIS-IV performance because it identifies strong and weak areas of cognitive functioning relative to both same-age peers from the normal population (inter-individual or normative approach) and the person's own overall ability level (intra-individual or ipsative approach); (p. 146)
> … our current method for the WAIS-IV links ipsative analysis with normative analysis, rather than focusing exclusively on either one or the other. (Lichtenberger & Kaufman, 2009, p. 147)

Thus, the guiding principles that we will employ in interpreting the WAIS-IV rest upon: (1) a theoretically well-grounded definition of intelligence; (2) a comprehensive assessment approach that takes into consideration not just the test scores, but also the clinical presentation of the client; and (3) an assessment approach, which is both normative as well, as ipsative.

How Do We Interpret the WAIS-IV Profile?

The scoring criterion for the WAIS-IV presents upwards of 50 values and the approach to this wealth of information must therefore be systematic rather than by a random selection. This process can take place in seven steps.

Step 1: Interpret the Full Scale Intelligence Quotient (FSIQ)

The FSIQ is the most reliable score on the WAIS-IV. It has a mean split half coefficient of .98 and a stability coefficient of .96, it has a standard error of measurement of 2 points and is the best overall measure of ability. It thus represents the most sensible measure of overall functioning; however, the neuropsychological meaningfulness of full-scale IQ as an index of behaviour in the real world is much less compelling (Lezak, 1988). There certainly are situations in which full-scale IQ is not just a desirable score to have but one necessary for the purposes of eligibility determinations. We will explore this issue in some detail when we address the issue of eligibility determinations in the context of intellectual disability in Chapter 5. In the meantime, however, the probative value of full-scale IQ is really more for the purposes of comparison to other aspects of the performance of the individual as it is the most reliable score on the scale.

Step 2: Determine the Best Way to Summarise Overall Intellectual Level

The next step in our analysis is to ask: what is the best global measure of intellect? The WAIS-IV provides two possible approaches as the answer to this question. The first of these is the use of the FSIQ as we have discussed above. While in many circumstances this is sufficient, the situation of a client with acquired brain impairment (ABI) presents a more complex set of issues as, if we use the FSIQ as the estimate of present-day functioning, this measure may be contaminated by the very brain impairment we would seek to describe. In this situation, the General Ability Index (GAI) provides a summary score less sensitive than FSIQ to working memory and processing speed (i.e., the skills most affected by ABI). It is thus more appropriate to use the GAI when a deficit in WMI or PSI or both of these exist. Such cases would include a significant and unusual discrepancy between: VCI and WMI, PRI and PSI, WMI and PSI or any discrepancy between subtests within WMI and/or PSI. In these circumstances, GAI is a more accurate measure of ability and should be used in preference.

Before it is possible to employ the GAI, however, quality assurance checks on the data need to occur to ensure that the index is measuring what we say it is. Thus, to ascertain that the GAI can usefully be calculated we must consider the four indices, subtract the lowest from the highest and determine if the size of the standard score difference is less than 1.5 SDs (< 23 points). If it is, then FSIQ can be interpreted and should be employed. If it is not, then FSIQ should not be interpreted as the summary, and the GAI should be employed in its stead.

The next step in the analysis is to determine if the GAI is interpretable. Specifically, we must determine if the size of the standard score difference between VCI and PRI is less than 1.5 SDs (< 23 points). If it is, then GAI can be interpreted and should be employed. If it is not, then GAI should not be interpreted as the summary as it is not meaningful.

Once we have determined the interpretability of the FSIQ and the GAI, the next step in the analysis is to calculate the GAI. To undertake this, we must add together the scores for similarities, vocabulary, information, block design, matrix reasoning and visual puzzles. To undertake this step you will need to consult the appropriate table in the manual (see Table C.1 in the manual, Wechsler, 2008c, p. 169). I am a big fan of the computer scoring programs, and the new platforms for the WAIS-IV, the WMS-IV, the WIAT-II and the Advanced Clinical Solutions (ACS) package all integrate well with each other allowing the maximal yield of data with the minimum of wading through the tables and calculations from the manual. Note well however, it is important that you score the first few assessments that you conduct by hand so that you are aware of the processes that are being undertaken by the scoring programs and to ensure that you know what you are actually presenting in your reports;

after all, if garbage is inserted into the program it is unlikely that anything other than garbage will come out!

Step 3: Determine Whether the GAI/Cognitive Proficiency Index (CPI) is Unusually Large

The next step in Lichtenberger and Kaufman's interpretive approach is to examine the CPI. The CPI is a person's proficiency for processing certain types of information, most notably those functions that are measured by the WMI and PRI. Weiss and colleagues (Weiss, Saklofske, Schwartz, Prifitera, & Courville, 2006) note 'proficient processing, through quick visual speed and good mental control, facilitates fluid reasoning and the acquisition of new material by reducing the cognitive demands of novel tasks' (p. 170). Thus, the CPI represents the obverse of the GAI, a measure of those functions that are most directly affected by ABI: working memory and processing speed.

There is not, as yet, 100% agreement about whether the interpretation of this index is a useful one, for example Hebben (2009) has argued that the measure does not make neuropsychological sense and, in essence, is attempting to combine two aspects of performance that are quite distinct from each other. It is legitimate to ask whether it would be better and more appropriate to treat Working Memory and Processing Speed as separate constructs and thus not to combine them into a single CPI score. Certainly, they represent quite different aspects of performance and have quite different neural determinants. Nonetheless, it is clear that both indices are the ones most sensitive to change as a consequence of injury (as if it was not the case, why would it make sense to generate the GAI?) and, as a global measure of deficit they do represent a useful parameter. It is also interesting to speculate that this is the first iteration of the Wechsler scales that has eschewed the direct comparison of the constructs of Verbal versus Performance IQ; yet here we are developing a similar style of distinction (i.e., GAI versus CPI) that cuts across these more traditional constructs. Clearly, this issue will ultimately be decided by clinicians such as yourself and how useful this sort of information proves in the long run in accurately characterising performance in the clinic.

Step 4: Do the GAI and the CPI Constitute Unitary Abilities?

The next step in our analysis is to determine whether the newly fashioned super scores constitute unitary constructs. For GAI, we must determine whether the size of the difference between VCI and PRI is less than 1.5 SDs (< 23 points). If it is, then the GAI can be calculated and interpreted; if it is not then the comparison cannot be made and the individual indices should be interpreted separately. Similarly, for the CPI we must determine whether the size of the difference between WMI and PSI is less than 1.5 SDs (< 23 points). If it is, then the CPI can be calculated and interpreted; if it is not then comparison cannot be made.

To compute the CPI we must sum the scaled scores for the subtests in the WMI and the PSI (you can use the scoring program to calculate the index, percentile rank and confidence intervals of all measures that are useful in interpreting the reliability and implication of the scores, but if you do not have one, the manual [Wechsler, 2008b] clearly outlines how to calculate these scores). We then must determine whether the indices are different from each other. Inevitably, this raises the issue of how different the two scores need to be to actually represent 'real' differences. A statistical difference between the indices is observed at $p < .05$ with a difference of 8.8, and for $p < .01$ with a difference of 11.6. It is also important for us to go beyond just statistical significance to determine whether the differences are clinically significant (i.e., unusually large and rare) in the standardisation sample. If the difference is 19 points, the base rate — the number of nonimpaired individuals — in the normative sample that featured such a difference was only 10% or less; if the difference is 23 or more only 5% of the normative sample featured such a difference. Perhaps at this point it is useful for us to examine more fully the notion of clinical versus statistical significance, as this distinction is crucial in any discussion of the nature of the observed result.

Clinical Versus Statistical Significance: How Much Difference Between Scores is Enough to be *Really* Different?

Often, differences between indices may be statistically significant but may not be rare events in the normative population. Statistical significance and clinical significance are different issues and will have different implications for the interpretation of the result. The reliability of a test is a measure of its accuracy, consistency and stability as determined in various situations (Anastasi & Urbina, 1997; Sattler, 2008). The overall reliability coefficients of subtests on the WAIS-IV range from 0.78 to 0.93, with the Vocabulary, Digit Span, Information, Matrix Reasoning and Figure Weights subtests having very high reliabilities (> .90) and the Cancellation and Symbol Search subtests having the lowest reliabilities (0.78 and 0.81, respectively). The IQ and Index Scores of the WAIS-IV range in reliability from 0.90 to 0.98. You can thus see that these latter figures are consistently higher than the reliability index of any subtest, thus the composite scores (i.e., the IQ scores or the index scores) are *more reliable* than any of the constituent subtest scores. This is not surprising, as the composite scores are composed of more data points than the single point estimates of the subtest scores. Thus, error and variability of the single point estimate (i.e., the subtest score) is reduced when we combine these estimates together to make up the composite scores, culminating in the greater reliability of the index.

The technical manual for the WAIS-IV notes that:

> the reliability of a test refers to the accuracy, consistency, and stability of test scores across situations (Anastasi & Urbina, 1997; Sattler, 2008). Classical test theory posits that a test score is an approximation of an individual's hypothetical true score, that is, the score he or she would receive if the test were perfectly reliable. The difference between the hypothetical true score and an individual's obtained test score is measurement error. A reliable test will have relatively small measurement error and consistent measurement results within one administration and on different occasions. The reliability of a test should always be considered in the interpretation of obtained test scores and differences between an individual's test scores on multiple occasions. (Wechsler, 2008a, p. 41)

The upshot of this issue is that in any clinical context it is always better to use the most reliable indicator of a particular construct, as this is the one that is subject to the least error. In interpretation of the WAIS-IV and WMS-IV, the most reliable indicators (i.e., the FSIQ or the index scores rather than the constituent subtest scores) should always be used as the principal focus of interpretation of the performance as they are the best indicators of the cognitive constructs and therefore the ones least prone to error. For your purposes, this means that you are less likely to make an error in your clinical diagnosis if you use the most reliable indicators.

How then do we know how much difference between scores is enough to constitute meaningful difference? A statistically significant difference between scores (e.g., between the WMI and the PSI for example) refers to the likelihood that obtaining such a difference by chance alone is very low (e.g., by convention, $p < .05$, but a more stringent criterion of $p < .01$ could also be legitimately employed) if the true difference between the scores is 0 (Matarazzo & Herman, 1985). To all intents and purposes, this implies that there is no difference between the scores, which goes beyond the error of the measurement of the instrument. To state the obvious, if there is no statistically significant difference between the scores, then they are not different from each other. What this means in the clinic is that if there are no significant differences between scores, then the client's performance must be considered to be intact with regard to this function.

Often, however, differences between scores may be statistically significant but may not be rare in the general population. Clearly, if marked differences between scores occurred frequently in normal individuals, we would not want to impute pathology from them. After all, this finding occurred commonly in individuals without anything wrong with them (most probably even if we conducted the test with you or me). Statistical significance and clinical significance are separate issues and each will have different implications for interpretation of the obtained results.

The prevalence or frequency of an observed score difference in the general population is referred to as the *base rate* (Gouvier, 1999). Often the difference between an individual's composite scores (e.g., WMI and PSI or VCI and PRI) is significant in the statistical sense, but does not occur infrequently in the standardisation sample. Base rate information provides a basis for estimating the rarity or commonness of the obtained difference between scores within the normal adult population. If the difference, although statistically significant, is relatively common in normal participants, then the degree to which we would be convinced that this was a pathological finding would be significantly diminished. Thus, we need an index or rule of thumb to allow us to be able to determine what is both statistically significant and rare. Lichtenberger and Kaufman (2009), for example, suggest that the best score to use for base rate estimation of rarity is that observed in less than 10% of the normal sample, that is, one and a half standard deviations below or above the normal score. Thus, if the two scores are noted to be significantly different by a conventional significance test, and the frequency with which this difference occurs is relatively rare (i.e., occurs in less than 10% of the normative sample) then the difference is both statistically and clinically significant. The conclusion to be drawn from such a difference then is that it constitutes a clinically as well as statistically meaningful impairment of the individual.

It should be reiterated that these clinical rules of thumb are guides only and it may be the case that individuals with neural pathology do not perform in as profoundly an impaired fashion as the frequency of these indices would indicate. For example, in his manual for interpretation of the WAIS-III, Kaufman recommended a more lax criterion for clinical significance (i.e., one standard deviation below the normals; i.e., occurring in 16% of the standardisation sample; Kaufman & Lichtenberger, 1999). The failsafe that you have available to you, by using the analysis procedure proposed, is that while the difference itself is statistically reliable, the observed scores *are not the same as each other*. At the very least, this is a difference that needs to be explained in any interpretation of the result. The interpretation of the observed difference, however, is always a function of the clinical skill and acumen of the clinician him/her self. Rules of thumb are just that, helpful devices, but not definitive in diagnosing pathology and, harking back to our discussion of the work of Miller as discussed in the beginning of this chapter, while there is a difference between the scores, it may be the case that our large animal with four legs *is* a horse but nonetheless it could still be a zebra or a hippopotamus. Determining which large animal with four legs it is, is the job of the clinician, not the job of the test.

Two Paths for Interpretation

At this stage in the analysis of the result it is possible for the clinician to opt for two possible approaches to the interpretation of the performance: (1) to interpret the four indices of the WAIS-IV or (2) to interpret the performance in terms of the five factor model developed by Keith (as described in Lichtenberger & Kaufman, 2009). Keith's approach addresses the constructs that have been proposed by the Cattell-Horn-Carroll (CHC) theory of intelligence (Carroll, 1993, 1997; Horn, 1989) and interprets the WAIS-IV in terms of the CHC factors (Crystallised intelligence [*Gc*] = vocabulary + information; Short-term memory [*Gsm*] = digit span + letter number sequencing [LNS]; Fluid reasoning [*Gf*] = matrix reasoning + figure weights [FW]; Visual processing [*Gv*] = block design + visual puzzles; and Processing speed [*Gs*, 2000] = symbol search + coding). In fact, this is one of the reasons why they gave you all the extra stuff in the test kit. It is possible for you to use the Keith model, if the client is 16–69, and you have done the LNS and FW subtests. The interpretation of the WAIS-IV in terms of the CHC model is beyond the scope of this text, which is more introductory, but if you are keen to do further reading on this topic (which I strongly recommend), the Lichtenberger and Kaufman text (2009) is the best place to begin.

As we noted in our discussion of the issue of the relative reliabilities of indices versus subtests, the most statistically reliable and clinically meaningful focus of our interpretation of the WAIS-IV should be at the level of the indices rather than of the subtests. To do this most effectively, however, we must first determine whether the index represents consistent measures of the construct in question.

Step 5: Are the Indices Unitary?

At this stage it is necessary to determine whether there is a substantial difference between the scaled scores composing each index (VCI, WMI, PRI and PSI), as if there is undue subtest scatter then the index cannot be interpreted as a unitary construct. Consideration of intra subtest scatter is crucially important to ensure that the index represents a consistent and integrated measure of the construct under consideration, as opposed to one conflated by other aspects of functioning. Intersubtest variability of the subtests constituting the index is thus an important measure of the degree to which a particular index consistently measures one, rather than more than one, construct.

A good example of this point is to consider how frequently individuals feature a scaled score of 10 on each of the subtests of the WAIS-III, as we discussed previously in Chapter 3. As you would be aware, the WAIS-III was standardised to produce a mean IQ score of 100 with standard deviations of 15. Similarly, each subtest was standardised to have a population mean score of 10 and a standard deviation of 3. An idealised average individual then would be expected to perform with a score of 10 on each of the subtests of the scale, culminating in IQ scores of 100. Of the 2450 individuals who completed the WAIS-III for the standardisation study, however, no individual performed the test with a score of 10 on each of the subtests. Variability in score profile is intrinsic to each individual's performance. As a consequence, we need to be ever watchful to ensure that any conclusions that we draw about a given individual is substantiated by the data that we have gathered from them, rather than our biases and preconceptions about what they should be.

It is thus important to check for significant scatter between the subtests constituting the respective index scores to determine whether each is measuring a unitary construct. This range can be computed by subtracting the lowest score from the highest score to obtain a range. For example, if the subtest constituting the PRI (i.e., Block Design, Matrix Reasoning and Visual Puzzles) indicated that the client had a Block Design scaled score of 12, a Matrix Reasoning scaled score of 6 and Visual Puzzles scaled score of 9, then the scatter could be determined by subtracting the Matrix Reasoning scaled score (6) from the Block Design scaled score (12) to yield a product of 6. If the discrepancies between the subtest scaled scores are greater than 5 points (i.e., 1.5 SDs), then the index cannot be considered unitary and therefore should not be interpreted as a unitary construct. In our example, as the discrepancy is 6 (i.e., greater than 5) we should not interpret the PRI as a unitary index.

What this actually means is that the PRI construct is composed on more than one process, which means that it cannot be interpreted as if it represented a single factor. The determination of what this means clinically is really up to you, but in our example the fact that the individual has a difficulty with the Block Design subtest but not other aspects of the index may indicate that the unique features of the Block Design subtest may be contributing to the problem. So, for example, you might like to propose that both the other subtests do not feature the fine-motor coordination necessary for manipulating the blocks to produce the designs, suggesting that the mental processing necessary to successfully execute the designs are intact (as demonstrated by adequate performance with the Matrix Reasoning and the Visual Puzzles subtests) but that the motor execution is impaired. Such an interpretation must be supported by other evidence gathered during the assessment, for example, compromise of motor execution on purely motor tasks (e.g., the Grooved Pegboard task or some other estimated of motor coordination and execution).

The cumulative percentages of intersubtest scatter within the various scales of the WAIS-IV are provided in the administration and scoring manual in Table B.6, and this allows for the determination of whether the level of scatter is common or rare in the general population (Wechsler, 2008b). An evaluation of the variability helps the practitioner identify the strengths and weaknesses of the client's cognitive functioning, as well is to determine the consistency and reliability of the index in question, which may be useful in qualitative interpretations of the pattern of performances produced by the client.

Step 5a: Is the VCI Versus the PRI Difference Interpretable?

The factor VC and PRI indices are considered to be pure measures of verbal and visuo-spatial functions respectively, as VCI excludes tasks thought to measure sequential processing, working memory and number ability and instead measures conceptual thought and verbal expression; and PRI excludes the two subtests that measure mental and motor speed and thus more precisely captures nonverbal thinking and the application of visuo-spatial skill. Thus, comparing these indices allows us to conduct analysis of the difference of the person's performance on the purer measure of verbal versus visuo-spatial reasoning, rather than the one contaminated by the other factors.

Step 5b: Is the WMI Versus the PSI Difference Interpretable?

As we noted in Chapter 3, working memory is a term that has come into currency in the contemporary neuropsychological literature and is best thought of as a person's information processing capacity (Baddeley, 2000; Baddeley & Hitch, 1974). Analysis of the WMI allows us to ascertain whether the client is performing in an appropriate way on measures of this important skill in comparison to other aspects of their performance (i.e., contrasts between WMI and VCI, PRI and PSI).

Another important development, which occurred with the advent of the WAIS-III (Wechsler, 1997a, 2002) and continues with the WAIS-IV, is a much more comprehensive understanding of how various components of the performance could be independently assessed. Speed of information processing has been an important theoretical construct, particularly within cognitive psychology, but many of the measures that constituted earlier versions of the WAIS did not measure this construct separately from other aspects of the performance. Within the WAIS-III and WAIS-IV speed of information processing is measured as a phenomenon in its own right, particularly in the context of a very important work by Tim Salthouse (Salthouse, 2000; Salthouse & Babcock, 1991) who has emphasised the importance of speed of information processing as an important variable in explaining the deterioration in performance as a consequence of ageing across the lifespan. This measure is also particularly sensitive to the changes associated with traumatic brain injury with its associated compromise of cortical integrity.

A good demonstration of this point is provided by the Wechsler Adult Intelligence Scale — Revised (WAIS-R; Wechsler, 1981). On the WAIS-R, the Object Assembly subtest allotted 29 points for correct answers, but awarded an additional 12 bonus points for the speed of the performance (i.e., 29% of the total score). As a result, nearly one third of the score on the subtest was contributed to by a factor that was distinct from visuo-constructional functioning. The benefit of the way in which the WAIS-III and the WAIS-IV deals with this problem is that speed of information processing is measured as a construct in its own right and can be compared with other aspects of the performance to determine strengths and weaknesses of the client's performance (i.e., comparisons of PSI with VCI, PRI and WMI).

Step 6: Determining Normative Strengths and Weaknesses
As we discussed in the justification for the 'intelligent testing' system advocated by Kaufman and his colleagues (Kaufman, 1990; Kaufman & Lichtenberger, 1999, 2006; Lichtenberger & Kaufman, 2009), the comprehensive assessment of intelligence should be both normative (i.e., comparing the individual to the normative sample) and ipsative (comparing the individual's performance to his/her own performance). This involves the evaluation of the exact value of the interpretable indices. Thus, if the standard score of the index is greater than 115, the ability is considered a normative strength and if the index is less than 85, then it is considered a normative weakness.

Step 7: Determine Personal Strengths and Weaknesses
In this step, the individual is compared to his or her own profile of performances. The performances are compared to the mean performance across all of the subtests in the profile (or by index). The determination of whether the performance represents a personal strength or weakness is based on its uncommonness, using a 10% base rate criterion. This allows the examiner to identify key assets and high priority concerns in the individual's cognitive profile.

Step 8: Interpret Significant Strengths and Weaknesses
          on the Subtest Profile
Once the heavy lifting of the analysis of the performance has been done with the IQ and index scores, using the appropriate statistical analysis to determine whether they are different to each other, it is then possible to start to examine

qualitative aspects of the performance with a view to exploring possible explanations of the observed outcome. One means of doing this is by individual analysis of the performances on the subtests as a means of determining the quality of aspects of the performance for the individual. It should be noted that there is increasing scepticism on the part of clinicians as to whether this form of analysis is appropriate. For example, in their book on the WAIS-III, Kaufman and Lichtenberger (1999) commend this approach, whereas in their guide to interpretation of the WAIS-IV (Lichtenberger & Kaufman, 2009) they are considerably more cautious regarding the approach.

> Subtest-level interpretation obscures the contribution of item response patterns, item clusters, or individual items to subtest performance, assuming the variation in item-level performance represents random fluctuation that are unimportant or impossible to interpret meaningfully in an empirically valid manner. Clinicians seeking to interpret WAIS-IV assessment from a neuropsychological perspective are on somewhat firmer ground when attention is focused at the subtest level. The need for subtest-level interpretation is clear when significantly large differences are present between or among the subtests that comprise an index. In these instances, a clear pattern of difference in the use of cognitive capacity might be readily apparent. (p. 213)

As with difference between the index scores, the interpretation of a particular subtest score as especially high or low should take into account the statistical significance of the observed difference and estimates of population base rates. These can be statistically calculated from the standardisation sample data and allow determination of individual strengths and weaknesses in comparison to the individual themselves and with the standardisation sample overall. This comparison can be done for the mean of each index (i.e., VCI, PRI, WMI or PSI), or for the mean of all of the subtests. Undertaking this type of analysis must ensure that it takes into account attributes other than intelligence when interpreting test results. People with similar test scores may not cope well with similar environmental challenges, and people with different underlying levels of intellectual ability may achieve similar scores. But once again, the serial analysis of the performance with the most powerful indices compared statistically as the first step in the process provides the most careful and measured way of ensuring that erroneous clinical diagnoses are not made.

Step 9: Hypothesise About Fluctuations in the Profile

This step allows the opportunity for the clinician to apply their clinical skill and acumen to create a consistent story between the client's presenting problems, their background history and the pattern of performances on the WAIS-

IV. This allows for the analysis of qualitative aspects of the performance (Darby & Walsh, 2005; Kaplan, 1990; Lezak et al., 2004) to come into play, as well as the previous experience of the clinician with particular subtest indicators of particular behavioural patterns. Once again, it should be stipulated that qualitative aspects of the performance must ensue only after quantitative evaluation has taken place.

It is worthwhile to leave the further consideration of the WAIS-IV scores here, but we will take this issue up again in with a worked example in our next chapter with a view to examining specific hypotheses regarding the individual's test performances in our first clinical case. The next stop on our journey however is the interpretation of the performance on the Wechsler memory scale.

Memory and New Learning

As we noted in Chapter 3, one of the principal distinctions drawn in memory research is the difference between memory that is a subject to conscious recall (i.e., declarative memory including episodic and semantic memory) and memory that can occur in the absence of awareness (i.e., nondeclarative or implicit memory including skill learning, priming and conditioning). All standard tests of memory focus on the measurement of declarative memory. A further distinction is drawn in the context of declarative memory, a construct originally described by Endel Tulving (1972). Tulving divides declarative memory into two components: semantic memory, knowledge of words and other aspects of facts and information obtained about the world that are context-free; and episodic memory, the ability to be able to recall particular events and episodes that are defined by the context in which the episode occurred. While it is possible that the two constructs represent a continuum of learning experiences (i.e., that all semantic memories must, at some stage in their evolution, have been episodic memories), they can be clinically and functionally delineated from each other as most aspects of semantic memory are generally preserved following brain injury, while episodic memory is considerably more subject to change as a consequence of injury.

Almost all commonly employed memory tests and memory batteries (Delis et al., 1999; Delis et al., 1987; Malec et al., 1991; Meyers & Meyers, 1995; Rey, 1964; Wechsler, 1987, 1997b, 2009c) have a principal, if not exclusive, focus on episodic memory. This is not to say that other forms of memory testing are not available (e.g., tests of semantic memory such as the Boston Naming Test; Kaplan et al., 1976), tests of procedural memory (e.g., the Pursuit Rotor Task and Star Mirror Task; Lafayette Instrument Company, Lafayette, Indiana) and increasingly the focus upon working memory (Baddeley, 2000; Baddeley &

Hitch, 1974), but that what most clinicians and most of the general public speak about when discussing memory deficit is the construct of episodic memory. As we have previously discussed in Chapter 3, the WMS-IV represents the most comprehensive and well normed memory battery available in the contemporary clinical sphere.

Interpreting the WMS-IV Profile

Analysis of the performance on the WMS-IV can answer a number of questions about the client's current performance, particularly with regard to their memory, new learning and attention and concentration. It allows answers to specific questions such as: Can the person attend? How well do they learn? Is there any difference between the memory performance for different modalities of information input, such as audio-verbal versus visuo-spatial? Is there any difference between the working memory performance of the individual for different modalities of information input such as audio-verbal versus visuo-spatial? How quickly do they learn? How well is information maintained after a delay? Do they benefit from cues or choices in a recognition format?

As with our discussion of the WAIS-IV, the model of interpretation of the WMS-IV should be systematic, hypothesis-driven and cautious. In fact, it should be undertaken with all of those features considered worthwhile in the discussion of the WAIS-IV as outlined by Lichtenberger and Kaufman (Lichtenberger & Kaufman, 2009; Lichtenberger et al., 2002). It should be theoretically well grounded; it should take into consideration not just the test scores, but also the clinical presentation of the client and it should be both normative (i.e., comparing the individual to the standardisation sample), as well as ipsative (comparing the individual to his or her own performances across the profile of tests). How then do we interpret the performance on the WMS-IV in a cautious and step-wise fashion?

Most theorists and investigators in the area of memory functioning consider that the processing of a memory takes place in three distinguishable steps. These are: encoding, taking the information into the memory system in the first place; storage, retaining that information over time; and retrieval, recovering the information from the memory store. The retrieval stage of memory formation can be accessed in a variety of different formats, including free recall, retrieval of the information without any aid of cueing; cued recall; and recognition, recall that is prompted by stimulus triggers to remembering. Each of the stages of the memory processing train is comprehensively assessed by the WMS-IV.

Once again, in the interpretation of the performance on the WMS-IV, we will draw upon the method proposed by Kaufman and his colleagues with the WMS-III (Lichtenberger et al., 2002) in association with the guide to interpretation provided in the *WMS-IV Technical and Interpretive Manual* (Wechsler, 2009b, see pp. 156–172) and I again strongly recommend that you consult Kaufman's excellent texts on this topic for a more comprehensive and extensive discussion of the various issues. The approach to the interpretation of the WMS-IV takes place in nine steps.

Step 1: Is There an Attentional Problem?

Attention is the cognitive process through which a person concentrates on some features of the environment to the exclusion (for the most part) of all others and is a crucial aspect of encoding information for subsequent recall. While attention is at the heart of most aspects of cognitive processing, it continues to be a poorly measured and poorly described aspect of cognitive functioning. The principal problem, I believe, in appropriately measuring and describing attention is due to the pervasiveness of attention as a crucial aspect of all processes of cognition. Perhaps a parallel can be drawn with our discussion above of the issue of speed of information processing. Clearly, the speed with which we process information is a crucially important and distinct aspect of cognitive functioning and, as a result, should be measured in its own right. Certainly the same argument applies to attention. However, ability to be able to concisely and systematically measure attention and to disentangle it from all other aspects of cognition has largely eluded most accounts of mental processing. Particularly in the context of the measurement of memory, the contribution of attentional processes to the performance is pivotal. If there is a problem with attention, all further examination of memory is compromised, thus there is little point in further examination of other aspects of memory if there is attentional compromise. At some level, therefore, determination of whether the individual is appropriately attending to the information that you are presenting to them must transpire. Within the remit of the WMS-IV, it is possible to employ some of the supplementary assessment procedures to ascertain, at a basic level, the neurobehavioural integrity of the client. If you are concerned that the client may not be able to follow and attend to the assessment process, it may be worthwhile to undertake the optional Brief Cognitive Status Examination (BCSE) of the WMS-IV as the first step in the assessment process. This new subtest within the WMS-IV includes measures that assess orientation (for day, date, month, year and current political context), time estimation, mental control (ability to recite automatic sequences such as counting backwards from 20 and reversing the months of the year), clock drawing (assessing visuo-constructional skills), a brief verbal memory test, and measures of executive functioning (inhibition of automatic motor sequencing and a verbal fluency task). Inclusion of this set of measures allows you to conclude that the client is sufficiently oriented, focused and attending to be able to usefully measure a construct such as memory. If they demonstrate significant compromise on such a set of measures, then the appropriateness of putting the client through the more arduous set of measures that constitute the full WMS-IV should be seriously questioned.

The information-processing models of memory indicate that registration is a crucial aspect of all subsequent recall: thus we need to insure that the client has taken in the information in the first place to ascertain whether in fact, they can recall it later on. Largely speaking then, within the WMS-IV attentional function is measured by the working memory index (see Step 8 below), which gives a score regarding the ability of the client to take information on in either the audio-verbal or visuo-spatial modality and to manipulate it in the short-term store. Once we have ascertained that employing the WMS-IV makes clinical sense (i.e., the client is not so severely impaired on the BCSE that the effort would not be worthwhile), then the next step in our processing of the data is to determine whether the indices are consistent.

Step 2: Do the Indices Represent Unitary Constructs?

As we noted in our discussion of the WMS-IV in Chapter 3, the full battery yields five indices: the Auditory Memory Index (AMI), the Visual Memory Index (VMI), the Immediate Memory Index (IMI), the Delayed Memory Index (DMI) and the Visual Working Memory Index (VWMI). To determine whether the indices represent unitary constructs we must compare each subtest within the index with the others to ascertain the level of intrasubtest scatter.

As with the WAIS-IV, the overall reliability coefficients of subtests on the WMS-IV range from 0.74 to 0.97, with the Verbal Paired Associates I, the Visual Reproduction I and II and the Spatial Addition subtests having very high reliabilities (> .90) and the Logical Memory I and II, Verbal Paired Associates II and the Designs I and II subtests having the lowest reliabilities (0.82, 0.85, 0.85, 0.85 and 0.85 respectively). The Index Scores of the WMS-IV range in reliability from 0.93 to 0.96. Once again, we can see that the latter figures are mostly higher than the reliability indices of the subtests (although in contrast to the WAIS-IV, there are some exceptions). It is also heartening to note that in this iteration of the WMS the performance of the indices has improved substantially (for the WMS-III the indices ranged in reliability from 0.74 to 0.93; and for those of the WMS-R ranges were from 0.71 to 0.86).

The critical values of intrasubtest scatter are provided in the *Administration and Scoring Manual* in Tables F.1–F.5 (Wechsler, 2009a). A similar clinical guide as that employed with the WAIS-IV can be used to assess intra-index scatter. If the subtests have a discrepancy of ≥ 5 scaled points (i.e., 1.5 SDs different) then the index should be cautiously interpreted as it features significant intra-index scatter. If you find an unusual result you need to determine whether it is appropriate to undertake the analysis at the level of the index, as was the case with the WAIS.

Step 3: How Well Does the Person Learn as a Function of Modality of Information?

The second link in a memory processing chain, storage, represents the ability of the individual to learn new information and is best measured by the use of the Immediate Memory Index (IMI) of the WMS-IV. This index is composed of both the auditory and visual immediate memory performances and represents a composite measure across both modes of presentation. The performance of the individual can be compared to performance on the WAIS-IV to determine whether the difference between the memory measure and intellectual measures differ. This allows of means of determining whether the individual's performance is differentially impaired with regard to their intellectual functioning in comparison to the standardisation sample, as well as in comparison to the individual him/herself as assessed by predicting memory performance by GAI, VCI or PRI. The possibility of comparing both to the VCI, the PRI as well as to the GAI allows for a more concise set of comparisons, taking into consideration the fact that the PSI and WMI may be affected as a consequence of the ABI that has brought the individual to the assessment.

Step 4: Is There a Difference Between Modalities?

The next step in the interpretation of the performance is to determine if the person performs equivalently on audio-verbal versus visuo-spatial material. While it was traditionally thought that lesions of the left temporal lobe culminated in audio-verbal memory compromise, and lesions of the right temporal lobe culminated in visuo-spatial ones (Milner, 1971), more recent investigation of this issue has yielded equivocal results. In patients with epilepsy, impairment of verbal memory has consistently been associated with resection of the dominant left temporal lobe, whereas nonverbal memory deficits have been less reliably observed following resection of the right temporal lobe (Pillon et al., 1999). The WMS-R was demonstrated to be sensitive to material-specific deficits after left temporal lobectomy, but was not so for resection of the right temporal lobe (Naugle, Chelune, Cheek, Luders, & Awad, 1993). In my view, the comparability of the measures of each modality is now much better than they were with the WMS-III. The nature of the tasks is more even and the levels of the performance also appear more comparable. With the WMS-IV the clinical group studies that compare left and right temporal lobectomy patients with matched controls revealed that all of the WMS-IV indices were lower in the right temporal lobectomy patients in comparison to the controls, with the exception of the AMI and the DMI. However, with the left temporal lobectomy group, only the VWMI was different. It should be noted that the sample sizes for these comparisons (as with all of the clinical comparison groups with the WMS-IV) represent relatively small groups (i.e., 15 right-sided and 8 left-sided) indicating that the comparisons do not have very much power. As a result, caution is recommended in the use of the WMS-IV (as with all other versions of the scales) for locating sided deficits.

Step 5: How Well Does the Person Recall Following a Delay?

The final link in the memory processing chain, retrieval (i.e., recovering the information from the memory store), is best measured by use of the Delayed Memory Index (DMI) of the WMS-IV. This index measures how much material from the initial exposure is recalled following a 25- to 30-minute delay. As with the IMI, this index is also composed of both the auditory and visual immediate memory performances and represents a composite measure across both modes of presentation. This index represents perhaps the most useful indicator of how an individual will perform in the real world with regard to their memory functioning, as it provides the opportunity for the learning of material and then the requirement to retrieve it after a variety of intervening mental operations, much as you or I would do in our day-to-day lives. While the inclusion of immediate and delayed recall trials in the WMS-IV has been supported on theoretical grounds, factor analytic studies evaluating the WMS-III have consistently failed to support the ability of the scale to reliably make this distinction (Bradley Burton, Ryan, Axelrod, Schellenberger, & Richards, 2002; Millis, Malina, Bowers, & Ricker, 1999; Price, Tulsky, Millis, & Weiss, 2002). Thus, while delayed recall may be the best real-world measure of memory functioning, significant psychometric and other issues may still preclude its useful interpretation arising from assessment with the WMS-IV. For an extensive discussion of the issues underlying these concerns see our recent paper on this topic (Brophy, Jackson, & Crowe, 2009).

Step 6: Do They Benefit from Cues or Choices?

As noted above, the distinction between consolidation deficits versus retrieval deficits has been a very important theoretical and practical issue in the context of defining memory deficit. If the client has consolidated a memory but cannot retrieve it, their performance should benefit from mechanisms that support recall, such as the cueing and recognition formats. If however, the memory has not been consolidated in the first place (i.e., no permanent trace has been formed), then the individual should not benefit from such retrieval cueing. As a result, the determination of the benefit to be obtained by the provision of making choices regarding previously presented material is informative as it allows us to be able to determine which aspect of the memory process is compromised and therefore, what possible means might be able to be applied to facilitate better memory performances in the real world.

With the WMS-IV, each subtest has both an immediate, delayed and recognition trial associated with the material; however, there is now no separation of the recall versus recognition measures as separate indices in the way they were in the WMS-III. In fact, these aspects of the WMS-III yielded so little valuable information that some investigators recommended that they not be reported at all. Tulsky and colleagues for example note: 'For these reasons, we recommend that the recognition variables no longer be used in the same manner as the other index scores that are core to the WMS-III' (Tulsky, Chiaravallotti, Palmer, & Chelune, 2003, pp. 129–130). Thus, while the measurement of recognition is much better conducted in the WMS-IV and is done so more comprehensively and rigorously, the specific measures regarding this aspect of performance must be undertaken with qualitative and quantitative interpretation of the recognition subtest scores and are not included as a separate index.

Step 7: How Well Does the Person Recall in Comparison
to Other Aspects of Their Performance?

As we have discussed throughout this chapter, the interpretation of the client's performance should be both normative and ipsative. With regard to this latter concern, one thing that we are interested in doing in our interpretation of the performance is to ascertain whether the person's performance is at the level we should expect, as based upon other aspects of their own performance. Most notably, it is useful to compare the client's functioning with what should be expected on the basis of their overall level of cognitive function. To undertake this step we must first determine what the right measure to compare their memory performances to might be. As we noted in our discussion of the WAIS-IV, the FSIQ is the most reliable and valid indicator of performance and should be used as the measure of choice. The caveats to this suggestion, however, are those noted in the discussion of the issue of the appropriate use of the GAI in those cases in which there are deficiencies in the WMI or PSI. A second issue is whether, in fact, the most appropriate comparison for the contemporary memory performance might be with the estimate of the function of the individual preceding the brain impairment. Specifically, what I suggest is that estimates of pre-injury functioning such as the NART, WTAR or the instrument that has been developed to predict performance on the WAIS-IV and WMS-IV, the Test of Premorbid Function (TOPF) from the Advanced Clinical Solutions for the WAIS-IV and the WMS-IV (PsychCorp, 2009) might represent the best point of comparison for the individual with regard to their memory functioning. It is my suggestion that the memory performances be compared both to measures of present ability (i.e., GAI) as well as to estimates of functioning predating the injury (i.e., TOPF) to allow the most comprehensive comparison to both the pre-injury as well as the current levels of performance.

Step 8: Is There a Difference Between the Working Memory Indices?

The literature on working memory functioning has indicated that individuals can have sound episodic memory function independent of deficits in short-term (i.e., working) memory and, although these patients are rare, it can be the case that impairment of phonological loop (i.e., the auditory short-term memory) can exist without disruption of episodic memory. Shallice and Warrington's (Shallice & Warrington, 1970) patient KF, had impaired short-term memory but intact explicit (i.e., episodic and semantic) memory as a consequence of left parieto-occipital damage following a motor cycle accident at age 17. He had a normal IQ and normal memory and new learning ability but was capable of only a repeating a digit span of one item. While some investigators have argued that the tasks (i.e., digit span and episodic memory tasks) were not of equivalent levels of difficulty and therefore were not dissociable, the case clearly raises the point that measurement of this important function is necessary, prior to determining whether other aspects of the performance are intact.

As we considered in our discussion above regarding the issue of measurement of attention, it is worthwhile to compare how the client performs with respect to (Auditory) Working Memory from the WAIS-IV versus Visual Working Memory (VWM) from the WMS-IV. The direct comparison of these two indices is now possible, adding an extra aspect to the interpretation of this important construct.

Step 9: How Well is Information Retained After Delay?

The WMS-IV also provides a number of supplementary procedures that are useful for elucidating the nature of the client's memory compromise. These include: subtest discrepancy comparison (e.g., Spatial Addition versus Symbol Span), subtest-level contrasts (e.g., recognition versus recall measures as a function of modality), index-level contrasts (e.g., VMI versus VWMI) as well as the individual subtest profile across the whole instrument. The further elucidation of the clinical presentation of the client can be significantly enriched by this further analysis, which should, however, only take place after the statistical comparisons of the various aspects of the performance have occurred.

Final Thoughts on the WMS-IV

We are still in the early days with regard to this version of this clinical stalwart and we all still have a lot to learn. Nonetheless, so far the new edition demonstrates strong incremental improvement from the previous versions and it is clear that the WMS-IV is a much stronger instrument than any of its predecessors (a point on which I strongly disagree with the recent observations of Drs Loring and Bauer, 2010). One concern that I do have, however, is that the lengthy administration time will mean that many clinicians may not administer the full test consistently, which creates a situation in which selective administration of the instrument, with the associated problems of partial practice effects complicating the picture for anyone who follows up such an a assessment with the full battery.

Testing Clinical Hypotheses

As we noted in Chapter 1, the hypothesis testing assessment (the technique advocated by this book) follows a technique that rests upon successive elimination of alternative diagnostic possibilities. It begins with the clinician formulating the first set of hypotheses based upon the qualitative data presented by the examinee. Hypotheses formulated at this stage of the assessment, derived from the direct observations of the psychological dysfunction, often determine the shape of the quantitative assessment. In my view, the focus of the questions that we can ask about the patient's clinical presentation can be categorised into three groups: determining the client's current status, determining the client's status prior to the insult or injury, and determining the client's future status. While numerous referral questions could arise in the context of a cognitive assessment, these three categories of enquiry allow us to approach the assessment process in the most systematic way. What specific questions therefore, is it possible for us to ask?

Table 4.1 outlines the nature of the clinical questions you might be interested to pursue and then provides a statement of the sorts of evidence that you might require to endorse or refute these hypotheses.

Questions Regarding Current Status

As you can see from the Table 4.1, most of the questions that you will be interested in pertain to the current presentation of the client. The questions

---

Table 4.1
Possible Hypotheses Regarding the Client's Cognitive Status

Category	Hypothesis	Analysis
Current status	Are the findings abnormal?	Compare the scores of the client with the average scores obtained by similar, demographically matched individuals in the standardisation sample (see Chapter 5).
	Is the compromise global or specific?	Compare the scores of the client across the various domains of function to determine whether the compromise is global, or only in specified cognitive areas (see Chapter 6).
	Which pathological process is at work here?	Compare the scores of the client with the average scores of clients known to have the disorder (see Chapters 6 and 9).
	Is there only one or more than one pathological processes at work?	This is a little bit more difficult to disentangle and requires a comparison of the usual patterns observed with each of the two putative conditions to determine whether either or both is the culprit (see Chapter 9).
	Is the patient's presentation a genuine one, or is it due to some other cause, including the possibility of less than genuine effort?	Compare the patient's performance on measures of effort and symptom validity with those exerting less than genuine effort to determine the genuineness of the deficits (see Chapter 7).
Prior status	Do the findings represent a change from the prior level of functioning of this individual?	Compare performance in the present with those predating the current clinical presentation (see Chapter 7).
Future status	Do the findings represent a change from an assessment conducted earlier in the evolution of the condition?	Compare the present test scores with those gathered in earlier assessments to determine whether these are reliably different (see Chapter 9).

---

within this category include: Are the client's performances abnormal? Which pathological process is at work? Is the compromise global or specific? Is the client's presentation a genuine one, or is it due to some other cause, including the possibility of less than genuine effort? As we move through the clinical cases that constitute chapters 5–9 we will address each of these issues in turn. As we move through the clinical cases we will use the approaches that we have presented in chapters 1–4 as the framework on which we will evaluate the clinical hypotheses that we have generated and determine whether they apply to each of the clinical presentations.

Conclusion

In this chapter we have presented a method of evaluation using the WAIS-IV and the WMS-IV that allows us to specifically address a series of hypotheses that we can generate regarding the client's clinical presentation. We will use this approach as the principle under which we evaluate clinical hypotheses regarding the clients presented in the ensuing chapters.

CHAPTER FIVE

ARE THE FINDINGS NORMAL?
The Case of Ms Rosalie Ruby Red

If we think of assessment as the systematic collection, organisation, and interpretation of information about the person and his or her situation (Lichtenberger & Kaufman, 2009), then different assessment procedures will be indicated for different purposes. These might include: neuropsychological assessment, behavioural assessment or psychometric assessment for the purposes of determination of eligibility, particularly with regard to access to the support services provided by government and other bodies.

The first and most obvious reason that we are conducting an assessment is to ascertain the answer to the question: are the client's performances normal? More specifically, to what degree is the performance of the client within the normal variability of the instruments themselves and to what degree to some other process? The best place to begin with an analysis of the nature of intellectual abnormality therefore is the study of the intrinsic variation within the whole population and particularly the lowest reaches of that distribution, the intellectually disabled. This issue will be the focus of this chapter.

What is Intellectual Disability?

The Diagnostic and Statistical Manual of the American Psychiatric Association 4th Edition Text Revision (DSM-IV-TR; APA, 2000) notes that:

> … the essential feature of mental retardation is significantly subaverage general intellectual functioning (Criterion A) that is accompanied by significant limitations in adaptive functioning in at least two of the following skill areas: communication, healthcare, home living, social/ interpersonal skills, use of community resources, self-direction, func-

tional academic skills, work, leisure, health, and safety (Criterion B). The onset must occur before 18 years (Criterion C). Mental retardation has many different etiologies and may be seen as a final common pathway of various pathological processes that affect the functioning of the central nervous system. (p. 41)

In the DSM-IV-TR (APA, 2000) the level of intellectual functioning requisite to make a diagnosis of mental retardation is described as follows:

General intellectual functioning is defined by the intelligence quotient (IQ or IQ-equivalent) obtained by assessment with one or more of the standardised, individually administered intelligence tests (e.g., Wechsler Intelligence Scale for Children, 3rd edition; Stanford-Binet, 4th edition; Kaufman Assessment Battery for Children). Significantly sub average intellectual functioning is defined as an IQ of about 70 or below (approximately 2 standard deviations below the mean). It should be noted that there is a measurement error of approximately 5 points in assessing IQ, although this may vary from instrument to instrument (e.g., the Wechsler IQ of 70 considered to represent a range of 65–75). Thus, it is possible to diagnose mental retardation in individuals with IQs between 70 and 75 who exhibit significant deficits in adaptive behaviour. Conversely, Mental Retardation would not be diagnosed in an individual with an IQ lower than 70 if there are no significant deficits or impairments in adaptive functioning. (pp. 41–42)

The definition of mental retardation, as developed by the American Association on Mental Retardation (AAMR), was first proposed in 1983 and was subsequently refined in 1992 and once again in 2002. The definition states 'mental retardation is a disability characterised by significant limitations both in intellectual functioning and in adaptive behavior as expressed in conceptual, social, and practical adaptive skills. The disability originates before age 18' (p. 1). This definition is very similar to those of the DSM-IV-TR (2001) and feature a similar two-part definition that combines 'significant sub-average intellectual functioning' with 'concurrent deficits or impairment in adaptive functioning' (p. 37). Due to the nature of the focus of this text, we will not discuss the assessment of adaptive behaviour in any detail, as this often involves observation and situational evaluation of the client (see for example the Vineland Adaptive Behavior Scales: Second Edition; Sparrow, Cicchetti, & Balla, 2005), usually undertaken by someone who has close and ongoing contact with the client, improving the validity and reliability of these instruments.

With regard to the clinical decision-making criteria of intellectual disability, the Committee on Disability Determination for Mental Retardation (Reschly, Myers, & Hartel, 2002) have made the following recommendation related to intelligence and assessment:

Recommendation: A client must have an intelligence test score that is two or more standard deviations below the mean (e.g., a score of 70 or below, if the mean = 100 and the standard deviation = 15).

- Composite score is 70 or below: If the composite or total test score meets this criterion, then the individual has met the intellectual eligibility component.
- Composite score is between 71 and 75: If the composite score is suspected to be an invalid indicator of the person's intellectual disability and falls in the range of 71–75, a part score of 70 or below can be used to satisfy the intellectual eligibility component.
- Composite score is 76 or above: No individual can be eligible on the intellectual criterion if the composite score is 76 or above, regardless of part scores. (p. 5)

Certainly within Australia, and now much more broadly in the international context, the use of the term 'mental retardation' has become outdated and the more acceptable and appropriate terminology 'intellectual disability' (ID) is to be preferred. As Salvador-Carulla and Bertelli (2008) note:

ID may be regarded not as a disease or as a disability but as a syndrome grouping (metasyndrome) similar to the construct of dementia. It includes a heterogeneous group of clinical conditions, ranging from genetic to nutritional, infectious, metabolic or neurotoxic conditions. The ID metasyndrome is characterized by a deficit in cognitive functioning prior to the acquisition of skills through learning. The intensity of the deficit is such as to interfere in a significant way with individual's normal functioning as expressed in limitations in activities and restriction in participation (disabilities). (p. 10)

Thus intellectual disability is characterised by significantly below average general intellectual functioning with an IQ less than 70, the deficits occur in more than one domain and the aetiology of the condition may be genetic, such as in Down syndrome or the Fragile X syndrome; biological arising from metabolic conditions such as phenylketonuria; environmental as a result of exposure to teratogens *in utero* (e.g., foetal alcohol syndrome); on the basis of environmental deprivation resulting from familial retardation occurring in one parent and one or more siblings culminating in so-called cultural/familial retardation, or as a consequence of the location on the natural distribution of intelligence.

As can be seen in Figure 5.1, the bell-shaped distribution of intelligence scores means that 2.3% of the population will feature an intelligence score of 70 IQ points or less.

Based on the natural distribution of scores it is possible for us to be able to compare individuals within the population to determine if they are two or more standard deviations below the mean (i.e., their IQ is of 70 or below).

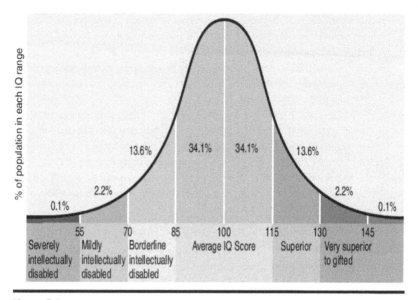

Figure 5.1
Percentage of the population in each range of IQ score.

This constitutes a statistical decision that an individual is significantly lower than the population mean (i.e., an IQ of 100). Thus, in answering the question posed by this chapter: 'are the findings normal?', we can answer this in the affirmative if the IQ is greater than or equal to two standard deviations below the mean (taking into consideration the caveats about variability surrounding the score raised above).

The Legal Context for Determination of Intellectual Disability in Australia

As we have noted in the context of the international definitions of intellectual disability, in particular those definitions found in legislation ('statutory definitions'), there is some diversity of view surrounding what constitutes a diagnosis and the criteria that need to be fulfilled to make a diagnosis of intellectual disability. The most clearly defined description of this issue in the Australian context is provided by the *Disability Act 2006* Victoria (No. 23 of 2006). Section 6, subsection 3 of the Act outlines that for the purpose of determining whether or not a person over the age of 5 years has an intellectual disability the following criteria apply:

    (a) if a standardised measurement of intelligence is used to assess general intellectual functioning and it—

(i) indicates that the person has an intelligence not higher than 2 standard deviations below the population average, then he or she must be taken to have significant sub-average general intellectual functioning;

(ii) indicates that the person has an intelligence not lower than 2 standard deviations below the population average, then he or she must be taken not to have significant sub-average general intellectual functioning;

(iii) is inconclusive as to whether or not the person has an intelligence higher or lower than 2 standard deviations below the population average, then the Secretary[1] may take into account other indicators of general intellectual functioning in determining whether or not the person has significant sub average general intellectual functioning;

(b) if a standardised measurement of adaptive behaviour is used to assess adaptive behaviour and it indicates a score at or below the second percentile of people of the same age and cultural group, then he or she must be taken to have significant deficits in adaptive behaviour.

(4) In applying a standardised measurement of intelligence for the purposes of subsection 3(a), the Secretary must consider the test result within the 95% confidence level as determined by the standard error of measurement of the test.

(5) Nothing in subsection 3 requires the Secretary to use a standardised measurement in the assessment of intellectual disability.

(6) Section 55 provides for planning for persons with an intellectual disability.

(7) Sections 86 to 88 provide for residential services for persons with an intellectual disability who require admission to a residential institution.

(8) Part 8 provides for persons with an intellectual disability who require compulsory treatment.

(9) If the Secretary is satisfied that a person has an intellectual disability, the Secretary may for the purposes of any Act or regulation provide a statement that a person has an intellectual disability within the meaning of this Act.

Thus, for our purposes, the determination of the intelligence component of the definition of ID indicates that the individual should feature a level of intelligence of 70 or below with the error estimate surrounding the score within the 95% confidence interval. Specific stipulation of which IQ score is involved (i.e., FSIQ, VIQ or PIQ) is not made, but certainly it would be fair to assume that FSIQ would be the most likely choice for such a determination. There is also no stipulation within the Act as to which form of instrument is indicated for the determination of the level of intellectual functioning, but as noted in the guidelines from the DSM-IV an individually administered intelligence test (e.g., Wechsler Intelligence Scale for Children, 3rd edition; Stanford-Binet, 4th edition; Kaufman Assessment Battery for Children), is suggested by the manual.

The clinical cases that I will present in this discussion are the actual data arising from real clients; however, various aspects of the presentation, background history and clinical description have been modified to ensure the confidentiality of the clients in question. So let us begin the discussion with the case of Ms Rosalie Ruby Red.

CASE STUDY 1: Rosalie Ruby Red

BACKGROUND

Name:	Ms Rosalie Ruby Red
Age:	25
Sex:	Female
Marital status:	Defacto with one child, Sebastian aged 14 months
Occupation:	Unemployed

ASSESSMENT

Date of Assessment:	October 10, 2009
Name of Assessor:	Simon Crowe
Type of Assessment:	Neuropsychological
Previous Assessment:	None noted, although it is most likely that Ms Ruby Red would previously have been assessed by the Department of Human Services for access to support from intellectual disability services.

NEUROPSYCHOLOGICAL EVALUATION

Description of Injury

Ms Ruby Red notes that the concerns that have brought her to the assessment include the fact that she has had a child about one year ago and the Department of Human Services in Victoria are concerned that she may not be capable of safely caring for the child.

Presentation

Ms Ruby Red is a woman of 158 cm in height and a weight of 75 kgs. She had short, brown hair. Her eyes were blue. She was casually dressed wearing a T-shirt, slacks and runners. She had earrings in each ear. Examination of her hands revealed no ingrained dirt or callusing, nor any evidence of recent physical work. She was neither depressed nor anxious on presentation. Her reality orientation seemed to be good and her cooperation was appropriate.

Present History

Ms Ruby Red's present activities include the fact that she has access to the child four days per week for five hours at a time and the rest of the time she spends with her de facto. Ms Ruby Red complained of no problems with her activities of daily living including dressing, washing, toileting or feeding herself but did note that she does not manage her own finances and the control of her finances is currently managed by the State Trustees as there is a guardianship order currently in place.

Past History

Ms Ruby Red notes no previous history of loss of consciousness nor any fits, faints, falls or funny turns. Her only previous hospitalisation was for the delivery of the child, which was undertaken by emergency caesarean section. She drinks only rarely and has not smoked cigarettes for two years. Her current medications include Fluoxetine (a serotonin-specific re-uptake inhibitor [SSRI]) for the treatment of depression. She was given a diagnosis of postnatal depression after the birth of the child. She takes no nonprescribed medications, according to her report. Ms Ruby Red has not received any psychological treatment.

Ms Ruby Red's mother and father are alive and well, respectively aged 58 and 60. There is no family history of dementia of the Alzheimer type, Parkinson's disease, alcoholism or psychiatric disorder. Ms Ruby Red, although she noted 'no trouble learning how to read or write' as a child, has had a learning disability diagnosed while she was in primary school aged nine and was transferred from the mainstream primary school to a special needs school at that stage. Ms Ruby Red indicated her most stressful life experience was having the baby.

Ms Ruby Red attended a mainstream primary school until age nine, and a special needs school until age 18 and finished there in 2001. She has only been briefly employed. In 2007 she worked as a process worker for about six months and discontinued this work when she became pregnant.

Tests Administered

I gave Ms Ruby Red the Wechsler Adult Intelligence Scale Version IV to ascertain whether she had a level of intelligence that was in the intellectually disabled range.

Test Results

To determine whether Ms Ruby Red has a level of intelligence within the intellectually disabled range we will conduct the systematic interpretation of the WAIS-IV as outlined in Chapter 4. As we noted in Chapter 4, the interpretation of the WAIS-IV takes place in nine steps.

Step 1: Interpret the full scale intelligence quotient (FSIQ). The first step in this process is to ascertain whether the FSIQ is interpretable (see Table 5.1). In this instance, the lowest index standard score VCI (70) is subtracted from highest index standard scores PSI (79) yielding a product of 9. The difference in scores is less than 1.5 standard deviations (i.e., < 23 points) indicating that the FSIQ can be interpreted as a reliable and valid estimate of Ms Ruby Red's overall intellectual ability. As can be seen from Table 1, the pattern of performances revealed by Ms Ruby Red employing the WAIS-IV indicated that she had a Full Scale IQ of 68, 95% confidence interval between 65 and 73 at the 2nd percentile rank in the mildly intellectually disabled range.

Step 2: Determine the best way to summarise overall intellectual level. Our next step is to ascertain whether Ms Ruby Red's FSIQ or her GAI should be most effectively used to summarise her overall intellectual level. Thus we will need to calculate the difference between the VCI (70) and the PRI (71), a difference of 1. The difference in scores is less than 1.5 standard deviations (i.e., < 23 points) indicating that the GAI can be interpreted as a reliable and valid esti-

---

Table 5.1
WAIS-IV Composite Score Summary

Scale	Sum of scaled scores	Composite score	Percentile rank	95% confidence interval	Qualitative description
Verbal Comprehension	14	VCI 70	2	66–77	Borderline
Perceptual Reasoning	15	PRI 71	3	66–79	Borderline
Working Memory	11	WMI 74	4	69–82	Borderline
Processing Speed	12	PSI 79	8	73–89	Borderline
Full Scale	52	FSIQ 68	2	65–73	Extremely low
General Ability	29	GAI 68	2	64–74	Extremely low

Note: Table of assessment results derived from *Wechsler Adult Intelligence Scale, Fourth Edition (WAIS-IV).*

Table 5.2
Index Level Discrepancy Comparisons

Comparison	Score 1	Score 2	Difference	Critical value .05	Significant difference Y/N	Base rate overall sample
VCI—PRI	70	71	−1	8.32	N	49.3
VCI—WMI	70	74	−4	8.81	N	38.8
VCI—PSI	70	79	−9	10.99	N	29.9
PRI—WMI	71	74	−3	8.81	N	42
PRI—PSI	71	79	−8	10.99	N	31.4
WMI—PSI	74	79	−5	11.38	N	39.5
FSIQ—GAI	68	68	0	3.51	N	

Note: Base rate by overall sample. Statistical significance (critical value) at the .05 level.
Table of assessment results derived from *Wechsler Adult Intelligence Scale, Fourth Edition (WAIS-IV)*. Copyright © 2008 NCS Pearson, Inc. Reproduced with permission. All rights reserved.

mate of Ms Ruby Red's overall intellectual ability. The next step is to undertake a comparison of the FSIQ and the GAI (see Table 5.2), which indicates that there was no difference between the two measures (i.e., both scores are 68), thus it is appropriate to use either the FSIQ or the GAI as the best summary measures of the performance for any further comparison. As the FSIQ is the more reliable measure (i.e., is composed of more subtests and as a result is less subject to error) then this should be the measure we use in preference to GAI in this instance.

Step 3: Determine whether the GAI/Cognitive Proficiency Index (CPI) is unusually large. To compute the CPI you must sum the two core subtest of the WMI and the two core subtests of the PSI. These figures can then entered into Appendix A.2 of the CD provided with *Essentials of WAIS-IV Assessment*, by Lichtenberger and Kaufman (2009). Thus, in the case of Ms Ruby Red, she had a DS (6), LN (5), SS (7), CD (5), if we add these together it produces a sum of 23, which as determined from Lichtenberger and Kaufman produces a CPI of 74.

Step 4: Do the GAI and the CPI constitute unitary abilities? The absolute difference between the GAI (68) and the CPI (74) was 6 (i.e., difference required for significance: 8.8 for $p < .05$; 11.6 for $p < .01$), indicating that the score is interpretable and that the difference was not statistically significant nor uncommon. This indicates that there is no discrepancy between these measures on this occasion.

Step 5: Are the indices unitary? The profile of index scores is presented in Figure 5.2. The profile of subtests scores by index is presented in Figure 5.3. To deter-

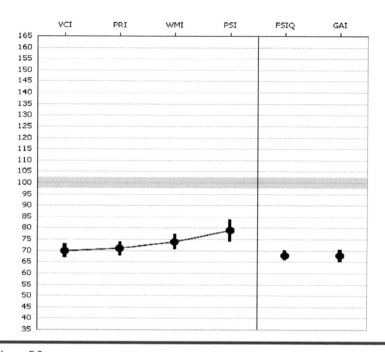

Figure 5.2

Composite score profile.

Note: The vertical bar represents the standard error of measurement (SEM).

Table of assessment results derived from *Wechsler Adult Intelligence Scale, Fourth Edition (WAIS-IV)*. Copyright © 2008 NCS Pearson, Inc. Reproduced with permission. All rights reserved.

mine whether the indices are unitary we must subtract the lowest scaled score from the highest. If the discrepancy is less than 5 points then the indices can be considered to be unitary factors. Examination of the subtest constituting the indices of the WAIS-IV (see Table 5.3) indicated that all of the discrepancies between the subtests constituting each index were all less than 5, indicating that the subtests constituting the indices were within normal limits for estimates of scatter and could be viewed as single measures of the functions of interest.

Step 5a–d: Are the index scores differences interpretable? Ms Ruby Red proved to have a Verbal Comprehension Index of 70, 95% confidence interval between 66 and 77 at the 2nd percentile rank in the borderline range, a Perceptual Reasoning Index of 71, 95% confidence interval between 66 and 79 in the borderline range, a Working Memory Index of 74, 95% confidence interval between 69 and 82 at the 4th percentile rank in the borderline range, and a Processing Speed Index of 79, 95% confidence interval between 73 and 89 in the borderline range. Comparisons between the indices indicated that there were no significant differences (see Table 5.2) between any of the

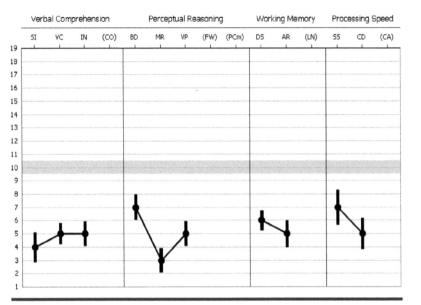

Figure 5.3

Subtest scaled score profile.

Note: The vertical bars represent the standard error of measurement (SEM).
Table of assessment results derived from *Wechsler Adult Intelligence Scale, Fourth Edition (WAIS-IV)*. Copyright © 2008 NCS Pearson, Inc. Reproduced with permission. All rights reserved.

indices, indicating that she consistently performed these within normal limits of each other in all cases.

Step 6: Determining normative strengths and weaknesses. Determination of the normative strengths and weaknesses (i.e., comparison of the performance to the normative sample) occurs by determining whether the index scores are normative weaknesses (i.e., < 85), are within normal limits (i.e., between 85 and 115) or normative strengths (> 115). In this instance, Ms Ruby Red's index scores are all below 85 thus they constitute normative weaknesses in each case.

Table 5.3
Determining the Quality of the Indices

Index	Highest subtest score	Lowest subtest core	Difference	Is the index unitary?
VCI	5	4	1	Yes
PRI	7	3	4	Yes
WMI	6	5	1	Yes
PSI	7	5	2	Yes

Step 7: Determine personal strengths and weaknesses. The personal strengths and weaknesses of the individual represent indices or factors that differ significantly from the person's own mean indices. So, in the case of Ms Ruby Red, her mean of index factors was 73.5 (i.e., 70 + 71 + 74 +79 = 294, divided by 4 = 73.5). The critical differences need for significance ($p < .05$) are VCI (5.5), PRI (5.5), WMI (5.8), PSI (7.5). Thus in no case do the score differences (i.e., VCI [–3.5], PRI [–2.5], WMI [0.5], PSI [5.5]) exceed the critical difference for significance, indicating that there were no particular strengths or weaknesses in the profile.

Step 8: Interpret significant strengths and weaknesses on the subtest profile. As we noted above, it is wise to be cautious in the interpretation of any subtest fluctuations and to reserve such an analysis of the performance until after the more reliable comparisons are made by contrasting the index and IQ scores. The reasons for fluctuations in the profile of subtest performances can be difficult to define, so use of this type of evidence should be reserved to explain differences noted by the formal analysis, rather than acting as the formal analysis itself. Nonetheless, this is a technique that has a long tradition within neuropsychology and continues to be one of value, particularly for those assessors who tend to favour a process approach. As we see from Table 5.4, examination of the subtests of the WAIS-IV indicated that Ms Ruby Red had no particular strengths or weaknesses in comparison to her mean score on all of the

Table 5.4
Differences Between Subtest and Overall Mean of Subtest Scores

Subtest	Subtest scaled score	Mean scaled score	Difference	Critical value .05	Strength or weakness	Base rate
Block design	7	5.20	1.8	2.85		>25%
Similarities	4	5.20	–1.2	2.82		>25%
Digit span	6	5.20	0.8	2.22		>25%
Matrix reasoning	3	5.20	–2.2	2.54		>25%
Vocabulary	5	5.20	–0.2	2.03		>25%
Arithmetic	5	5.20	–0.2	2.73		>25%
Symbol search	7	5.20	1.8	3.42		>25%
Visual puzzles	5	5.20	–0.2	2.71		>25%
Information	5	5.20	–0.2	2.19		>25%
Coding	5	5.20	–0.2	2.97		>25%

Note: Overall: Mean = 5.2, Scatter = 4, Base rate = 96.1.
Base rate for intersubtest scatter is reported for 10 full scale subtests.
Statistical significance (critical value) at the .05 level.
Table of assessment results derived from *Wechsler Adult Intelligence Scale, Fourth Edition (WAIS-IV)*. Copyright
© 2008 NCS Pearson, Inc. Reproduced with permission. All rights reserved.

other subtests, indicating that she consistently operates in the mildly intellectually disabled to borderline range on all measures.

Step 9: Hypothesise about fluctuations in the profile. As there were no clear fluctuations in the profile presented in Step 8, there is no need for any hypothesis generation regarding the performance. Overall, the pattern of performances revealed by Ms Ruby Red on this occasion indicates a woman of 25 years and 4 months who has had a longstanding intellectual disability who performs at this level in the present.

Conclusion

The analysis of performance conducted with Ms Ruby Red indicates that she has an intellectual disability in the mildly intellectually disabled range. Diagnostic tests on the quality of the performance revealed that there was no undue interindex or intersubtest scatter and that her performance was consistently in the mildly intellectually disabled range (i.e., full scale IQ of 68, 95% confidence interval between 65 and 73 at the 2nd percentile rank). In Chapter 6 we will develop the theme we have presented in Chapter 5 and ask the question: Is the compromise global or specific?

Endnote

1   The Secretary of the Victorian Department of Human Services.

CHAPTER SIX

Is the Compromise Global or Specific?
The Case of Colonel Keen As

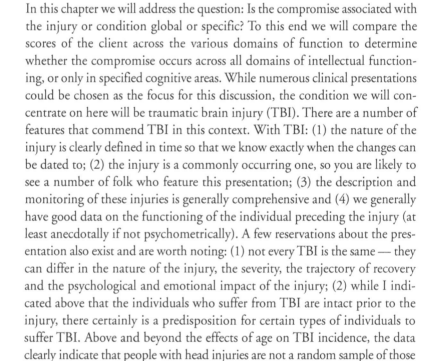

In this chapter we will address the question: Is the compromise associated with the injury or condition global or specific? To this end we will compare the scores of the client across the various domains of function to determine whether the compromise occurs across all domains of intellectual functioning, or only in specified cognitive areas. While numerous clinical presentations could be chosen as the focus for this discussion, the condition we will concentrate on here will be traumatic brain injury (TBI). There are a number of features that commend TBI in this context. With TBI: (1) the nature of the injury is clearly defined in time so that we know exactly when the changes can be dated to; (2) the injury is a commonly occurring one, so you are likely to see a number of folk who feature this presentation; (3) the description and monitoring of these injuries is generally comprehensive and (4) we generally have good data on the functioning of the individual preceding the injury (at least anecdotally if not psychometrically). A few reservations about the presentation also exist and are worth noting: (1) not every TBI is the same — they can differ in the nature of the injury, the severity, the trajectory of recovery and the psychological and emotional impact of the injury; (2) while I indicated above that the individuals who suffer from TBI are intact prior to the injury, there certainly is a predisposition for certain types of individuals to suffer TBI. Above and beyond the effects of age on TBI incidence, the data clearly indicate that people with head injuries are not a random sample of those in their age group (Jennett, 1990). Rather, they include '... an undue proportion of people with some kind of social deviancy. Some are risk-takers in cars and on motorcycles, and some are drinkers or declared alcoholics' (p. 5). These issues are discussed in considerable length in my book: *The Behavioural and Emotional Complications of Traumatic Brain Injury* (Crowe, 2008), which I recommend to you for more detail.

The consequences of a brain injury are directly dependent on the severity of the initial injury sustained (i.e., mild, moderate, severe or very severe). However, each individual case will result in a different structural and behavioural pathology depending on the nature of the injury and the physical forces of the impact, as well as the age, sex, genetic endowment and experience of the individual at the time of injury (Bigler, 2001). Thus, while TBI can be treated as if it were a common diagnostic entity, the nature of the individual component in terms of the blow, the neural substrate and the unique psychology of the individual who sustains the injury, each contribute variance to the explanation of the postinjury outcome.

The most common neurological symptoms following TBI include headache, pain, nausea, dizziness or vertigo, unsteadiness or poor coordination, tinnitus, hearing loss, blurred vision, diplopia, convergence insufficiency, increased light and noise sensitivity, and altered sense of taste and smell. The most common neuropsychological deficits include memory difficulties, decreased attention and concentration, decreased speed of information processing, compromise in working memory functioning, communication difficulties, difficulties with executive functions (including initiation and planning, concrete thinking, lack of initiative, inflexibility, the dissociation between thought and action, impulsivity, irritability and temper outbursts, interpersonal communication problems, socially inappropriate behaviours, self centredness, changes in affect, lack of insight and of self-awareness and alterations in judgment and perception), fatigue, and increased sensitivity to lack of sleep, stress, drugs and alcohol (Groher, 1977; Levin, Grossman, Rose, & Teasdale, 1979; Lezak, 1995; Morse & Montgomery, 1992; Pollens, McBrantie, & Burton, 1988; Ponsford, Sloan, & Snow, 1995).

The published research indicates that cognitive functioning recovers most rapidly during the first few weeks following a mild traumatic brain injury (MTBI) and effectively returns to baseline by one to three months postinjury in nonsports-related injuries (e.g., Iverson, 2005; Schretlen & Shapiro, 2003). The restitution of functioning in the latter group is more rapid with decrements in neuropsychological test performance resolving in 5–10 days (Iverson, 2005). Cognition also improves over the first two years after moderate to severe TBI but these individuals almost all continue to show compromise beyond this time.

Depending on the focal point and severity of the injury, more specific deficits in visual, perceptual or language processing may also be added to this list. The language deficits following TBI may include naming difficulties and diminution in fluency of speech (Bittner & Crowe, 2006a, 2006b).

Behavioural and characterological changes following TBI are often described in terms of loss of initiative, apathy, increased dependency, irritability, impulsivity, disinhibition, insensitivity to the need of others, childishness, poor judgment in social and financial matters and either hyposexuality (less commonly) or hypersexuality (more commonly) (Crowe & Ponsford, 1999), with an overall lack of insight into these personality changes (e.g., Brooks, 1984; Wood, 1990).

Neuropsychiatric illness is also a common concomitant of TBI (Jorge, 2005). Fann, Burington, Leonetti, Jaffe, Katon, and Thompson (2004) compared the frequency of psychiatric diagnoses in 939 TBI patients and 2,817 controls. The presence of any psychiatric diagnosis in the first year following the TBI was 49% in the moderate to severe group, 34% following a MTBI and 18% in the controls. In patients without a prior diagnosis of psychiatric disorder, the adjusted relative risk for psychiatric illness in the first six months following a moderate to severe TBI was 4.0 (95% CI, 2.4–6.8), (i.e., the TBI patients were four times more likely to feature psychiatric illness than were the non-injured participants). Following a MTBI it was 2.8 (95% CI, 2.1–3.7) in comparison to the noninjured controls. For those patients with a psychiatric diagnosis prior to the injury, the adjusted relative risk in the first six months postinjury was 2.1 (95% CI, 1.3–3.3) for moderate to severe TBI and 1.6 (95% CI, 1.2–2.0) for MTBI. Prior psychiatric illness proved to be a significant predictor of psychiatric morbidity post-TBI, and these problems tended to persist for these patients. This was particularly the case for patients with a previous history of mood or anxiety disorders or with a history of alcohol abuse (Dikmen, Bombadier, Machamer, Fann, & Temkin, 2004; Jorge, 2005; Wilde et al., 2004).

Behaviour disturbances such as impulsivity, poor self-control, inability to organise oneself to complete daily activities and lack of flexibility (Proctor, Wilson, Sanchez, & Wesley, 2000) can have a devastating impact upon the individual in terms of reintegrating into their pre-injury lives and functioning adequately and independently in society. In addition, these individuals may have diminished awareness and understanding of their impairments, which can affect their ability to engage in rehabilitation and learn compensatory strategies to enhance their ability to live independently.

The most common emotional difficulties following TBI include: emotional lability, irritability and aggression, change in personality, fatigue, decreased energy, anxiety, depression, apathy, disordered sleep, loss of libido and poor appetite (Anderson, 1995). Fatigue, emotional distress and pain are each very common following TBI irrespective of severity.

As a result of the cognitive impairments such as slowed speed of information processing and attentional difficulties, many tasks that were once automatic for the individual — such as concentrating, monitoring ongoing performance and warding off distractions — can only be completed with deliberate effort (Lezak et al., 2004). The extra effort required to complete these once automatic tasks leads to the individual becoming more easily fatigued, reducing yet further the amount of energy that the individual has to expend to undertake the task in hand. The increasing effort required to complete tasks and the resulting fatigue often leads to the individual becoming irritable, frustrated and angry.

TBI can also result in a variety of neuropsychiatric disturbances ranging from subtle deficits through to severe intellectual and emotional disturbances. In rare cases, it can result in chronic vegetative states. The neuropsychiatric disturbances associated with TBI include cognitive impairments, mood disorders, anxiety disorders, psychosis and behavioural problems (Rao & Lyketsos, 2000).

Researchers have observed increased rates of depression, mania, generalised anxiety disorder, psychosis, behavioural dyscontrol, and cognitive deficits following TBI when compared to the rates in the general population. Others have also suggested increase rates of obsessive–compulsive symptoms, post-traumatic stress disorder, depersonalisation and personality disorder. Many of these syndromes are common both with the severely brain injured, as well as in the mildly injured subjects. While these disorders occur in the acute phase of TBI, delayed onset of symptoms also occurs and how these neuroanatomical, psychological, cognitive medical and social factors interact to determine the resulting psychopathology is still in need of clarification (Fann, 1997).

The residual emotional and behavioural difficulties that occur for individuals who have sustained a traumatic brain injury have been well documented in the contemporary literature (Crowe, 2008). Lishman. for example, estimates that 'the psychiatric consequences and their social repercussions may be judged to be significant in upwards of a quarter of patients who survive' (Lishman, 1997, p. 161). These issues encompass a complex and interdependent set of variables that can lead on to a number of pathological states including substance abuse, depression, anxiety, chronic suicidal or homicidal ideation and action, poor impulse control, significant increase of frustration and poor insight into behavioural and emotional processes as well as the numerous psychosocial complications associated with the injury (Delmonico, Hanley-Peterson, & Englander, 1998).

The majority of patients with mild TBI recover fairly quickly and are usually completely restored to their pre-injury level of functioning in a relatively brief period of time following the initial injury (Mooney & Speed, 2001). However, a significant minority have prolonged, complicated or incomplete recoveries and display outcomes disproportionately worse than would have been predicted on the basis of the objective factors associated with the biomechanics of the injury. It is those individuals who, as a consequence of the injury or the interaction of the injury with their pre-injury state, have the disproportionately worse outcomes that constitute the principal focus of this discussion.

So let us begin the discussion with the case of Colonel Kevin Keen As.

CASE STUDY 2: Colonel Kevin Keen As

BACKGROUND

Name:	Colonel Kevin Keen As
Age:	53
Sex:	Male
Marital status:	Married with two children, a son aged 24 and a daughter aged 26
Country of birth:	Australia
Language spoken:	English
Interpreter used:	No
Occupation:	Plumber
Employer:	Comprehensive Waterworks P/L
Handedness:	Right

ASSESSMENT

Date of Assessment:	12/03/2010
Name of Assessor:	Simon Crowe
Type of Assessment:	Neuropsychological
Previous Assessment:	I had previously examined Colonel Keen As twice before the current assessment. The first of these assessments occurred 24 months after the initial injury and the more recent one 58 months following the initial injury. At that stage I noted by way of conclusion that, 'The pattern of performances revealed by Colonel Keen As on this occasion indicates a man of 47 years and five months who was subjected to a severe to very severe

closed head injury some four years and 10 months ago, who presents with attenuation of his speed of processing and perceptual organisation in association with deficits of the frontal executive functions including poor ability to be able to control his responses both verbally and visuospatially, as well as deficits in fine motor coordination of both his right and left hand. These deficits exist in association with moderate levels of self-reported depression, severe levels of self-reported anxiety and moderately severe levels of self-reported abnormal illness behaviour. Colonel Keen As has considerably improved since my previous assessment of him and now his memory functions are within the normal range, considerably better than they were in my previous assessment, and his other functions do not demonstrate as severe a compromise as they had on my last assessment. This improvement in performance seems to be associated with the better control of his emotional state (either due to his medication regime or the counselling he has been having or both) in the present that has resulted in some diminution of his level of psychopathology as reflected by the self-reported measures of depression and anxiety. He continues to have a post-injury personality change with coarsening of his personality, a much more disinhibited style of response, as well as inability to be able to plan and anticipate at the same level he was capable of before his injury and explosiveness'.

NEUROPSYCHOLOGICAL EVALUATION
Description of Injury
Colonel Keen As was working on the roof of a factory, installing spouting, when he fell backwards from a height of about 10 metres to the concrete pavement below.

Presentation
Colonel Keen As is a man of 161 cm in height and a weight of 88.7 kgs. He had red hair flecked with grey and was male patterned bald stage one. His eyes were brown and he wore glasses throughout the interview. He was casually dressed wearing a flannelette shirt, jeans and boots. He presented as clean-shaven and rosy cheeked. Examination of his hands revealed no ingrained dirt

or callusing, consistent with the fact that he had not recently been involved in hard physical work.

Present History

Colonel Keen As's last recall of events before the accident taking place was slipping from the roof. His first recall of events afterwards was about one to two weeks later. He noted he could not remember much from the first week following the accident and his first recall of events was while he was in Head Injury Hospital some several days later. This indicates that Colonel Keen As had a loss of consciousness and associated posttraumatic amnesia in the vicinity of about one week and a very brief period of retrograde amnesia (loss of recall of events preceding the injury), consistent with the notion of a very severe closed head injury.

Since his injury, Colonel Keen As notes that he feels much more nervous and frustrated, he has diminution of his memory, he has to write things down and keeps a diary to remember things, he has loss of sense of smell and some attenuation of his sense of taste. He has diminution of sexual functioning and notes that he cannot ejaculate, and has had some personality changes. He also notes problems finding his words and is much more circumlocutory in his conversational style. Colonel Keen As's wife, Carla, who attended with him, notes that living with Colonel Keen As is like having another child to look after. She has to be with him all the time. She has to go everywhere with him and if she cannot attend any function, he will not go by himself.

Colonel Keen As's current activities indicate that he does his chores at home. He maintains his role as a father and enjoys cooking. The children are able to cope with Colonel Keen As but they treat him as if he were just another sibling. When he manages to infuriate them (which occurs often) they take off and allow the situation to pass. Colonel Keen As complained of no problems with his activities of daily living including dressing, washing, toileting or feeding himself, but he no longer manages his own finances, which are now cared for by his wife.

Past History

Colonel Keen As attended primary school at the Top Notch Primary School and secondary school at the Urban and Industrial Technical School, where he completed Year 10. He commenced Year 11 in the following year but discontinued halfway through to take up an apprenticeship in plumbing. Colonel Keen As indicated he was an average student; his best subjects were English and geography and his worst subject mathematics. Colonel Keen As worked as a subcontract plumber from 1981 up to the time of the injury in 1999. He was never in the military and his commission is honorary. Colonel Keen As is still taking Aropax (paroxetine, a serotonin specific re-uptake inhibitor [SSRI] for depression), Serenace (haloperidol, an typical antipsychotic agent for agitation), Epilim (sodium valproate, an anti-epileptic agent and mood stabiliser, for mood stabilisation) and Inderal (propranolol, for hypertension) and he takes nonprescribed Nurofen (ibuprofen) for headache. He has had no return to work or any return to work attempts since his injury.

Tests Administered

I gave Colonel Keen As the Wechsler Adult Intelligence Scale Version IV (WAIS-IV), the Wechsler Memory Scale Version IV (WMS-IV) and the Test of Premorbid Function (TOPF) from the Advanced Clinical Solutions for WAIS-IV and WMS-IV (PsychCorp, 2009) to test the following hypotheses:

- Did Colonel Keen As have intelligence in the normal range?
- Were there any areas of weakness in Colonel Keen As's profile of intellectual skills?
- Did Colonel Keen As have memory functions equivalent to the level we would expect from someone of his current level of ability and in comparison to estimates of his ability preceding his injury?

Test Results

To conduct the systematic interpretation of the WAIS-IV and WMS-IV we need to undertake the steps we outlined in Chapter 4.

Step 1: Interpret the full scale intelligence quotient (FSIQ). The first step in this process is to ascertain whether the FSIQ is interpretable (see Table 6.1). In this instance, the lowest index standard score PSI (71) is subtracted from highest index standard scores WMI (86) yielding a product of 15. The difference in scores is less than 1.5 standard deviations (i.e., < 23 points) indicating that the FSIQ can be interpreted as a reliable and valid estimate of Colonel Keen As's overall intellectual ability. As can be seen from Table 6.1, the pattern of performances revealed by Colonel Keen As employing the WAIS-IV indicated that he had a Full Scale IQ of 74, 95% confidence interval between 70 and 79 at the 4th percentile rank in the borderline range.

Step 2: Determine the best way to summarise overall intellectual level. Our next step is to ascertain that Colonel Keen As's GAI can be effectively used to summarise his overall intellectual level. Thus we will need to calculate the difference between the VCI (76) and the PRI (81), an absolute difference of 5. The difference in scores is less than 1.5 standard deviations (i.e., < 23 points) indicating that the GAI can be interpreted as a reliable and valid estimate of his overall intellectual ability.

Table 6.1
WAIS-IV Composite Score Summary

Scale	Sum of scaled scores	Composite score	Percentile rank	95% CI	Qualitative description
Verbal Comprehension	17	VCI 76	5	71–83	Borderline
Perceptual Reasoning	20	PRI 81	10	76–88	Low average
Working Memory	15	WMI 86	18	80–94	Low average
Processing Speed	9	PSI 71	3	66–82	Borderline
Full Scale	61	FSIQ 74	4	70–79	Borderline
General Ability	37	GAI 76	5	72–82	Borderline

Note: Table of assessment results derived from *Wechsler Adult Intelligence Scale, Fourth Edition (WAIS-IV)*. Copyright © 2008 NCS Pearson, Inc. Reproduced with permission. All rights reserved.

The next step is to undertake a comparison of the FSIQ and the GAI (see Table 6.2), which indicates that there was a difference of 2 points between the two measures (i.e., GAI 76; FSIQ 74; pcrit [i.e., critical difference between scores at $p \leq .05$] = 3.29, base rate [i.e., frequency in which this difference occurred in the normative sample] = 37.6), thus the difference does not exceed the critical difference, hence it is appropriate to use either the FSIQ or the GAI as the best summary measures of the performance for any further comparison. As the FSIQ is the more reliable measure (i.e., is composed of more subtests and as a result is less subject to error) then this should be the measure we use in preference to GAI in this instance.

Step 3: Determine whether the GAI/Cognitive Proficiency Index (CPI) is unusually large. To compute the CPI you must sum the two core subtests of the WMI

Table 6.2
Index Level Discrepancy Comparisons

Comparison	Score 1	Score 2	Difference	Critical value .05	Significant difference Y/N	Base rate overall sample
VCI—PRI	76	81	−5	7.78	N	37.1
VCI—WMI	76	86	−10	8.31	Y	22.1
VCI—PSI	76	71	5	11.76	N	39.1
PRI—WMI	81	86	−5	8.81	N	37.1
PRI—PSI	81	71	10	12.12	N	25.6
WMI—PSI	86	71	15	12.47	Y	16
FSIQ—GAI	74	76	−2	3.29	N	37.6

Note: Base rate by overall sample. Statistical significance (critical value) at the .05 level.
Table of assessment results derived from *Wechsler Adult Intelligence Scale, Fourth Edition (WAIS-IV)*. Copyright © 2008 NCS Pearson, Inc. Reproduced with permission. All rights reserved.

and the two core subtests of the PSI. These figures can then entered into Appendix A.2 of the CD provided with Lichtenberger and Kaufman (2009). Thus, in the case of Colonel Keen As, he had a DS (9), LN (6), SS (4), CD (5), if we add these scores together it produces a sum of 24, which as determined from Lichtenberger and Kaufman produces a CPI of 75.

Step 4: Do the GAI and the CPI constitute unitary abilities? The absolute difference between the GAI (76) and the CPI (75) was 1 (i.e., the difference required for statistically significant differences between scores is 8.8 with $p \leq$ .05 and 11.6 with $p \leq .01$), indicating that the score is interpretable and that the scores are not significantly different from each other and that the frequency of the difference is not uncommon. This indicates that there is no discrepancy between these measures on this occasion.

Step 5: Are the indices unitary? The profile of index scores is presented in Figure 6.1. The profile of subtests scores by index is presented in Figure 6.2. To determine whether the indices are unitary we must subtract the lowest scaled score from the highest. If the discrepancy is less than 5 points (i.e., the standard devi-

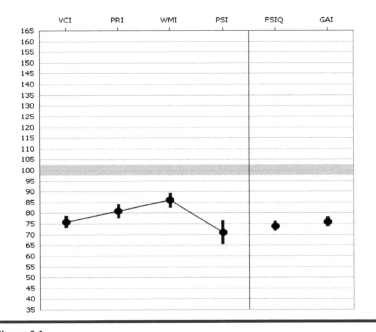

Figure 6.1

Composite score profile.

Note: The vertical bars represent the standard error of measurement (SEM).

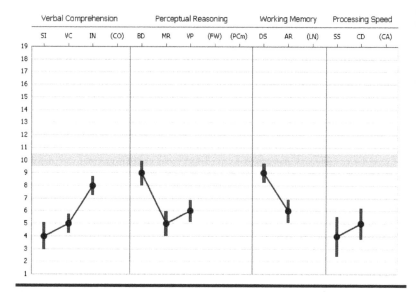

Figure 6.2

Subtest scaled score profile.

Note: The vertical bars represent the standard error of measurement (SEM).
      Assessment results derived from *Wechsler Adult Intelligence Scale, Fourth Edition (WAIS-IV)*.
      Copyright © 2008 NCS Pearson, Inc. Reproduced with permission. All rights reserved.

ation (sd) for each subtest = 3, therefore 1.5sds = 4.5, rounded up to 5 to ensure that the score is clearly in the rejection range) then the indices can be considered to be unitary factors. Examination of the subtest constituting the indices of the WAIS-IV (see Table 6.3) indicated that all of the discrepancies between the subtests constituting each index were less than 5, indicating that the subtests constituting the indices were within normal limits for estimates of scatter and could be viewed as single measures of the functions of interest.

Step 5a-d: Are the index scores differences interpretable? Colonel Keen As proved to have a Verbal Comprehension Index of 76, 95% confidence interval between

Table 6.3
Determining the Quality of the Indices

Index	Highest subtest score	Lowest subtest core	Difference	Is the index unitary? (i.e., difference < 5)
VCI	8	4	4	Yes
PRI	9	5	4	Yes
WMI	9	6	3	Yes
PSI	5	4	1	Yes

71 and 83 at the 5th percentile rank in the borderline range, a Perceptual Reasoning Index of 81, 95% confidence interval between 76 and 88 at the 10th percentile in the low average range, a Working Memory Index of 86, 95% confidence interval between 80 and 94 at the 18th percentile rank in the low average range, a Processing Speed Index of 71, 95% confidence interval between 66 and 82 at the 3rd percentile rank in the borderline range and a General Ability Index of 76, 95% confidence interval between 72 and 82 at the 5th percentile rank in the borderline range. Comparisons between the indices indicated that there were significant differences ($p \leq .05$; see Table 6.2) in the case of the VCI–WMI comparison and for the WMI–PSI comparison. The base rates of these differences were relatively uncommon (i.e., 22.1% in the overall sample in the case of the VCI–WMI comparison and 16% in the case of the WMI–PSI comparison). This indicates that Colonel Keen As performs better on tests of working memory than he does on some other aspects of the assessment conducted on this occasion.

Step 6: Determining normative strengths and weaknesses. Determination of the normative strengths and weaknesses occurs by deciding whether the index scores are normative weaknesses (i.e., < 85), are within normal limits (i.e., between 85 and 115) or normative strengths (> 115). In this instance, Colonel Keen As's index scores for VCI, PRI and PSI were all below and 85 thus constitute normative weaknesses in each case. Colonel Keen As's index score for WMI was within the normal range.

Step 7: Determine personal strengths and weaknesses. The personal strengths and weaknesses of the individual represent indices or factors that differ significantly from the person's own mean indices. So in the case of Colonel Keen As, his rounded mean of index factors was 78.5 (i.e., 76 + 81 + 86 +71 = 314, divided by 4 = 78.5). The critical differences needed for significance ($p < .05$) are VCI (5.1), PRI (5.5), WMI (5.9), PSI (8.3). Thus, in only in the case of WMI (7.5) (i.e., VCI [–2.5], PRI [2.5], PSI [–7.5]), do the score differences exceed the critical difference for significance, indicating that WMI constitutes a personal strength in Colonel Keen As's profile.

Step 8: Interpret significant strengths and weaknesses on the subtest profile. As we noted above, it is wise to be cautious in the interpretation of any subtest fluctuations and to reserve such an analysis of the performance until after the more statistically reliable comparisons are made by contrasting the index and IQ scores. The reasons for fluctuations in the profile of subtest performances can be difficult to specify, so use of this type of evidence should be reserved to explain differences noted with the formal analysis, rather than acting as the formal analysis itself. Nonetheless, this is a technique that has a long tradition within neuropsychology and continues to be one of value, particularly for those

Table 6.4
Differences Between Subtest and Overall Mean of Subtest Scores

Subtest	Subtest scaled score	Mean scaled score	Difference	Critical value .05	Strength or weakness	Base rate
Block Design	9	6.10	2.9	2.85	S	15–25%
Similarities	4	6.10	–2.1	2.82		> 25%
Digit Span	9	6.10	2.9	2.22	S	15–25%
Matrix Reasoning	5	6.10	–1.1	2.54		> 25%
Vocabulary	5	6.10	–1.1	2.03		> 25%
Arithmetic	6	6.10	–0.1	2.73		> 25%
Symbol Search	4	6.10	–2.1	3.42		> 25%
Visual Puzzles	6	6.10	–0.1	2.71		> 25%
Information	8	6.10	1.9	2.19		> 25%

Note: Overall: Mean = 6.1, Scatter = 5, Base rate = 85.4.
 Base Rate for Intersubtest Scatter is reported for 10 full scale subtests.
 Statistical significance (critical value) at the .05 level.
 Table of assessment results derived from *Wechsler Adult Intelligence Scale, Fourth Edition (WAIS-IV)*.
 Copyright © 2008 NCS Pearson, Inc. Reproduced with permission. All rights reserved.

assessors who tend to favour a process approach. As we see from Table 6.4, examination of the subtests of the WAIS-IV indicated that Colonel Keen As had particular strength in comparison to his mean score on all other subtests for the Block Design and Digit Span subtests in comparison to his performance on the other measures.

Step 9: Hypothesise about fluctuations in the profile. As there were fluctuations in the profile presented in Step 8, we can speculate about what these particular measures might constitute in Colonel Keen As's profile. The subtest-level comparisons of the WAIS-IV allow us to make comparisons at the level of subtest score and at the level of cognitive process (see Tables 6.5 and 6.6). As we can see from Table 6.4, Colonel Keen As has strengths in both Block Design and Arithmetic.

With regard to the cognitive processes involved the analysis presented in Table 6.5 indicates that Colonel Keen As performs significantly better on the Digit Span subtest in comparison to his performance on the Arithmetic subtest. If we examine this finding more closely with the data presented in Table 6.6, we can see that Colonel Keen As is performing much better on the reversal of digit spans than he does on sequencing the spans. Combining the finding of the relatively lower performance on Arithmetic and the performance on Digit Span sequencing, we might suggest that Colonel Keen As is performing at an attenuated level on tasks involving numerical calculation and number processing, perhaps due to educational deprivation of long standing.

Table 6.5

Subtest Level Discrepancy Comparisons

Subtest Comparison	Score 1	Score 2	Difference	Critical value .05	Significant difference Y/N	Base rate
Digit Span–Arithmetic	9	6	3	2.57	Y	17.5
Symbol Search–Coding	4	5	-1	3.41	N	40.1

Note: Statistical significance (critical value) at the .05 level.
Table of assessment results derived from *Wechsler Adult Intelligence Scale, Fourth Edition (WAIS-IV)*.
Copyright © 2008 NCS Pearson, Inc. Reproduced with permission. All rights reserved.

Table 6.6

Process Level Discrepancy Comparisons

Process Comparison	Score 1	Score 2	Difference	Critical value .05	Significant difference Y/N	Base rate
Block Design–Block Design No Time Bonus	9	9	0	3.08	N	
Digit Span Forward–Digit Span Backward	9	11	–2	3.65	N	31.5
Digit Span Forward–Digit Span Sequencing	9	7	2	3.6	N	31.3
Digit Span Backward–Digit Span Sequencing	11	7	4	3.56	Y	12.5
Longest DS Forward–Longest DS Backward	6	6	0	—	—	
Longest DS Forward–Longest DS Sequence	6	4	2	—	—	39.5
Longest DS Backward–Longest DS Sequence	6	4	2	—	—	5

Note: Statistical significance (critical value) at the .05 level.
Table of assessment results derived from *Wechsler Adult Intelligence Scale, Fourth Edition (WAIS-IV)*.
Copyright © 2008 NCS Pearson, Inc. Reproduced with permission. All rights reserved.

In our generation of hypotheses regarding Colonel Keen As's performance we generated two specific hypotheses:

- Did Colonel Keen As have intelligence in the normal range?
- Were there any areas of weakness in Colonel Keen As's profile of intellectual skills?

In response to the first hypothesis it is clear that Colonel Keen As does not have intelligence in the normal range as both his FSIQ and his GAI are in the borderline range of functioning. While we would need further evidence to determine whether it is reasonable to expect that he would have been performing at a level superior to this preceding his injury, this is a question that must be addressed in its own right. The investigation relative to the second hypothesis indicates that Colonel Keen As features weaker performances on VCI and PSI than he does on PRI and WMI, and WMI represents a normative strength for the Colonel.

Colonel Keen As's Performance on the WMS-IV

As we noted in our discussion of the effects of TBI on neuropsychological functioning above, memory processes represent the most sensitive indicator of compromise following TBI. As a result, it seems worthwhile for us to examine this function in Colonel Keen As's case.

Step 1: Is there an attentional problem? As we see from our discussion above regarding Colonel Keen As's performance on the WAIS-IV, he is capable of attending, concentrating and focusing on the assessment in a sufficient way not to require specific evaluation of attentional focus on the task. As a result, it was deemed unnecessary to undertake the Brief Cognitive State Examination in this case, and the assessment immediately moved to the evaluation of memory functioning.

Step 2: Do the indices represent unitary constructs? As we noted in our discussion of the WMS-IV in Chapter 3, the full battery yields five indices: the Auditory Memory Index (AMI), the Visual Memory Index (VMI), the Immediate Memory Index (IMI), the Delayed Memory Index (DMI) and the Visual Working Memory Index (VWMI). In the assessment of Colonel Keen As, due to the constraints of time, the subtests constituting the VWMI were not administered.

To determine whether the indices represent unitary constructs we must compare each subtest within the index with the others to ascertain the level of intrasubtest scatter. The data surrounding this analysis in the case of Colonel Keen As are presented in Tables 6.7–6.10.

Table 6.7
Auditory Memory Index

Subtest	Scaled score	AMI mean score	Difference from mean	Critical value	Base rate
Logical Memory I	8	5.75	2.25	2.64	15–25%
Logical Memory II	7	5.75	1.25	2.48	> 25%
Verbal Paired Associates I	4	5.75	−1.75	1.90	> 25%
Verbal Paired Associates II	4	5.75	−1.75	2.48	> 25%

Note: Statistical significance (critical value) at the .05 level.
  Table of assessment results derived from *Wechsler Memory Scale, Fourth Edition (WMS-IV)*.
  Copyright © 2009 NCS Pearson, Inc. Reproduced with permission. All rights reserved.

Table 6.8
Visual Memory Index

Subtest	Scaled score	VMI mean score	Difference from mean	Critical value	Base rate
Designs I	5	6.50	−1.50	2.38	> 25%
Designs II	8	6.50	1.50	2.38	> 25%
Visual Reproduction I	6	6.50	−0.50	1.86	> 25%
Visual Reproduction II	7	6.50	0.50	1.48	> 25%

Note: Statistical significance (critical value) at the .05 level.

Table 6.9
Immediate Memory Index

Subtest	Scaled score	IMI mean score	Difference from mean	Critical value	Base rate
Logical Memory I	8	5.75	2.25	2.59	> 25%
Verbal Paired Associates I	4	5.75	−1.75	1.82	> 25%
Designs I	5	5.75	−0.75	2.42	> 25%
Visual Reproduction I	6	5.75	0.25	1.91	> 25%

Note: Statistical significance (critical value) at the .05 level.

Table 6.10
Delayed Memory Index

Subtest	Scaled score	DMI mean score	Difference from mean	Critical value	Base rate
Logical Memory II	7	6.50	0.50	2.44	> 25%
Verbal Paired Associates II	4	6.50	−2.50	2.44	15–25%
Designs II	8	6.50	1.50	2.44	> 25%
Visual Reproduction II	7	6.50	0.50	1.57	> 25%

Note: Statistical significance (critical value) at the .05 level.

As we can see from the analysis, in no case do Colonel Keen As's scores indicate a significant subtest difference from the mean score on the subtests constituting the index, thus the index scores do represent unitary factors. You will also note that this approach to assessing the consistency of the index is slightly different to the way that we approached this issue with the WAIS-IV in which we determined a spread of scores, rather than a difference from the

Table 6.11
Index Score Summary

Index	Sum of scaled scores	Index score	Percentile rank	95% CI	Qualitative description
Auditory Memory	23	AMI 75	5	70–82	Borderline
Visual Memory	26	VMI 80	9	75–86	Low Average
Immediate Memory	23	IMI 72	3	67–80	Borderline
Delayed Memory	26	DMI 76	5	71–84	Borderline

Note: Table of assessment results derived from *Wechsler Memory Scale, Fourth Edition (WMS-IV)*.
Copyright © 2009 NCS Pearson, Inc. Reproduced with permission. All rights reserved.

means score, but either approach is quite appropriate. It is also possible to apply this method with the WMS-IV. In no instance was the difference between the largest scaled score minus the smallest scaled score 5 or more, indicating that there was no undue scatter. Choice of method here is up to you. It is worthwhile to note in this context that in the case that we do observe significant subtest variability within an index, it does not preclude interpretation of the index nor invalidate the finding, but does suggest caution in its interpretation as it may represent more than one component operating within the profile of index performance. This may be influenced by a specific form of memory difficulty in the index and the clinician should account for this discrepancy in the reporting of their result (Wechsler, 2009b).

Step 3: How well does the person learn as a function of modality of information? As we have now determined that the indices indicate unitary factors in Colonel Keen As's case we can move on to the examination of the components of his memory functioning. The performance of Colonel Keen As on each of the indices is presented in Table 6.11 and in Figure 6.3.

This indicated that he had an Auditory Immediate Memory Index of 75, 95% confidence interval between 70 and 82 at the 5th percentile rank in the borderline range; a Visual Immediate Memory Index of 80, 95% confidence interval between 75 and 86 at the 9th percentile rank in the low average range; an Immediate Memory Index of 72, 95% confidence interval between 67 and 80 at the 3rd percentile rank in the borderline range and a Delayed Memory Index of 76, 95% confidence interval between 71 and 84 at the 5th percentile rank in the borderline range.

Step 4: Is there a difference between modalities? The comparison between the AMI and VMI is presented in Table 6.12. Here we see that the comparison between AMI and the VMI indicate a contrast scaled score of 8. As noted in the *Technical and Interpretive Manual of the WMS-IV* (Wechsler, 2009b):

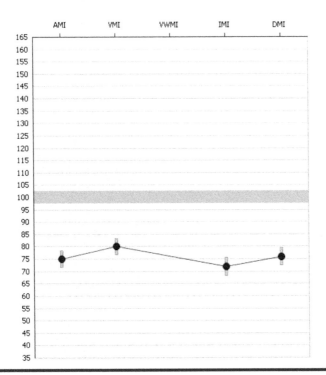

Figure 6.3
Index score profile.

Note: The vertical bars represent the standard error of measurement (SEM).
   Assessment results derived from *Wechsler Memory Scale, Fourth Edition (WMS-IV)*.
   Copyright © 2009 NCS Pearson, Inc. Reproduced with permission. All rights reserved.

Contrast scaled scores test hypotheses about the degree to which common variance may account for performance of one score on a related score … The resulting scaled score is interpreted in the same manner at all ability levels on the control variable (i.e., if the delayed memory score controlling for immediate memory is a scaled score of 6, then the examinee is at the 9th percentile on delayed memory when compared to individuals of similar immediate memory ability [see Table 5.1]). For contrast scores, values between 8 and 12 are in bold or highlighted in the conversion table to denote that performance on the control and dependent variables do not differ from one another. That is, performance on the dependent measure is primarily due to common variance rather than due to the unique processes measured by the dependent measure. (p. 153)

As we see in the case of Colonel Keen As, the comparison of the AMI and the VMI is in the range between 8 and 12 indicating that they do not differ.

Step 5: How well does the person recall following a delay? The comparison of immediate versus delayed memory is also presented in Table 6.12. Colonel Keen As proved to have a contrast scaled score on this comparison of 11 (i.e., a score between 8 and 12), once again indicating that the two scores did not differ.

Step 6: Do they benefit from cues or choices? The primary subtests scaled score performance of Colonel Keen As is presented in Table 6.13.

The performance is described in terms of percentile rank. As noted in the *Technical and Interpretive Manual* (Wechsler, 2009b):

> Percentiles are based on a *z* transformation to determine where the scores fall relative to a normal distribution. Cumulative percentages indicate the percentage of examinees who obtain specific scores and are minimally smoothed for reversals across age groups. The interpretation for a cumulative percentage and a percentile are slightly different. For example, a score at the 9th percentile is interpreted to mean that the examinee's score is better than 9% of age peers. A cumulative percentage of 9% is interpreted to mean that 9% of the examinees in the age group have the same or lower score. (p. 153)

Table 6.12
Index-Level Contrast Scaled Scores

Score	Score 1	Score 2	Contrast scaled score
Auditory Memory Index vs. Visual Memory Index	75	80	8
Immediate Memory Index vs. Delayed Memory Index	72	76	11

Note: Table of assessment results derived from *Wechsler Memory Scale, Fourth Edition (WMS-IV)*. Copyright © 2009 NCS Pearson, Inc. Reproduced with permission. All rights reserved.

Table 6.13
Primary Subtest Scaled Score Summary

Subtest	Domain	Raw score	Scaled score	Percentile rank
Logical Memory I	AM	20	8	25
Logical Memory II	AM	15	7	16
Verbal Paired Associates I	AM	11	4	2
Verbal Paired Associates II	AM	3	4	2
Designs I	VM	48	5	5
Designs II	VM	47	8	25
Visual Reproduction I	VM	28	6	9
Visual Reproduction II	VM	16	7	16

Note: Table of assessment results derived from *Wechsler Memory Scale, Fourth Edition (WMS-IV)*. Copyright © 2009 NCS Pearson, Inc. Reproduced with permission. All rights reserved.

Thus, in our interpretation of Colonel Keen As's performance, we see that he performs in a manner at less than the 10th percentile for the Verbal Paired Associate (VPA) I and II, for the Designs I and for the Visual Reproduction I. He performs at a better level than this on each of the other subtests. We could conclude from this information that he performs worse for immediately presented information, but once he has been exposed to the information (i.e., following delay) his recall is better (although obviously this is not the case with regard to the VPA-II).

How then does he perform, relatively speaking, with regard to cued recall? In Tables 6.14 and 6.15, we can see that Colonel Keen As performs adequately (i.e., at > 10th cumulative percentage) for each of the recognition measures, with the exception once again of the VPA. It would appear that his recall is aided by recognition with the single exception of his performance on VPA, which indicates that even with the facilitation provided by recognition cueing, he did not improve his performance. This probably indicates that he had no record of the associates available in memory for them to be aided by recognition cuing.

Table 6.14
Auditory Memory Process Score Summary

Process score	Raw score	Scaled score	Percentile rank	Cumulative percentage (base rate)
LM II Recognition	21	—	—	10–16%
VPA II Recognition	22	—	—	≤ 2%

Note: Table of assessment results derived from *Wechsler Memory Scale, Fourth Edition (WMS-IV)*.
Copyright © 2009 NCS Pearson, Inc. Reproduced with permission. All rights reserved.

Table 6.15
Visual Memory Process Score Summary

Process score	Raw score	Scaled score	Percentile rank	Cumulative percentage (base rate)
DE I Content	30	7	16	—
DE I Spatial	14	8	25	—
DE II Content	27	7	16	—
DE II Spatial	14	12	75	—
DE II Recognition	11	—	—	10–16%
VR II Recognition	6	—	—	51–75%

Note: Table of assessment results derived from *Wechsler Memory Scale, Fourth Edition (WMS-IV)*.
Copyright © 2009 NCS Pearson, Inc. Reproduced with permission. All rights reserved.

Step 7: How well does the person recall in comparison to other aspects of their performance? As we have discussed in Chapter 5, the interpretation of the client's performance should be both normative and ipsative. With regard to this latter concern, one thing that we are interested in doing in our interpretation of the performance is to ascertain whether the person's performance is at the level we should expect, based upon other aspects of their performance. To undertake this step we must first determine the right measure to which we should compare the memory performances. In the case of Table 6.16, we can compare Colonel Keen As's performance to his GAI. As we discussed in Step 2 of the WAIS-IV Colonel Keen As performed equivalently on the FSIQ and the GAI indicating either measure is appropriate for comparison purposes. This indicates that he performs in a manner less than would be expected by his GAI for the AMI and for the IMI. While these differences are statistically significant, they are only moderately rare, occurring in 15–20% and 15% of the standardisation sample respectively in each case. Thus, it is clear that Colonel Keen As is performing at a level less than would be expected on the basis of his ability, and the level of compromise is in the mild to moderately impaired range particularly for auditory and immediate memory.

It is also possible for us to compare Colonel Keen As's performances to what we should have expected of him preceding his injury, as based upon estimations of his premorbid functioning. As we noted in Chapter 3, the Test of Premorbid Function (TOPF) from the Advanced Clinical Solutions for the WAIS-IV and WMS-IV package is the updated revision of the WTAR, which predicts performance on the WAIS-IV and the WMS-IV (PsychCorp, 2009). As we can see in Table 6.17 and 6.18, Colonel Keen As is performing below estimates, as based upon the performance on the word reading test as modi-

---

Table 6.16
Ability-Memory Analysis

Predicted Difference Method

Index	Predicted WMS–IV Index score	Actual WMS–IV Index score	Difference	Critical value	Significant difference Y/N	Base rate
Auditory Memory	87	75	12	9.38	Y	15–20%
Visual Memory	86	80	6	9.36	N	
Immediate Memory	84	72	12	10.29	Y	15%
Delayed Memory	86	76	10	10.13	N	

Note: Ability Score Type:　GAI
　　　 Ability Score:　　　 76
　　　 Statistical significance (critical value) at the .01 level.
　　　 Table of assessment results derived from *Wechsler Memory Scale, Fourth Edition (WMS-IV)*. Copyright © 2009 NCS Pearson, Inc. Reproduced with permission. All rights reserved.

Table 6.17

Test of Premorbid Functioning Actual–Predicted Comparison

	Actual score	Predicted score	Prediction interval	Difference	Critical value	Significant difference	Base rate
Actual–Predicted	75	93	64–122	-18	5.47	Y	6.7%

Note: Actual–Predicted Comparison based on Simple Demographics Predictive Model.
Prediction intervals reported at the 95% level of confidence.
Statistical significance (critical value) at the .01 level.
Table of assessment results derived from *Advanced Clinical Solutions for WAIS-IV and WMS-IV (ACS)*. Copyright © 2009 NCS Pearson, Inc. Reproduced with permission. All rights reserved.

Table 6.18

WAIS–IV Actual–Predicted Comparison

Composite	Actual	Predicted	Prediction interval	Difference	Critical value	Significant difference	Base rate
FSIQ	74	84	60–108	-10	6.99	Y	13.2%
VCI	76	81	59–103	-5	8.08	N	29.8%
PRI	81	91	61–121	-10	8.44	Y	20.8%
WMI	86	87	59–115	-1	9.46	N	48.3%
PSI	71	88	54–122	-17	14.22	Y	10.2%

Note: Actual–Predicted Comparison based on Simple Demographics with Test of Premorbid Functioning Predictive Model.
Prediction intervals reported at the 95% level of confidence.
Statistical significance (critical value) at the .01 level.
Table of assessment results derived from *Advanced Clinical Solutions for WAIS-IV and WMS-IV (ACS)*. Copyright © 2009 NCS Pearson, Inc. Reproduced with permission. All rights reserved.

fied by the simple demographics model (i.e., demographics of Melbourne as equated to the north east of the United States, sex, ethnicity, highest level of education and highest occupational level) on this occasion.

More specifically, as we see in Table 6.18, Colonel Keen As is performing below premorbid estimates for his FSIQ, his PRI and his PSI (also see Figure 6.4). Clearly, on these aspects of functioning Colonel Keen As demonstrates a decline on what would be expected by the predictions of his performance preceding his injury.

It is also possible for us to use the TOPF to determine predictions of his performance on the WMS-IV. As we can see from Table 6.19 and Figure 6.5, Colonel Keen As is performing below expectation as based upon his word reading and the simple demographic correction in the case of the IMI but not the DMI. This supports our previous qualitative observations regarding his performance on the subtests analysis.

Step 8: Is there a difference between the working memory indices? As we noted in the discussion above, we did not administer the VWMI index so it is not possible to make this comparison. While in Colonel Keen As's case we would

Table 6.19
WMS–IV Actual–Predicted Comparison

Index	Actual	Predicted	Prediction interval	Difference	Critical value	Significant difference	Base rate
IMI	72	85	52–118	–13	9.9	Y	19.1%
DMI	76	84	50–118	–8	9.81	N	28.3%

Note: Actual–Predicted Comparison based on Simple Demographics with Test of Premorbid Functioning Predictive Model
Prediction Intervals reported at the 95% Level of Confidence.
Statistical significance (critical value) at the .01 level.
Table of assessment results derived from *Advanced Clinical Solutions for WAIS-IV and WMS-IV (ACS)*.
Copyright © 2009 NCS Pearson, Inc. Reproduced with permission. All rights reserved.

not anticipate a specific compromise in verbal versus visual working memory, due to the absence of data it is not possible to definitively provide an answer to this question.

Step 9: How well is information retained after delay? The comparison of IMI versus DMI is presented in Table 6.12. Colonel Keen As performs in a manner consistent with what should be expected on each measure and no significant difference was noted.

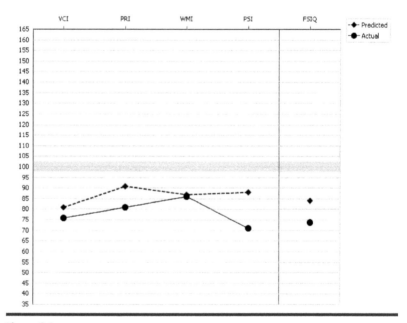

Figure 6.4
WAIS–IV actual–predicted score profile.

Note: Assessment results derived from *Advanced Clinical Solutions for WAIS-IV and WMS-IV (ACS)*.
Copyright © 2009 NCS Pearson, Inc. Reproduced with permission. All rights reserved.

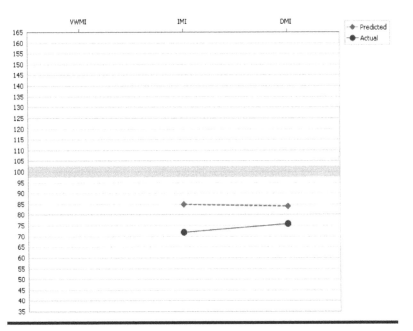

Figure 6.5
WMS–IV actual–predicted score profile.

It is now possible for us to provide an evaluation of our third hypothesis regarding Colonel Keen As's memory functioning: Did Colonel Keen As have memory functions equivalent to the level we would expect from someone of his current level of ability and in comparison to estimates of his ability preceding his injury? The assessment indicated that the Colonel had an Auditory Immediate Memory Index of 75, 95% confidence interval between 70 and 82 at the 5th percentile rank in the borderline range; a Visual Immediate Memory Index of 80, 95% confidence interval between 75 and 86 at the 9th percentile rank in the low average range; an Immediate Memory Index of 72, 95% confidence interval between 67 and 80 at the 3rd percentile rank in the borderline range and a Delayed Memory Index of 76, 95% confidence interval between 71 and 84 at the 5th percentile rank in the borderline range. These figures were significantly different from his contemporary levels of intelligence as determined using the General Ability Index, which were discrepant at the one in 100 chance level in the case of the Auditory Memory and Immediate Memory Indices. This indicates that Colonel Keen As shows significant memory decline for both auditory memory and immediate memory in comparison to estimates of his contemporary intellectual ability. This observation was also noted for his performance on the Immediate Memory Index in comparison to estimates of his pre-injury level of function as determined using the Test of Premorbid Function, which was discrepant at the one in 100 chance level on this occasion.

Conclusion

The pattern of performances revealed by Colonel Keen As on this occasion indicate a man of 53 years who was subjected to a severe to very severe closed head injury some 10 years ago. He presents at this point in time as having weakness in the area of processing speed and perceptual organisation and some compromise of function on tests of memory function, with particular weakness in the area of auditory and immediate memory. These performances are virtually identical to those noted in the two previous assessments of the Colonel. Colonel Keen As continues to demonstrate ongoing personality change in association with coarsening of his emotional responses, disinhibition and inability to be able to respond in an appropriate way, which has resulted in explosiveness and aggression both towards his wife and children. He is now infantilised in the family situation and it does not look like there will be any change in the foreseeable future. We are now some 10 years subsequent to the initial injury and I consider that the Colonel's condition is quite stable at this point in time.

CHAPTER SEVEN

Is the Patient's Presentation a Genuine One?
The Case of Mrs Peahen

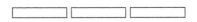

The clinical neuropsychologist has a particular attraction for lawyers in those cases where the neurological and/or neurodiagnostic examinations reveal no abnormality. Ironically, Russell (1990) has attributed the increased use of neuropsychology in the courts to the fact that neuropsychology can easily diagnose brain damage where there is none. As there are no pathognomonic tests of brain damage, Russell attributes many of the false positives identified with cognitive testing to the false belief that cognitive tests are tests for brain damage when actually they are tests of cognitive ability. As noted above, it is not tests that diagnose brain damage, it is the interpretation of the performance by the trained clinician that does.

At some point in the evaluation of every examinee referred for assessment the clinician must ask him or herself: are the responses and the behaviour of this individual in this circumstance consistent with an actual psychiatric or neurological disorder or are the observed deficits due to some other cause? In the context of medico-legal disputation, in which considerable periods of incarceration or sizeable sums of money are at stake, this issue culminates in the question from the barrister: 'Tell me Doctor, isn't it possible that people can either consciously or unconsciously fake brain damage?' While one would like to be able to instantly retort that any clinician worth his or her salt should be able to easily detect malingering, the literature and most experienced clinicians are aware that the problem is not quite so simple.

As Guilmette and Guiliano (1991, p. 208) have observed:

> ... regardless of the assumptions or convictions that clinical neuro-
> psychologists may have about their ability to detect malingering, at the
> present time the expert witness must concede that, at best, there is lit-
> tle to no scientific evidence that supports clinician's ability to detect
> malingering with traditional measures of cognitive functioning.

Thankfully, this is now less the case than it was when they first made these observations, due to the massive developments in this area of practice that have arisen from the seminal work of David Faust and Jay Ziskin (1995) and its culmination in the various papers published by the 'method sceptics' and their respondents.

A number of definitional issues surround this area and it seems worthwhile to clarify a number of these before we go further. DSM IV-TR (American Psychiatric Association [APA], 2000) defines somatoform disorders as 'a pattern of recurring multiple, clinically significant somatic complaints' (p. 486). This description is reserved for those conditions in which the physical symptoms suggest a general medical condition but are not fully explained by that general medical condition. The manual draws a distinction between somatoform disorders and factitious disorders and malingering in that, in the former case, the symptoms are not intentional or under voluntary control.

The manual indicates that the common features of the somatoform disorders include: (a) the presence of subjective physical symptoms that suggest a medical illness or syndrome that is not fully explained by or attributable to a general medical condition, substance abuse or other type of mental disorder and (b) the absence of voluntary control over symptomatology (APA, 2000).

The manual indicates that there are a number of entities under the umbrella of somatoform disorders, including somatisation disorder, undifferentiated somatoform disorder, conversion disorder, pain disorder, hypochondriasis, body dysmorphic disorder, and those somatoform disorders not otherwise specified. Consult DSM IV-TR (APA, 2000) for a full description of these conditions.

Somatisation disorder features a history of multiple unexplained symptoms and complaints, beginning before the age of 25, which can often be traced to events and circumstances that emerge in childhood and adolescence (APA, 2000). The symptoms of the condition can mimic other syndromes such as PCS or PTSD or may be more florid with an atypical or bizarre pattern of quality, location or duration (L. Miller, 2001). Insofar as it is possible to ascertain the underlying motivation for this presentation, the behaviour is frequently inferred to be a 'cry for help' (i.e., a plea for support and reassurance), manipulation of the affection of a significant other or in quest of the satisfaction of dependency needs by reliance on caretakers (L. Miller, 2001).

Miller (2001) contends that the unconscious motivation underlying conversion disorder involves the attempt to resolve intrapsychic conflicts such as dependency issues by channelling them into physical impairment. There may also be an actual symbolic 'conversion' of the intrapsychic conflict that is represented by a somatic expression, for example the paralysis of an arm in a patient who fears acting upon a hostile impulse (L. Miller, 2001) or hysterical aphonia in the patient who fears the outcome of what may come from the mouth.

Conversion disorder can be difficult to discern from actual illness and common misdiagnoses may emerge in conditions that are relatively ambiguous on presentation, such as myasthenia gravis, idiopathic dystonia or multiple sclerosis (APA, 2000). Typically, the presence of actual neurological disorder does not preclude the diagnosis of conversion disorder and up to one third of individuals with conversion symptoms have a previous diagnosis of a neurological condition (Binder, 2005; Binder & Campbell, 2004). The distinction between conversion disorder and malingering may merely be the absence of intentional production of the symptoms.

One of the interesting features of conversion disorder is that the symptoms typically do not conform to the usual anatomical or physiological distributions. For example, a paralysis may be in the form of a glove or stocking distribution and may be delimited by perceived boundaries rather than by anatomical ones (the wrist for example), while the distribution of the anaesthesia and their responsivity to particular forms of sensory stimulation do not accord with anatomical reality. The patient may also show little apparent anxiety or concern about the apparently massively debilitating nature of their presented problems, a situation that Charcot referred to as *la belle indifference* (or beautiful indifference).

Factitious disorders are characterised by either psychological or physical symptoms that are intentionally produced with a view to fulfilling a sick role. The DSM-IV-TR (APA, 2000) divides the factitious disorders into factitious disorder with predominantly physical signs and symptoms and factitious disorder with predominantly psychological signs and symptoms. The former category includes chronic factitious disorder with physical symptoms, which has been historically referred to as Munchausen Syndrome, a presentation named after the legendary Baron Munchausen, who undertook fantastic travels and celebrated extravagant tales of his own prowess as described in the book by Rudolph Raspe. This condition is characterised by an 'illness' that revolves around a lifestyle focusing on hospitalisation, surgeries and contentious battles with physicians (Cunnien, 1997).

The diagnosis of factitious disorder with psychological symptoms denotes a presentation of intentionally produced psychological symptoms without any identifiable external incentive (APA, 2000). It is the issue of 'external incentive' that is used to differentiate the condition from malingering; however, as noted by Cunnien (1997, p. 25) 'The mere presence of external gains cannot negate the primacy of psychological motives'. Clearly, both psychological and other incentives can co-exist and behaviours can be motivated by both external and internal gain.

Chronic factitious disorder with psychological symptoms has been historically referred to as Ganser Syndrome, a mixture of organic, affective and psychotic symptoms (L. Miller, 2001) that includes clouding of consciousness, hallucination, hysterical conversion and a strange pattern of cognitive impairment featuring 'approximate answers' (e.g., 2 + 2 = 5). Nowadays, the full spectrum of the presentation is rarely seen, and the diagnosis is made based largely on the presence of the approximate answers alone (L. Miller, 2001).

This syndrome was originally described in 1898 by Ganser after attending three patients who featured the characteristic 'Ganser' response. These are sometimes referred to as answers past the point or approximate answers. The patient's responses to questions are markedly inaccurate and often absurdly so. However, by the nature of the response, the patient betrays knowledge as to the purpose of the question by their close approximation to the correct answer, implying that this too is at some level available.

In an attempt to prevent massive overdiagnosis, the proviso that the false response, although wrong is never far wrong and bears a definite and obvious relationship to the question — indicating clearly that the patient has grasped the question — was added. The apparent dementia that accompanies the approximate answers is usually incomplete, inconsistent and often self-contradictory. Disorientation is invariably present, but the apparently gross disturbance of intellect fails to be reflected in the patient's overall behaviour.

Prevalence and Incidence of Abnormal Illness Behaviour

The reported frequency of neurological and neuropsychological symptoms in healthy controls is quite high with normal subjects commonly reporting: fatigue (33%), headaches (58%), forgetfulness (58%) and poor concentration (35%) (Paniak et al., 2002). Similarly, the level of reported frequency of pain in community dwellers is common (Kroenke & Price, 1993), with normal subjects reporting generalised pain (37%), back pain (32%), headache (25%), chest pain (25%), arm or leg pain (24%), and abdominal pain (24%). People who view themselves as able bodied do not allow these symptoms to disable them. However, some people see these commonly occurring symptoms as signs of serious illness; made worse by the oft noted social isolation of these folk, which means they do not get significant-other feedback on the frequency of these complaints (Binder, 2005; Binder & Campbell, 2004).

Half of the patients seen by neurologists have comorbid psychiatric disorders (Fink, Hansen, & Sondergaard, 2003). Fink and colleagues (2003) questioned 198 consecutive patients referred to a neurologist for the first time and found that 61% had at least one medically unexplained symptom and 33.8% met criteria for one of the somatoform disorders. Two recent papers (Carson, Ringbauer, & Stone, 2000; Fink, Rosendal, & Olesen, 2005) indicate that up to one third of new patients referred to neurologists fulfil criteria for somatoform disorder. Worse still, 70% of neurologists often do not recognize common psychiatric conditions such as somatoform disorders (Bridges & Goldberg, 1984; Fink et al., 2005). A retrospective review of more than 13,000 psychiatric consultations found that somatization disorder resulted in more disability and unemployment than any other psychiatric diagnosis (Thomassen, van Hemert, Huyse, van der Mast, & Hengeveld, 2003). Somatization has an estimated incidence in primary care settings of 0.2–0.7% (Escobar & Canino, 1989).

Nonetheless, the factitious disorders are diagnosed in less than 1% of referrals to psychiatric services (Cunnien, 1997). The lifetime prevalence for somatization disorder ranges between 0.2 and 2% among women and in less than 0.2% of men (APA, 2000), while conversion disorder occurs in about 1–3% of outpatient referrals to mental health clinics. These figures compare very unfavourably with the frequency with which a diagnosis of malingering is made (see below) and the number of cases diagnosed with the various factitious and somatization disorders a literal drop in the ocean when compared to the estimated and guesstimated numbers of cases of malingering.

Evolution of Abnormal Illness Behaviour

The factitious disorders are distinguished from malingering by the fact that in the latter case, the individual is producing the symptoms intentionally and has a clear goal in mind (i.e., financial gain, evading imprisonment), whereas in factitious disorders overt incentives are absent.

Cullum, Heaton and Grant (1991) have proposed that the distinction between primary and secondary gain is somewhat artificial and they prefer the notion of gain of itself, irrespective of whether the benefit is conscious or unconscious. It follows from their suggestion that all psychologically determined symptoms involve gain. In somatoform disorders this involves anxiety reduction, and a symbolic restatement of the disorder that is unconsciously determined. In the case of factitious disorders there is a conscious attempt to adopt the sick role to avoid an emotional conflict. In malingering the activity is again under conscious control and is directed towards a demonstrable and tangible benefit.

These conditions are characterised by the fact that they do not have a biological origin. The malady is, by definition, a misinterpretation or embellishment of the usually observed pattern of disorder associated with a given diagnosis. The tendency for the invocation of the notion of the subconscious or the unconscious tends to be popular in explanations of these phenomena. It is difficult to ascertain how informative these approaches actually are, as rarely does this area result in extensive research, exploration or theory generation. This problem has not prevented a huge explosion of studies reported in the literature on the issue of malingering and impaired effort, but much of this literature focuses upon the identification of nongenuine response sets, rather than in trying to come to grips with the mechanism of the behaviour. This problem is exacerbated as the gold standard for identification of malingering, for example, can only occur on the basis of self-report, and the number of individuals prepared to 'crack' under Perry Mason's incisive interrogation on the witness stand is relatively low.

In these types of cases, the evidence is obtained from neuropathology and structural and functional imaging results in a diagnosis by exclusion. It is the X-ray, CT, MRI or SPECT scan that indicates no abnormality in the examinee, who is to all intents and purposes severely impaired, that raises the index of concern.

One matter on which all investigators who study these conditions do agree is that conversion symptoms occur much more frequently in women than they do in men (Boffeli & Guze, 1992). Whether this observation occurs as a consequence of sex differences at a biological, psychological or social level is as yet undefined.

Due to the fact that the somatoform, factitious and dissociative disorders are each due to an interpretation on the part of the client as to what neurological and neuropsychological symptoms should look like, they generally do not conform in any consistent way to the usual patterns of neuropsychological disorder. Description in the literature has indicated a tendency by patients to focus on particular aspects of cognitive functioning.

Lesion Location and Mechanism of the Abnormal Illness Behaviour

To understand the mechanism of the action of these disorders, it is necessary to understand the knowledge and the sophistication of the subject who suffers from them. Clearly, the more experienced and knowledgeable the subject is, the more likely that their symptomatology will look real. The examinee who has had previous exposure to a friend or relative with Broca's aphasia is likely to present with agrammatism and halting speech, the client who has seen Alzheimer's disease at close quarters is more likely to present with amnesia, aphasia, apraxia and agnosia.

This is not to gainsay the fact that even relatively naïve individuals with relatively little motivation can manufacture convincing evidence of psychiatric disorder at least on self-report measures. Lees-Haley and Dunn (1994) have found that 99% of untutored undergraduates could achieve a performance satisfying DSM-IV criteria for PTSD on a symptom checklist. A similar level of endorsement was noted by Burges and McMillan (2001) who observed that 94% of their sample of 136 night class further education college students could satisfy the criteria of PTSD after being read a vignette. Clearly, it is possible for relatively untrained participants with little or no knowledge of PTSD to fake responses on symptom checklists sufficient to achieve the diagnosis. Similar levels of performance pertain to other diagnoses including MTBI (Panayiotou, Jackson, & Crowe, 2010). It is anyone's guess what a highly motivated individual facing a large settlement or avoidance of prison or military duty might be capable of achieving.

With regard to the issue of the tendency of clients to embroider their clinical symptomatology, the technique of assessment, reassessment and assessment yet again that are characteristic of our adversarial legal system almost begs the client to overpresent and embroider his or her symptoms. Most assessors will ask the same set of questions as each other and generally, as the assessor has asked the question so often before, the answers are virtually written down before the client has responded.

The traumatically brain injured client, for example, invariably complains of problems with memory, attention, irritability, tiredness and vague depressive and anxious mentation. The assessor is astounded if the subject does not complain of these and if he or she does not, the assessor will invariably ask why not? In this context it is quite easy for the injured subject to learn how to play the game and present the most 'convincing' set of symptoms to achieve the desired outcome.

As noted above, the likelihood of an increase in the presentation of psychologically based factitious disorders is a growing clinical reality. If we consider these symptoms a cry for help, then the fact that a glove or stocking anaesthesia can be immediately dismissed by the general practitioner (GP) as a clear attempt at attention-seeking, will result in the lessened likelihood of the presentation of such a symptom due to its ineffectiveness in eliciting the desired outcomes. The presence of ongoing compromise following MTBI, chronic unremitting tiredness, ongoing pain, prolonged reactions to commonly encountered products and chemicals or the presence of migrainous headaches may result in a more sympathetic hearing on the part of the GP and, as a consequence, validation of the problems by the world.

Dissociative disorders are characterised by the disruption of the flow of consciousness, memory, identity or perception of the environment, including such patterns of disorder as dissociative amnesia, dissociative fugue, dissociative identity disorder and depersonalisation disorder. (Consult DSM-IV-TR for a full description of these conditions.) Dissociation occurs most commonly in the context of the anxiety disorders, most notably PTSD, but it can also occur in other contexts.

Malingering

As Richard Rogers (1999) has cogently argued:

> Diagnoses of the mental disorders and the evaluation of psychopathology rely heavily on the honesty, accuracy, and completeness of patients' self-reporting. Most symptoms of disorders are not directly observable by others. Therefore each patient's presentation becomes a critical component of the clinical assessment. Distortions, both intentional and unintentional, complicate the assessment process. (p. 1)

Mankind has been interested in the notion of malingering from our earliest history and reports of malingering go back at least as far as the ancient Greeks (Brussel & Hitch, 1943) and the ancient rabbis of the second century BCE (Nies & Sweet, 1994). The word 'malingering' was first defined in *Grove's Dictionary of the Vulgar Tongue* in 1785 (Brussel & Hitch, 1943) in the military context as 'one who under the pretence of illness evades his duty'. Bailey (1998) contends that the word malingerer derives from the term *malingroux*, a word used to describe the practices of 18th century French beggars who injured themselves for financial gain.

The DSM-IV-TR (APA, 2000) includes malingering as a V-Code under the category of 'Other Conditions which may be a Focus of Clinical Attention'. Thus, while the condition is considered to be worthy of clinical attention, it is not considered a mental disorder *per se* (Slick, Sherman, & Iverson, 1999).

The manual defines malingering as:

> ... the intentional production of false or grossly exaggerated physical or psychological symptoms, motivated by external incentives such as avoiding military duty, avoiding work, obtaining financial compensation, evading criminal prosecution, or obtaining drugs ... Malingering should be strongly suspected if any combination of the following is noted:

(1) medicolegal context of presentation (e.g., the person is referred by an attorney for examination)

(2) marked discrepancy between the person's claimed stress or disability and the objective findings

(3) lack of cooperation during the diagnostic evaluation and in complying with the prescribed treatment regimen

(4) the presence of Antisocial Personality disorder.

Malingering differs from Factitious Disorders in that the motivation for the symptom production in Malingering is an external incentive, whereas with the factitious disorders the external incentive is absent. Evidence of an intrapsychic need to maintain the sick role suggests Factitious Disorder. Malingering is differentiated from Conversion Disorder and other Somatoform Disorders by the intentional production of symptoms and by the obvious, external incentives associated with it. (p. 739–740)

Thus, the notion of malingering refers to a voluntary production or exaggeration of symptoms with a view to presenting oneself as worse than one actually is with a view to a demonstrable and predictable gain. In the psychoanalytic tradition, gain has generally been divided into primary versus secondary gain. Primary gain is considered to represent the reduction in anxiety and relief generated by the unconscious emotional conflict. Secondary gain describes the psychosocial benefit of the sick role including such things as release from unpleasant responsibility, increased personal attention and sympathy and financial reward. As noted above (Cullum et al., 1991), the actual basis on which determination of the source of the conflict can be made is at best tenuous, so acceptance of the fact that motivation to achieve a particular outcome by effecting abnormal illness behaviour is probably the most economical account of the behaviour.

There have, however, been a number of problems identified with regard to the criteria proposed by the manual. These include: difficulty with judging the difference between external versus psychological incentives and volitional versus unconscious behaviours; the specification that if the client presents with one of the other somatoform disorders (e.g., conversion or factitious disorder) that this precludes the dual diagnosis of somatoform disorder and malingering; and the fact that the criteria were developed in the context of psychiatric presentations, thus making the application of these in nonpsychiatric patients (e.g., patients with TBI) potentially inapplicable (Slick et al., 1999).

Most clinicians would agree that malingering can be regarded as unlikely if data from a variety of sources (i.e., serial testing) confirm the same test findings. Inconsistent results in the examination, evidence of lying or exaggeration during the interview, poor performance on tests of an autobiographical nature and a level of performance below that usually expected given the nature of the injury can be viewed as warning signs, but must of themselves be regarded as inconclusive.

Price and Stevens (1997, p. 79) have prepared a list of 10 signs and symptoms that they consider indicate increased likelihood of malingering in traumatically brain injured subjects. These include:

- an eagerness to discuss or call attention to symptoms in an overly dramatic manner
- making false imputations about valid symptoms
- endorsing symptoms rarely found in credible patients with head trauma and reporting improbable numbers of symptoms
- simulating positive symptoms more often than negative symptoms
- endorsing more blatant than subtle brain injury symptoms
- endorsing symptoms that are of unusually extreme severity, even if bizarre and ridiculous
- reporting symptoms, performing tasks, or failing to perform tasks that are inconsistent with their own previous reports, reports from others or observations of their behaviour in other situations
- presenting a constellation of signs and symptoms that are inconsistent with a recognisable brain injury and demonstrating a course of the alleged injury that is contrary to the development of actual injuries
- an eagerness to endorse new symptoms suggested by the neuropsychologist
- focusing on his or her perceived disability rather than the alleged injury and rarely mentioning or acknowledging his or her abilities or capacity.

Mittenberg, Patton, Canyock and Condit (2002) have noted a similar list of diagnostic impressions that support a diagnosis of probable malingering or symptom exaggeration including: a severity or pattern of cognitive impairment that is inconsistent with the condition; scores below cut-off on forced choice or other forms of malingering tests; discrepancies between records, self-report and observed behaviour; implausible symptoms reported in the interview; implausible changes in test scores over repeated examinations; scores above validity scale cut-offs on objective personality tests; and scores below chance on forced choice tests.

In the attempt to expand and formalise these criteria and in keeping with the style of the DSM, Slick et al. (1999, pp. 552–555) have proposed a set of research diagnostic criteria on which basis they contend, a diagnosis of malingering can be made.

For a diagnosis of definite Malingering Neurocognitive Deficit (MND) the authors propose:

> (1) the presence of a substantial external incentive [Criterion A].
>
> (2) definite negative response bias [Criterion B]
>
> (3) behaviors meeting necessary criteria for group B are not fully accounted for by Psychiatric, Neurological or Developmental Factors [Criterion D]. (p. 552)

For Probable MND:

> (1) the presence of a substantial external incentive [Criterion A].
>
> (2) two or more types of evidence from neuropsychological testing, excluding definite negative response bias [two or more of Criteria B2-B6],
>
> Or
>
> (3) one type of evidence from neuropsychological testing, excluding definite negative response bias, and one or more types of evidence from Self-Report [one of Criteria B2-B6 and one or more of Criteria C1-C5]
>
> (4) behaviors meeting necessary criteria for group B and C are not fully accounted for by Psychiatric, Neurological or Developmental Factors [Criterion D]. (p. 552–553)

And for Possible MND:

> (1) the presence of a substantial external incentive [Criterion A].
>
> (2) evidence from Self-Report [one of more of Criteria C1-C5]
>
> (3) behaviors meeting necessary criteria for group C are not fully accounted for by Psychiatric, Neurological or Developmental Factors [Criterion D]'
>
> Or
>
> (4) Criteria for Definite or Probable MND are met except for Criterion D (i.e. primary psychiatric, neurological or developmental etiologies cannot be ruled out). In such cases, the alternate etiologies that cannot be rules out should be specified. (p. 553)

For criterion A there must be evidence for at least one clear and identifiable incentive for exaggeration or fabrication; for example, a personal injury settlement, disability pension, evasion of criminal prosecution or release from military service. For criterion B there must be evidence of exaggeration or fabrication on neuropsychological testing as demonstrated by: (1) definite negative response, (2) probable negative responses bias, (3) a discrepancy between the test data and known patterns of brain functioning, (4) observed behaviour, (5) reliable collateral reports or (6) documented background history. Criterion C focuses on evidence from self-report that is noted to be discrepant from (1) documented history, (2) known patterns of brain functioning, (3) behavioural observations, (4) information obtained from collateral informants or (5) evidence of exaggerated or fabricated psychological dysfunction.

Criterion D indicates that the observed behaviours are not otherwise explained by intercurrent psychiatric, neurological or developmental factors.

Two possible means of identifying exaggeration or fabrication of cognitive dysfunction have been discussed in the literature. The first set of techniques involve the evaluation of exaggeration of the reporting of symptoms most commonly by the use of questionnaire measures such as the MMPI, and the second by identifying poor motivation and/or effort on tests of neuropsychological functioning (Larrabee, 2005).

The MMPI has long been regarded as a sensitive measure for the detection of deviant response sets. The F Scale, F-K index, the Gough Dissimulation Index, and the Fake Bad Scale, as well as checking the 16 repeated items all represent reasonable means of detecting exaggerated symptomatology, malingering and random or feigned responses (Etcoff & Kampfer, 1996).

A rich literature has developed on the use of the MMPI and MMPI-2 as a means of assessing malingering in forensic and brain injury settings (e.g., Arbisi & Ben-Porath, 1995; Berry et al., 1995; Berry, Baer, & Harris, 1991; Larrabee, 2005; Rogers, Sewell, & Salekin, 1994; Rogers, Sewell, & Ustad, 1995; Tsushima & Tsushima, 2001; Wetter, Baer, Berry, Smith, & Larsen, 1992), which should be consulted for more detailed discussion of the issues in establishing malingering in the context of traumatically brain-injured examinees.

Exaggeration of symptom reporting on the MMPI-2 can be assessed using the following scales: F, Back F, Variable Response Inconsistency Scale (VRIN), the True Response Inconsistency Scale (TRIN), Infrequency Psychopathology Scale and exaggerated somatic symptomatology can be assessed by noting elevations over T 79 on Scales 1 and 3, plus elevated Lees-Haley Fake Bad Scale (Larrabee, 2005).

Exaggerated psychopathology can be evaluated using the F, F-K, Back F, and the Arbisi and Ben-Porath's (1995) F(p) scale. The VRIN is useful for ruling out random responding as a cause of elevated F (Wetter et al., 1992). The exaggeration of psychopathology tends to occur more commonly in settings where malingering obviates responsibility for mandatory duties such as military service or the consequences of prosecution for alleged crimes (Larrabee, 2005).

Although exaggerated psychopathology does occur in personal injury settings, it is more typical for these patients to exaggerate their somatic, affective and cognitive complaints, producing significant elevations on MMPI-2 scales 1, 2 and 3 with secondary elevations on 7 and 8 (Larrabee, 1998, 2001). The F scale and related measures are not sensitive to this type of malingering (Larrabee, 1998; Millis, & Kler, 1995) and this type of exaggeration is most effectively detected using the Lees-Haley Fake Bad Scale (Lees-Haley, 1992). While some dispute regarding this measure has emerged in the literature it represents an important measure in forensic settings (Nelson, Parsons, Grote, Smith, & Sisung, 2006; Nelson, Sweet, & Demakis, 2006; Nelson, Hoelzle, Sweet, Arbisi, & Demakis, 2010).

The evaluation of poor motivation and/or effort on neuropsychological testing can be determined by three means: observation of poor performance on tasks that are easily performed by injured individuals who are not litigating, evaluation of patterns of responding characteristic of malingering and symptom validity testing using a forced-choice methodology (Larrabee, 2000, 2005).

The typical example of tasks that are easily performed by nonlitigating persons who have bona fide neurological disorder include the early malingering tests developed by the French neurologist André Rey, including the Rey 15-Item Test and the Dot Counting Test. These tasks were developed to appear as if they measured an actual cognitive function such as memory, but are consistently performed in an unimpaired fashion by nonlitigating patients who have brain impairment. While the principle underlying their development is sound, their sensitivity and specificity to malingering tends to be low as compared to other procedures (e.g., Greiffenstein, Baker, & Gola, 1996; Schretlen, Brandt, Krafft, & Van Gorp, 1991; Vallabhajosula & Van Gorp, 2001).

The second technique involves the application of pattern analysis. This approach determines impaired motivation by detecting score patterns that are atypical for the neurological disorder in question (Larrabee, 2000, 2005). Walsh (Darby & Walsh, 2005) for example has attempted to outline a number of strategies to determine faking by his inferential technique of syndrome analysis. The examinee's performance is evaluated not so much as a deviation from statistical normality as in terms of conformity with a recognised syndrome of cognitive deficit. This results in a series of error types that are inconsistent with organic dysfunction. The error types include frequent additions or omissions in digit span sequences, often involving the last number in a series, answering a question by simply restating the question, incorporation of the factual elements of a question in an answer, failure of performance to vary with difficulty level of the test (the sin of summation), regular omissions from the serial additions test and gross distortions in the reproductions of designs from memory. This work has been further taken up by Rawling and Brooks (1990) who have noted a number of error types specific to dissimulation in head-injured groups.

Unfortunately, the precision with which techniques such as those advocated by Walsh can be applied is notoriously unreliable, thus more concise formulations of these behaviours have been developed by a number of investigators.

Malingerers frequently show impairment on motor function tasks that are out of keeping with the nature of the injury and may perform more poorly on gross as compared to the fine motor tasks (Binder & Willis, 1991; Greiffenstein et al., 1996; Heaton, Smith, Lehman, & Vogt, 1978; Mittenberg, Rotholc, Russell, & Heilbronner, 1996; Rapport, Farchione, Coleman, & Axelrod, 1998). They will also show disproportionate impairment on measures of attention relative to other problem-solving and memory tasks, in particular, very impaired performance on Digit Span sequencing (Binder & Willis, 1991; Greiffenstein, Baker, & Gola, 1994; Heaton et al., 1978; Iverson & Tulsky, 2003; Millis, Ross, & Ricker, 1998; Mittenberg, Azrin, Millsaps, & Heilbronner, 1993; Mittenberg, Theroux-Fichera, Zielinski, & Heilbronner, 1995), often display marked impairment in recognition memory (Binder, Villanueva, Howieson, & Moore, 1993; Millis, 1992; Millis & Kler, 1995; Sweet et al., 2000), and may also demonstrate atypical error patterns on measures of problem-solving, such as the Category Test (DiCarlo et al., 2000; Tenhula & Sweet, 1996), the Wisconsin Card Sorting Test (Bernard, McGrath, & Houston, 1996), and a higher ratio of loss-of-set to categories achieved (Suhr & Boyer, 1999) than seen in nonlitigating closed head injury.

Mittenberg and his colleagues (Mittenberg et al., 1993, 1995) have reported discriminant function equations on the WAIS-R, the WMS-R and the HRB that have proven capable of differentiating noninjured simulators from bona fide head-injured patients with a hit rate of 91% of subjects based upon the discriminant function score derived from the WMS-R; 79% with the WAIS-R and 88.8% using the HRB. This approach using the WAIS has received further support in a subsequent validation study conducted by Greve, Bianchini, Mathias, Houston and Crouch (2003).

Another example of this type of approach is afforded by the intriguing technique developed by Killgore and DellaPietra (2000). Using a number of items from the recognition trail of Logical Memory Delayed Recognition items in the WMS-III these authors have developed a Rarely Missed Index (RMI). This represents the items that were correctly answered by participants who had not previously heard the passages and, as a result, had determined the correct response by the context of the questions. Using cut-off scores of less than 136, the RMI achieved a sensitivity of 97% and specificity of 100%. While the technique is an intriguing and promising approach, no further validation study has as yet taken place with the method to determine its reliability. Some concern that the necessity to infer the correct answer from the context of the other questions on the recognition format relies upon relatively intact levels of intellectual functioning could be raised and at this point in time the method should be viewed as worthwhile but not definitive. This form of assessment has been significantly expanded and developed in the qualitative aspects of the evaluation of the WMS-IV presented in the Advanced Clinical Solutions for WAIS-IV and WMS-IV (PsychCorp, 2009).

Symptom Validity Testing was originally developed by Loren Pankrantz (Pankratz, 1979; Pankratz, Fausti, & Peed, 1975) and these techniques invariably use a forced-choice recognition test format. The key assumption underlying symptom validity testing is that a person who performs at a level significantly worse than chance (i.e., performs outside the confidence interval for chance performance) must at some level have the correct answer available to them in order to perform so poorly and, consequently, must be malingering (Larrabee, 1992). Choosing by chance alone, the examinee would be expected to be correct about 50% of the time. A simulator, overestimating the degree of impairment may be induced to score below chance (Larrabee, 2001, 2005).

These procedures involve presenting a very large series of items such as multi-digit numbers (e.g., Portland Digit Recognition Test [PDRT], Binder & Kelly, 1996); Computerized Assessment of Response Bias (CARB; Allen, Conder, Green, & Cox, 1997; Conder, Allen, & Cox, 1992); Hiscock Digit Memory Test (HDMT) (Slick, Hopp, Strauss, Hunter, & Pinch, 1994), words (Recognition Memory Test [RMT], Warrington, 1984); Word Memory Test (WMT; Green, Allen, & Astner, 1996) or pictures (Test of Memory Malingering [TOMM], Tombaugh, 1996), which are evaluated by two-alternative forced-choice testing.

These tasks can be scored in two ways: first, is the obtained performance significantly worse-than-chance? The frequency with which such a response set occurs tends to be quite rare and, as a result, this tends not to be a very discriminating technique for identification. For example, in the comparison between the WMT, the CARB and the TOMM undertaken by Gervais, Rohling, Green and Ford (2004) they noted that only four TOMM protocols of the total 519 (i.e., 0.07% of cases) contained scores below chance (i.e., less than 18 on Trials 1, 2 or the recognition trial) on any trial of the TOMM. They noted only nine worse than chance performances on the CARB and only six on the WMT. Certainly, when such a performance does occur it is so compelling as to be tantamount to confession; however, on balance the frequency with which it would occur tends to be very low (i.e., in less than 2% of cases). Mittenberg and colleagues (2002) noted a similarly rare rate of identification of this response set (i.e., with such a score only observed in 30.04% of their respondents, the lowest level of endorsement noted in their list of nine possible indicators of probable malingering or symptom exaggeration).

Second, the responses can be scored by determining an objective cut-off that minimises false positive identification in nonlitigating clients with moderate-to-severe brain disease (Larrabee, 2005). In this instance the sensitivity of the task will contribute to the degree to which it is capable of determining failure rate. For example, in the study of Gervais et al. (Gervais et al., 2004) just discussed, these investigators noted that failure rates varied from 11% of claimants on the TOMM, to 17% on the CARB to 32% on the WMT. Clearly these tasks are not equally sensitive to response bias or suboptimal effort.

In their review, Etcoff and Kampfer (1996) evaluated a number of symptom validity tests and indicators and classified these according to their ability to reliably identify dissimulation in neuropsychological assessment. The instruments were classified according to a scheme developed by Rogers (1988) that postulates five levels of certainty as to whether a given test measures a characteristic reliably. These range from definite (accurately classifies 90% or more of individuals based on extensive cross-validated research), probable (research studies consistently established statistically significant results that accurately differentiate at least 75% of the criterion groups), tentative (shows statistically significance in expected direction but has little or no practical value in classifying subjects), little practical value, or no practical value at all.

Etcoff and Kampfer (1996) classified seven tests as meeting the criterion of a definite certainty of identifying malingering. These were the Hiscock Digit Recognition Test (72- and 36- item versions), the Portland Digit Recognition Test (72-item version and 54-item version with conservative scoring), the F scale and the F-K index on the MMPI, a WAIS Digit-Span age corrected scale score less than 4, and an error score of 24 or more on the Speech Sounds Perception Test.

Tests given a rating of probable included the Hiscock Digit Recognition Test (48-item Victoria version), the Portland Digit Recognition Test (the 54-item version with liberal scoring), the Rey 15-item test with a score of 7 or less, the Fake Bad Scale on the MMPI, Recognition Memory Score on the California Verbal Learning Test, a WAIS Digit-Span age corrected scale score less than 7, and an error score of 17 or more on the Speech Sounds Perception Test.

Clearly, the base rate with which such a response set occurs is a crucial aspect of the nature of this presentation and one that must make the clinician constantly aware. A sample of some of the frequency data presented in the literature to date, as summarised by Larrabee (2005), indicates that a weighted total for eight studies reported frequency counts that indicated the base rate of response bias and malingering in litigating and compensation seeking subjects was 41% of the 1177 subjects assessed.

Mittenberg and colleagues (2002) surveyed 131 neuropsychologists in the attempt to determine how frequently they encountered malingering in their practice. An incidence of probable malingering was noted in 29% of personal injury cases, 19% of criminal cases, 30% of disability cases and 8% of medical cases. These figures compare favourably to other similar studies (e.g., Binder, 1993; Green et al., 2001; Greiffenstein et al., 1994).

In their survey of expert's practices, Slick, Tan, Strauss and Hultsch (2004) noted that in their respective practices half of the experts indicated a base rate of possible malingering of at least 10% and one third of 20% or higher. Definite malingering was estimated to occur in at least 10% of cases in two thirds of the expert sample and in at least 20% by one third. Part of the explanation for this somewhat lower estimate than that noted by Larrabee (2001, 2005), Slick et al. (2004), Mittenberg et al., (2002) or Gervais et al. (2004), may stem from the fact that the experts reported that the Rey 15-item test and the TOMM were the most commonly used measures of malingering.

The 15-item test is consistently reported to lack sensitivity and specificity (e.g., Greiffenstein, Baker, & Gola, 1994; Vallabhajosula & Van Gorp, 2001), and the TOMM reported the lowest level of detection in comparison to the CARB and the WMT in the Gervais et al. (2004) study. Gervais et al. (2004) have indicated that the TOMM had the lowest failure rate because it was relatively less sensitive to exaggeration than the other two measures.

When asked how they presented their opinions regarding this diagnosis, most experts (i.e., more than 80%) indicated that in couching their opinion, they tended to indicate that their results were invalid, inconsistent with the severity of the injury or indicative of exaggeration. They tended to be cautious with the use of the term 'malingering' and 12.5% indicated that they never used the term, while 41.7% did so rarely.

The argument raised by Slick et al. (1999) is of particular interest here and their point that:

> Consistent with APA guidelines, euphemisms or descriptors such as 'poorly motivated' or 'poor effort' should not be used as synonyms for malingering, as persons who malinger may be highly motivated to appear realistically impaired, and expend a significant amount of effort in doing so. Similarly, it is technically incorrect and possibly misleading to refer to symptom validity tests and most other measures of response bias, exaggeration, or fabrication as measures of 'effort' or 'motivation', as these tests do not directly measure the motivation behind behavior or the level of effort expended. (p. 557)

Clearly this is not an irrelevant clinical problem and, as noted by Green and colleagues, the effects of response bias and malingering are several times more powerful in their disruption of cognition than are the effects even of TBI alone (Green et al., 2001), the condition which most assessments were probably set in train to diagnose.

As a general rule most examiners recommend that at least one and preferably two or more tests of symptom validity be administered (e.g., Gervais et al., 2004; Inman & Berry, 2002; Slick et al., 2004), to ensure as much consistency as possible in observing the behavioural pattern. Despite Slick and colleagues (1999), principled stand on this matter, I would strongly caution you against describing this behaviour when you detect it, as 'malingering'. In legal disputation, the determination of whether the plaintiff is telling the truth or not is the determination of the court, not the determination of the expert. Thus if the expert's evidence is accepted, the ultimate issue of the case (i.e., whether the person is telling the truth about the injury/illness and its effects upon them), is determined by the expert, not by the tribunal. As a consequence of this issue alone, I recommend that if you do determine that this is what is going on, that the behaviour should be described as demonstrating less than genuine effort, or that the client did not perform to the best of their ability or that they were showing inadequate effort, but describing this behaviour as malingering accuses the client of lying, with the associated concerns which flow from this charge. As a result, I suggest that a more conservative description of the behaviour, rather than the conclusion arising from it, seems more prudent way to present the opinion.

With this background information in mind it is now worthwhile to examine the case of Ms Priscilla Peahen

CASE STUDY 3: Mrs Priscilla Peahen
BACKGROUND

Name:	Mrs Priscilla Peahen
Age:	59
Sex:	Female
Marital status:	Separated with one child, a son aged 36
Handedness:	Right

ASSESSMENT

Date of Assessment:	16/10/2009
Name of Assessor:	Simon Crowe
Type of Assessment:	Neuropsychological
Previous Assessment:	It would seem that Mrs Peahen has previously been assessed by Dr Colleague shortly following the event. I did not have a copy of any of Dr Colleague's report(s) available to me at the time that I conducted my assessment of Mrs Peahen.

NEUROPSYCHOLOGICAL EVALUATION

Description of Injury

Mrs Peahen reports that she suffered a traumatic brain injury in a motor vehicle accident.

Presentation

Mrs Peahen is a woman of 168 cm in height and a weight of 75 kgs. She had mid-length black hair. Her eyes were blue and she wore glasses for reading. She was immaculately dressed and carefully made up wearing a stylish skirt, a shirt, jacket and flat shoes and had an earring in each ear. Her hair was well maintained. Examination of her hands revealed no ingrained dirt, callusing, nor any evidence of recent physical work. She was neither depressed nor anxious on presentation. Her reality orientation was good and her cooperation seemed appropriate.

Present History

Mrs Peahen indicates that she was conscious throughout the event. She was driving her car and had stopped at a traffic light. She was struck by a third party to the rear of her vehicle. She felt pain in her neck and felt that she may have experienced 'whiplash'. She was taken by her husband to the Country Rural Hospital. She stayed overnight and was discharged home. She saw her own doctor three days later who advised her not to return to work. She eventually went for rehabilitation, including return to work training, more than six months after the injury at the Back to Normal Rehabilitation facility and attended as an outpatient for one and half years subsequent to the injury. She did not make a claim regarding the injury until nearly a year after the injury, thus there was no inpatient rehabilitation.

The changes that Mrs Peahen has noted subsequent to her injury include the fact that she was always a worrier but is more so now. She notes that she is stressed much of the time and is often frustrated. She feels the need to apologise for herself. She shies away from things now. She notes that she sometimes says the wrong words. She also sometimes cannot get her words out. She occasionally says words in the wrong way. She has some confusion of spelling. She notes her memory is okay for some things. She notes that sometimes she goes blank. Her vision is deteriorating.

Mrs Peahen complained of no problems with her activities of daily living including dressing, washing, toileting or feeding herself. She notes that she needs to be careful in the shower. She continues to manage her own finances. Her present activities include the fact that she spends her time playing golf (she currently has a handicap of 16) and looking after her house. She and her husband have separated since the injury.

Past History

Mrs Peahen notes no previous history of loss of consciousness nor any fits, faints, falls or funny turns. She was only previously hospitalised for the delivery of her son. She drinks only lightly, perhaps a gin and tonic or a sherry two to three times per week. She does not smoke cigarettes. Her current medications include a blood pressure medication, an antidepressant, an anti-inflammatory for her back and hormone replacement therapy. She could not remember the specific names of the medications. She takes no nonprescribed medications. She is receiving psychological treatment and has been doing so since for nearly 12 years since the time of the injury. She sees Dr Colleague once per month and feels that her input has been very beneficial. Dr Colleague's approach is by way of supportive psychotherapy and some supportive case management with regard to the neurological stigmata.

There was no family history of dementia of the Alzheimer type, Parkinson's disease or psychiatric disorder, but her father did have problems with alcohol. Mrs Peahen indicated no difficulty learning how to read or write as a child and had never had a diagnosis of specific learning disability. She indicated that her most stressful life experience was the accident.

Mrs Peahen completed Year 11 in the 1960s. She indicated that she was a good student. She undertook various forms of office work at a high level including office manager and personal assistant roles. She has not had any substantive return to work since the injury.

Tests Administered

I gave Mrs Peahen the Wechsler Adult Intelligence Scale Version IV, the Wechsler Memory Scale Version IV, the Test of Premorbid Function from the Advanced Clinical Solutions for WAIS-IV and WMS-IV (PsychCorp, 2009), the Rey 15-Item Test (Rey, 1964) and the Test of Memory Malingering (Tombaugh, 1996). In most assessment (including the assessment with Mrs Peahen) quite a number of additional instruments would also be used as outlined in Chapter 2. For the purposes of not overwhelming the substantive issues within the assessment I will limit the description of the tests used to only those indicated above. In Chapter 8 I will discuss the instruments that I would commonly use in most of my assessments.

The assessment set out to test the following hypotheses:

- Did Mrs Peahen have intelligence in the normal range?
- Were there any areas of weakness in Mrs Peahen's profile of intellectual skills?
- Did Mrs Peahen have memory functions equivalent to the level that we should expect from someone of her current level of ability and in comparison to estimates of her ability preceding his injury?

- Are Mrs Peahen's performances consistent with what should be expected for someone who is making genuine effort to perform to the best of their ability?

Test Results

To conduct the systematic interpretation of the WAIS-IV and WMS-IV we need to once again systematically undertake the steps outlined in Chapter 4.

Step 1: Interpret the full scale intelligence quotient (FSIQ). The first step in this process is to ascertain whether the FSIQ is interpretable. In this instance, the lowest index standard score WMI (71) is subtracted from highest index standard scores WMI (102) yielding a product of 39 (see Table 7.1). The difference in scores is greater than 1.5 standard deviations (i.e. < 23 points) indicating that the FSIQ cannot be interpreted as a reliable and valid estimate of Mrs Peahen's current overall intellectual ability. As can be seen from Table 7.1, the pattern of performances revealed by Mrs Peahen employing the WAIS-IV indicated that she had a Full Scale IQ of 77, 95% confidence interval between 73 and 82 at the 6th percentile rank in the borderline range and a GAI of 92, 95% confidence interval between 87 and 97 at the 30th percentile rank in the average range. As a result, the FSIQ should be interpreted cautiously as a measure of current functioning.

Step 2: Determine the best way to summarise the overall intellectual level. Our next step is to ascertain that Mrs Peahen's GAI can be effectively used to summarise her overall intellectual level. Thus we will need to calculate the difference between the VCI (102) and the PRI (82), an absolute difference of 20. The difference in scores is less than 1.5 standard deviations (i.e. < 23 points)

Table 7.1
WAIS-IV Composite Score Summary

Scale	Sum of scaled scores	Composite score		Percentile rank	95% CI	Qualitative description
Verbal Comprehension	31	VCI	102	55	96–108	Average
Perceptual Reasoning	21	PRI	82	12	77–89	Low average
Working Memory	7	WMI	63	1	58–72	Extremely low
Processing Speed	7	PSI	65	1	60–77	Extremely low
Full Scale	66	FSIQ	77	6	73–82	Borderline
General Ability	52	GAI	92	30	87–97	Average

Note: Confidence Intervals are based on the Overall Average SEMs.
    Values reported in the SEM column are based on the examinee's
    Table of assessment results derived from *Wechsler Adult Intelligence Scale, Fourth Edition (WAIS-IV)*.
    Copyright © 2008 NCS Pearson, Inc. Reproduced with permission. All rights reserved.

Table 7.2
Index Level Discrepancy Comparisons

Comparison	Score 1	Score 2	Difference	Critical value .05	Significant difference Y/N	Base rate overall sample
VCI–PRI	102	82	20	8.31	Y	7.5
VCI–WMI	102	63	39	8.82	Y	0.2
VCI–PSI	102	65	37	10.19	Y	1.2
PRI–WMI	82	63	19	9.74	Y	7.4
PRI–PSI	82	65	17	11	Y	13.4
WMI–PSI	63	65	–2	11.38	N	46.5
FSIQ–GAI	77	92	–15	3.51	Y	0

Note: Base rate by overall sample.
   Statistical significance (critical value) at the .05 level.
   Table of assessment results derived from *Wechsler Adult Intelligence Scale, Fourth Edition (WAIS-IV)*.
   Copyright © 2008 NCS Pearson, Inc. Reproduced with permission. All rights reserved.

indicating that the GAI can be interpreted as a reliable and valid estimate of Mrs Peahen's overall intellectual ability.

The next step is to undertake a comparison of the FSIQ and the GAI (See Table 7.2), which indicates that there was a difference of 15 points between the two measures (i.e., GAI 92; FSIQ 72; critical difference (pcrit) at the .05 level = 3.51, base rate = < 1st percentile), thus the difference does exceed the critical difference, hence it is appropriate to use the GAI as the best summary measures of the performance for any further comparison.

Step 3: Determine whether the GAI/Cognitive Proficiency Index (CPI) is unusually large. To compute the CPI we must sum the two core subtests of the WMI and the two core subtests of the PSI. These figures can then entered into Appendix A.2 of the CD provided with Lichtenberger and Kaufman (2009). Thus in the case of Mrs Peahen, she had a DS (3), LN (4), SS (3), CD (4), if we add these scores together it produces a sum of 14, which as determined from Lichtenberger and Kaufman produces a CPI of 58.

Step 4: Do the GAI and the CPI constitute unitary abilities? The absolute difference between the GAI (92) and the CPI (58) was 34 (i.e., difference required for significance: pcrit = 8.8 at the .05 level and 11 at the .01 level), indicating that the score is interpretable and that the frequency of the difference is statistically significant. This indicates that there is a marked discrepancy between these measures on this occasion.

Step 5: Are the indices unitary? The profile of index scores is presented in Figure 7.1. The profile of subtests scores by index is presented in Figure 7.2. To determine whether the indices are unitary we must subtract the lowest scaled score

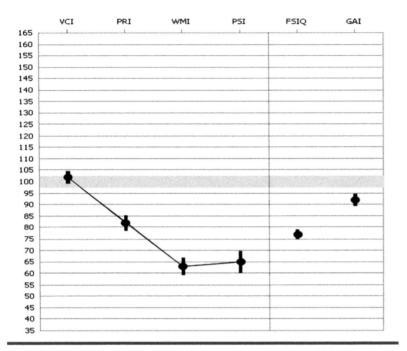

Figure 7.1

Composite score profile.

Note: The profile of subtests scores by index is presented in Figure 7.2.
Assessment results derived from *Wechsler Adult Intelligence Scale, Fourth Edition (WAIS-IV)*.

from the highest. If the discrepancy is less than 5 points then the indices can be considered to be unitary factors. Examination of the subtest constituting the indices of the WAIS-IV (see Table 7.3) indicated that the discrepancies between the subtests constituting each index for the PRI, WMI and PSI were all less than 5, indicating that the indices were within normal limits for estimates of scatter and could be viewed as single measures of the functions of interest. However, this was not the case for the VCI, indicating that the VCI was not a unitary index and thus interpretation of the construct as single factor should be cautiously undertaken.

Step 5a-d: Are the index scores differences interpretable? Mrs Peahen proved to have a Verbal Comprehension Index of 102, 95% confidence interval between 96 and 108 at the 55th percentile rank in the average range; a Perceptual Reasoning Index of 82, 95% confidence interval between 77and 89 at the 12th percentile rank in the low average range; a Working Memory Index of 63, 95% confidence interval between 58 and 72 at the 1st percentile rank in the extremely low range; and a Processing Speed Index of 65, 95%

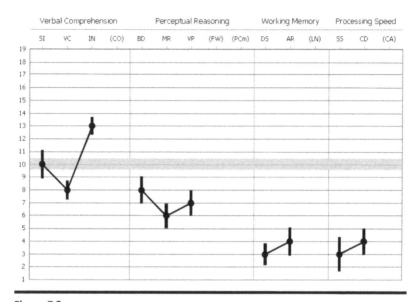

Figure 7.2
Subtest scaled score profile.

confidence interval between 60 and 77 at the 1st percentile rank in the extremely low range.

Comparisons between the indices indicated that there were significant differences ($p \leq .05$; see Table 7.2) in the case of all of the index comparison with the exception of the WMI-PSI comparison. The base rates of these differences were relatively uncommon (i.e., at < 10th% in the overall normative sample for VCI-PRI, VCI-WMI, VCI-PSI and PRI-WMI comparisons) and 13.4% in the case of the PRI-PSI comparison. This indicates that Mrs Peahen, if anything, performs best on the VCI and somewhat less than this on the PRI, but much worse than this still in the case of each of the other indices.

Step 6: Determining normative strengths and weaknesses. Determination of the normative strengths and weaknesses occurs by determining whether the index scores are normative weaknesses (i.e., < 85), are within normal limits (i.e., between 85 and 115) or normative strengths (> 115). In this instance, Mrs Peahen's index scores for PRI, WMI, and PSI were all below 85 and thus constitute normative weaknesses in her case. Mrs Peahen's index score for VCI was within the normal range.

Step 7: Determine personal strengths and weaknesses. The personal strengths and weaknesses of the individual represent indices or factors that differ sig-

Table 7.3
Determining the Quality of the Indices

Index	Highest subtest score	Lowest subtest core	Difference less than 5)	Is the index unitary (i.e., difference ≥ 5)
VCI	13	8	5	No
PRI	8	6	2	Yes
WMI	4	3	1	Yes
PSI	4	3	1	Yes

nificantly from the person's own mean indices. So in the case of Mrs Peahen, the rounded mean of the unitary index factors was 78 (i.e., 102 + 82 + 63 + 64 = 311, divided by 4 = 77.75). The critical differences needed for significance ($p < .05$) are VCI (5.0), PRI (5.8), WMI (6.2), PSI (7.2). Thus, in the case of VCI (24) we can see a personal strength, but in the case of WMI (–15) and PSI (–13), we see personal weaknesses. In fact, in the case of the WMI the base rate of this discrepancy was at less than the 10th percentile, indicating that it is a high priority concern in Mrs Peahen's profile of skills. Only in the case of the PRI (4), did the score differences not exceed the critical difference for significance.

Step 8: Interpret significant strengths and weaknesses on the subtest profile. As we noted above, it is wise to be cautious in the interpretation of any individual subtests fluctuations and to reserve such an analysis of the performance until after the more statistically reliable comparisons are made by contrasting the index and IQ scores. The reasons for fluctuations in the profile of subtest performances can be difficult to specify, so use of this type of evidence should be reserved to explain differences noted by the formal analysis rather than acting as that formal analysis itself.

As we see from Table 7.4, examination of the subtests of the WAIS-IV indicated that Mrs Peahen had particular strength in comparison to her mean score on all other subtests for the Similarities and Information subtests in comparison to her mean performance on the other measures. She had significant weaknesses for Digit Span and for Information.

Step 9: Hypothesise about fluctuations in the profile. As there were fluctuations in the profile presented in Step 8, we can speculate about what these particular measures might constitute in Mrs Peahen's profile. The subtest-level comparisons of the WAIS-IV allow us to make comparisons at the level of subtest score and at the level of cognitive process. The analysis of the process-level comparisons (not reported) did not yield any significant or rare findings, indi-

Table 7.4
Differences Between Subtest and Overall Mean of Subtest Scores

Subtest	Subtest scaled score	Mean scaled score	Difference	Critical value .05	Strength or weakness	Base rate
Block Design	8	6.60	1.4	2.85		> 25%
Similarities	10	6.60	3.4	2.82	S	5–10%
Digit Span	3	6.60	–3.6	2.22	W	5–10%
Matrix Reasoning	6	6.60	–0.6	2.54		> 25%
Vocabulary	8	6.60	1.4	2.03		> 25%
Arithmetic	4	6.60	–2.6	2.73		15–25%
Symbol Search	3	6.60	–3.6	3.42	W	10–15%
Visual Puzzles	7	6.60	0.4	2.71		> 25%
Information	13	6.60	6.4	2.19	S	< 1%
Coding	4	6.60	–2.6	2.97		15–25%

Note: Overall: Mean = 6.6, Scatter = 10, Base rate = 8.9.
  Base rate for Intersubtest Scatter is reported for 10 full scale subtests.
  Statistical significance (critical value) at the .05 level.
  Table of assessment results derived from *Wechsler Adult Intelligence Scale, Fourth Edition (WAIS-IV)*. Copyright © 2008 NCS Pearson, Inc. Reproduced with permission. All rights reserved.

cating that there was no additional diagnostic information in the qualitative analysis of performance that was not provided by the index score analysis.

In our generation of hypotheses regarding Mrs Peahen's WAIS-IV performance we generated two specific hypotheses:

• Did Mrs Peahen have intelligence in the normal range?
• Were there any areas of weakness in Mrs Peahen's profile of intellectual skills?

In response to the first hypothesis it is clear that Mrs Peahen does not have intelligence in the normal range as her FSIQ was in the borderline range of functioning. Interestingly, however, her GAI was in the normal range indicating that there has been a deterioration in performance for those tasks that are sensitive to the changes associated with brain injury (i.e., particularly the WMI and the PSI). While we would need further evidence to determine whether it is reasonable to expect that she would have been performing at a level superior to this preceding her injury, this is a question that must be addressed in its own right. The investigation relative to the second hypothesis indicates that Mrs Peahen features stronger performances on VCI ,which she performs in the average range. She performs somewhat lower than this for the PRI, which was in the low average range and lower still for the WMI and PSI, which were in the extremely low (i.e., borderline intellectually disabled) range.

As we noted in our discussion of the effects of TBI on neuropsychological functioning above, memory processes represent the most sensitive indicators of compromise following TBI. As a result, it seems worthwhile for us to examine this function in Mrs Peahen's case.

Mrs Peahen's Performance on the WMS-IV

Step 1: Is there an attentional problem? As we see from our discussion above regarding Mrs Peahen's performance on the WAIS-IV, she is capable of attending, concentrating and focusing on the assessment in a sufficient way not to require specific evaluation of attentional focus on the task. As a result, it was deemed unnecessary to undertake the Brief Cognitive State Examination in this case, and the assessment immediately moved to the evaluation of memory functioning.

Step 2: Do the indices represent unitary constructs? As we noted in our discussion of the WMS-IV in Chapter 3, the full battery yields five indices: the Auditory Memory Index (AMI), the Visual Memory Index (VMI), the Immediate Memory Index (IMI), the Delayed Memory Index (DMI) and the Visual Working Memory Index (VWMI). Due to the constraints of time, the subtests constituting the VWMI were not administered in the assessment of Mrs Peahen. However, I would recommend to all assessors that it is best to collect the data for this index if it is possible, but if time is limited and no specific hypotheses regarding the measure have been proposed, then other higher priority information may be gathered in its stead. To determine whether the indices represent unitary constructs we must compare each subtest within the index with the others to ascertain the level of intrasubtest scatter. In no case did Mrs Peahen's scores indicate significant subtest difference from the mean score on the subtests constituting the index (data not presented in the interests of brevity nor was any within index subtest score discrepancy ≥ 5 scaled score points), thus the index scores do represent unitary factors.

Step 3: How well does the person learn as a function of modality of information? As we have now determined that the indices represent unitary factors in Mrs Peahen's case we can move on to the examination of the components of her memory functioning. The performance of Mrs Peahen on each of the indices is presented in Table 7.5 and in Figure 7.3. These data indicated that she had an Auditory Immediate Memory Index of 57, 95% confidence interval between 53 and 65 at less than the 1st percentile rank in the extremely low range; a Visual Immediate Memory Index of 65, 95% confidence interval between 61 and 72 at the 1st percentile rank in the extremely low range; an Immediate Memory Index of 60, 95% confidence interval between 56 and 68 at less than the 1st percentile rank in the extremely low range; and a Delayed Memory Index of 56, 95% confidence interval between 52 and 65 at less than the 1st percentile rank in the extremely low range.

Table 7.5
Index Score Summary

Index	Sum of scaled scores	Index score		Percentile rank	95% CI	Qualitative description
Auditory Memory	12	AMI	57	0.2	53–65	Extremely low
Visual Memory	18	VMI	65	1	61–72	Extremely low
Immediate Memory	16	IMI	60	0.4	56–68	Extremely low
Delayed Memory	14	DMI	56	0.2	52–65	Extremely low

Note: Table of assessment results derived from *Wechsler Memory Scale, Fourth Edition (WMS-IV)*.

Step 4: Is there a difference between modalities? The comparison between the AMI and VMI is presented in Table 7.6. Here we see that the comparison between AMI and the VMI indicate a contrast scaled score of 5. As we can see in the case of Mrs Peahen, the comparison of the AMI and the VMI is not in the range between 8 and 12 indicating that the two scores do differ, demonstrating that she performed significantly worse on the AMI than she did on the VMI.

Step 5: How well does the person recall following a delay? The comparison of immediate versus delayed memory is also presented in Table 7.6. Mrs Peahen proved to have a contrast scaled score on this comparison of 4 (i.e., a score not between 8 and 12), once again indicating that the two scores differ and that Mrs Peahen was performing worse on the DMI in comparison to the IMI.

Step 6: Do they benefit from cues or choices? The primary subtest scaled score performance of Mrs Peahen is presented in Table 7.7. We see that Mrs Peahen performs in a manner at less than the 10th percentile for all of the measures, indicating a global impairment on each subtest. How then does she perform relatively speaking, with regarding to cued recall? In Tables 7.8 and 7.9, we can see that Mrs Peahen performs in an impaired way (i.e., all < 10th cumulative percentage) for each of the recognition measures with the exception the Designs II content and spatial scores. It would appear that her recall is largely not aided by recognition, with the single exception of her performance on the Designs delayed scores.

Step 7: How well does the person recall in comparison to other aspects of their performance? To undertake this step we must first determine the right measure to which we should compare the memory performances. In the case of Table 7.10, we can compare Mrs Peahen's performance to her GAI. This indicates that she performs in a manner less than would be expected by her GAI for all of the memory indices. These differences are both statistically significant and

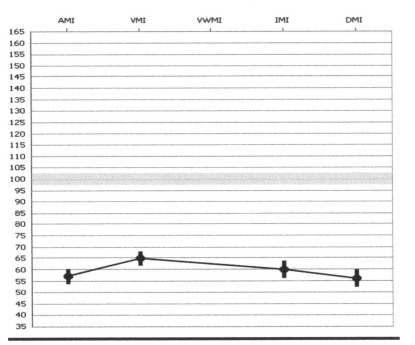

Figure 7.3

Index score profile.

Note: The vertical bars represent the standard error of measurement (SEM).

very rare, occurring in < 1st percentile of the standardisation sample in each case. Thus it is clear that Mrs Peahen is performing at a level less than would be expected on the basis of her current ability, and the level of compromise is in the very severely impaired range.

It is also possible for us to compare Mrs Peahen's performances to what we should have expected of her preceding her injury, as based upon estimations of her premorbid functioning using the Test of Premorbid Function

Table 7.6

Index-Level Contrast Scaled Scores

Score	Score 1	Score 2	Contrast scaled score
Auditory Memory Index vs. Visual Memory Index	57	65	5
Immediate Memory Index vs. Delayed Memory Index	60	56	4

Note: Table of assessment results derived from *Wechsler Memory Scale, Fourth Edition (WMS-IV)*. Copyright © 2009 NCS Pearson, Inc. Reproduced with permission. All rights reserved.

Table 7.7
Primary Subtest Scaled Score Summary

Subtest	Domain	Raw score	Scaled score	Percentile rank
Logical Memory I	AM	12	4	2
Logical Memory II	AM	5	3	1
Verbal Paired Associates I	AM	10	4	2
Verbal Paired Associates II	AM	0	1	0.1
Designs I	VM	36	2	0.4
Designs II	VM	37	6	9
Visual Reproduction I	VM	25	6	9
Visual Reproduction II	VM	5	4	2

Note: Table of assessment results derived from *Wechsler Memory Scale, Fourth Edition (WMS-IV)*.

(TOPF; PsychCorp, 2009). As we can see in Table 7.11, Mrs Peahen is performing on the word reading test (i.e., 101) at an equivalent level to estimates as based upon the simple demographics model (i.e., demographics of Melbourne as equated to the Northeast of the U.S., sex, ethnicity, highest level of education and highest occupational level [i.e., 95] on this occasion), indicating no differences. However, as we see in Table 7.12, Mrs Peahen is performing at her level of premorbid estimates for her VCI, but not so for the FSIQ, PRI, WMI and her PSI (also see Figure 7.4). Clearly, on these aspects of functioning Mrs Peahen demonstrates a decline in what would be expected by the predictions of her performance preceding her injury, and in all cases (with the exception of VCI) she is performing at a level at the 10th percentile or lower.

It is also possible for us to use the TOPF to generate predictions of her performance on the WMS-IV. As we can see from Table 7.13 and Figure 7.5, Mrs Peahen is performing below expectation as based upon her word reading and

Table 7.8
Auditory Memory Process Score Summary

Process Score	Raw score	Scaled score	Percentile rank	Cumulative percentage (base rate)
LM II Recognition	20	—	—	3–9%
VPA II Recognition	27	—	—	≤ 2%

Note: Table of assessment results derived from *Wechsler Memory Scale, Fourth Edition (WMS-IV)*.

Table 7.9
Visual Memory Process Score Summary

Process Score	Raw score	Scaled score	Percentile rank	Cumulative percentage (base rate)
DE I Content	22	4	2	—
DE I Spatial	10	5	5	—
DE II Content	26	7	16	—
DE II Spatial	9	8	25	—
DE II Recognition	10	—	—	3–9%
VR II Recognition	2	—	—	≤ 2%

Note: Table of assessment results derived from *Wechsler Memory Scale, Fourth Edition (WMS-IV)*.
Copyright © 2009 NCS Pearson, Inc. Reproduced with permission. All rights reserved.

the simple demographic correction in the case of the IMI, but not the DMI. This supports our previous qualitative observations regarding her performance on the subtest analysis.

Step 8: Is there a difference between the working memory indices? As we noted in the discussion above, we did not administer the VWMI index, so it is not possible to make this comparison. While in Mrs Peahen's case we would not anticipate a specific compromise in verbal versus visual working memory, due to the absence of data it is not possible to definitively provide an answer to this question, remember the name of the book!

Step 9: How well is information retained after delay? The comparison of predicted versus actual performance on the IMI and DMI is presented in Table

Table 7.10
Ability-Memory Analysis

Predicted Difference Method

Index	Predicted WMS–IV Index score	Actual WMS–IV Index score	Difference	Critical value	Significant difference Y/N	Base rate
Auditory Memory	96	57	39	8.95	Y	< 1%
Visual Memory	95	65	30	8.82	Y	< 1%
Immediate Memory	95	60	35	10.35	Y	< 1%
Delayed Memory	95	56	39	10.08	Y	< 1%

Note: Statistical significance (critical value) at the .01 level.
Ability Score Type: GAI
Ability Score: 92
Table of assessment results derived from *Wechsler Memory Scale, Fourth Edition (WMS-IV)*. Copyright © 2009 NCS Pearson, Inc. Reproduced with permission. All rights reserved.

Table 7.11

Test of Premorbid Functioning Actual–Predicted Comparison

	Actual score	Predicted score	Prediction interval	Difference	Critical value	Significant difference	Base rate
Actual–Predicted	101	95	66–124	6	5.47	Y	35.7%

Note: Actual–Predicted Comparison based on Simple Demographics Predictive Model.
  Prediction Intervals reported at the 95% Level of Confidence.
  Statistical significance (critical value) at the .01 level.
  Table of assessment results derived from *Advanced Clinical Solutions for WAIS-IV and WMS-IV (ACS)*. Copyright © 2009 NCS Pearson, Inc. Reproduced with permission. All rights reserved.

7.13 and Figure 7.5. Mrs Peahen performs in a manner less than what should be expected on each measure.

It is thus now possible for us to provide an evaluation of our third hypothesis regarding Mrs Peahen's memory functioning: Did Mrs Peahen have memory functions equivalent to the level we would expect from someone of her current level of ability and in comparison to estimates of her ability preceding her injury? The assessment indicated that she had an Auditory Immediate Memory Index of 57, 95% confidence interval between 53 and 65 at less than the 1st percentile rank in the extremely low range; a Visual Immediate Memory Index of 65, 95% confidence interval between 61 and 72 at the 1st percentile rank in the extremely low range; an Immediate Memory Index of 60, 95% confidence interval between 56 and 68 at less than the 1st percentile rank in the extremely low range; and a Delayed Memory Index of 56, 95% confidence interval between 52 and 65 at less than the 1st percentile rank in the extremely low range.

These figures were significantly different to her contemporary levels of intelligence as determined using the General Ability Index, which were dis-

Table 7.12

WAIS–IV Actual–Predicted Comparison

Composite	Actual	Predicted	Prediction interval	Difference	Critical value	Significant difference	Base rate
FSIQ	77	99	75–123	−22	6.99	Y	1.3%
VCI	102	97	75–119	5	8.08	N	27.4%
PRI	82	97	67–127	−15	9.29	Y	10.3%
WMI	63	99	71–127	−36	10.22	Y	0%
PSI	65	99	65–133	−34	11.93	Y	0.4%

Note: Actual–Predicted Comparison based on Simple Demographics with Test of Premorbid Functioning Predictive Model.
  Prediction Intervals reported at the 95% Level of Confidence.
  Statistical significance (critical value) at the .01 level.
  Table of assessment results derived from *Advanced Clinical Solutions for WAIS-IV and WMS-IV (ACS)*. Copyright © 2009 NCS Pearson, Inc. Reproduced with permission. All rights reserved.

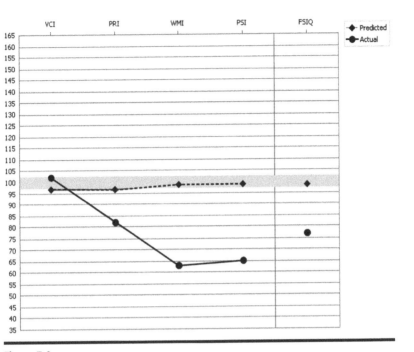

Figure 7.4

WAIS–IV Actual–Predicted score profile.

crepant at the five in 100 chance level in all cases. This indicates that Mrs Peahen shows profound memory decline for both auditory-verbal and visuo-spatial memory, auditory working memory, immediate and delayed memory in comparison to estimates of her contemporary intellectual ability. This observation was also noted in comparison to estimates of her pre-injury level of function as determined using the Test of Premorbid Function, which was discrepant at the five in 100 chance level on this occasion.

Our fourth hypothesis regarding Mrs Peahen surrounds the issue of the genuineness of her performance. Specifically: Are Mrs Peahen's performances consistent with what should be expected for someone who is making genuine effort to perform to the best of their ability?

A number of aspects of the assessment described so far necessitate concern regarding Mrs Peahen's level of effort.

1. With regard to the nature of the injury itself, given that Mrs Peahen suffered from a TBI yet did not suffer loss of consciousness, retrograde amnesia and was only admitted to hospital overnight, such an injury would not,

Table 7.13
WMS–IV Actual–Predicted Comparison

Index	Actual	Predicted	Prediction interval	Difference	Critical value	Significant difference	Base rate
IMI	60	99	66–132	-39	9.9	Y	0.2%
DMI	56	96	62–130	-40	9.81	Y	0.1%

Note: Actual–Predicted Comparison based on simple demographics with Test of Premorbid Functioning Predictive Model
 Prediction Intervals reported at the 95% level of confidence.
 Statistical significance (critical value) at the .01 level.
 Table of assessment results derived from *Advanced Clinical Solutions for WAIS-IV and WMS-IV (ACS)*.
 Copyright © 2009 NCS Pearson, Inc. Reproduced with permission. All rights reserved.

in the normal course of events, be expected to result in long-term neuropsychological sequelae. It should be noted that TBI has been reported to occur without loss of consciousness, but this is a very rare and controversial phenomenon (Crowe, 2000).

2. The various medical reports that were sent along with her referral (not discussed due to confidentiality concerns) did not present anything more on formal neurological examination beyond the indication that Mrs Peahen said that she had had a whiplash injury.

3. She was not subjected to any sustained attempt at rehabilitation until more than 6 months after the injury.

4. She has been having 'therapy' with Dr Colleague for more than 12 years and yet does not appear to be getting any better. It is, after all, the natural course of events for neurological injuries to improve as a function of time.

5. Despite the concerns raised by Mrs Peahen:
   - she features no overt neurological stigmata
   - she is immaculately presented on clinical interview, and
   - she plays golf and is off a handicap of 16 (better than mine by a considerable degree unfortunately!)

These issues exist in association with the levels of deficits that she features on neuropsychological testing, particularly her overtly dense amnesia (her memory indices are consistently in the mid 50s to the mid 60s, a level of memory impairment that would most commonly be noted with someone with moderately severe Alzheimer's disease) and the fact that her working memory functioning and her speed of processing are at a level commonly noted with a very severe TBI (see Colonel Keen As in Chapter 6). Thus, on a number of fronts, the consistency with which Mrs Peahen's cognitive profile presents itself suggests close scrutiny is warranted. To this end, I undertook a

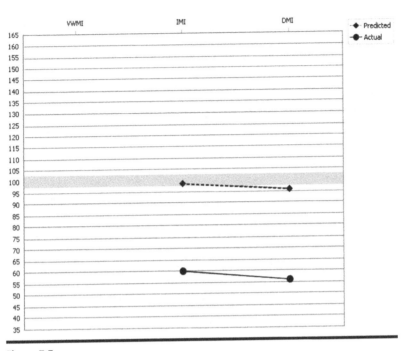

Figure 7.5

WMS–IV Actual–Predicted score profile.

Note: Assessment results derived from *Advanced Clinical Solutions for WAIS-IV and WMS-IV (ACS).*
Copyright © 2009 NCS Pearson, Inc. Reproduced with permission. All rights reserved.

number of commonly employed tests of symptom validity to ascertain the reliability of her effort.

This testing included performance on the Rey 15-Item Test, a qualitative analysis of her performance on the subtests of the Wechsler Memory Scale, the Word Choice subtest from the Advanced Clinical Solutions for WAIS-IV and WMS-IV (PsychCorp, 2009) as well as performance on the Test of Memory Malingering. Mrs Peahen correctly recalled 12 of the 15 items on the Rey 15-Item Test, a normal performance. As noted above, concerns regarding the reliability and validity of the 15-Item test has been commonly raised (e.g., Greiffenstein et al., 1996; Schretlen et al., 1991; Spreen & Strauss, 1998; Vallabhajosula & Van Gorp, 2001), but nonetheless Mrs Peahen does perform in an unimpaired manner on this measure.

The Test of Memory Malingering (TOMM; Tombaugh, 1996) employs a two-trial, visual recognition procedure. On each trial (i.e., trial 1, trial 2 and the recall trial), 50 line-drawn pictures are presented at four-second intervals that are followed by 50 two-item test panels containing a target and a foil. The task of the client is to determine which of the two choices was the one presented before. The test has been well validated to be capable of discriminating between less than genuine effort and genuine memory-impaired performances, as the recognition function assessed by the Test of Memory Malingering tends to be largely unaffected by acquired brain injury in most of its forms.

Mrs Peahen's performance on the TOMM indicated that she correctly recognised only 11 of the 50 items on the first trial of the task and recognised 24 of the 50 items on the second trial of the task. The manual for the Test of Memory Malingering indicates that any performance of less than 45 of 50 items on the second trial of the task is consistent with the notion of less than genuine effort. This observation does pertain in Mrs Peahen's case and supports the notion that she was not performing to the best of her ability. In the case of the first trial of the Test of Memory Malingering, Ms Peahen performs with a score of less than 18. A performance of less than 18 on any trial of the Test of Memory Malingering represents a less than chance performance and is consistent with the notion of someone who not only does not recall the previously presented material, but an examinee who is actively choosing the incorrect response, as this is the most likely explanation of why they are performing at a less than chance level. This indicates that Mrs Peahen has the correct answer available to her and is actively choosing the incorrect answer on this measure. This is a very disconcerting pattern of performances and raises significant concern that Mrs Peahen was not performing to the best of her ability and that she was faking bad.

The embedded symptom validity measures of the WMS-IV also proved to reveal further concerns with regard to Mrs Peahen's performances. As we can see from Table 7.14, Mrs Peahen performed at a level below the 25% base rate for all of the clinical samples on all five of the embedded measures on the

Table 7.14
Effort Score Summary

Score	Raw score	Overall clinical sample base rates					
		≤ 2%	≤ 5%	≤ 10%	≤ 15%	≤ 25%	> 25%
Word Choice	23	X	X	X	X	X	
LM II Recognition	20					X	
VPA II Recognition	27		X	X	X	X	
VR II Recognition	2		X	X	X	X	
Reliable Digit Span	5			X	X	X	
Totals	1	3	4	4	5	—	

Table 7.15
Effort Score Analysis

	Percentages with matching number of cut scores at cutoff				
	Number of scores at 10% cutoff				
lGroup of interest	1	2	3	4	5
No stimulus	100	100	96	60	–
Simulators	64	36	20	10	8
Overall clinicalsample	19	5	1	0	0
Traumatic brain injury	30	6	0	0	0
GAI	7	1	0	0	0

Note: Assessment results derived from *Advanced Clinical Solutions for WAIS-IV and WMS-IV (ACS)*.

WMS-IV. In fact for the Word Choice subtest (effectively a verbal analogue of the TOMM) she performs at a level less than the 2nd percentile.

Comparisons of Mrs Peahen's performance with a variety of clinical groups at the 10% cut-off level reveals a high index of concern in comparison to each of the clinical groups (see Table 7.15).

Thus, in response to our question: are Mrs Peahen's performances consistent with what should be expected for someone who is making genuine effort to perform to the best of their ability it is clear that she performs in a manner consistent with the notion of less than genuine effort on numerous measures of this construct, and in fact on some measures she performs in a manner consistent with the notion of actively choosing the incorrect answer.

Conclusion

The pattern of performances revealed by Mrs Peahen on this occasion indicates a woman of 59 years who was subjected to MTBI more than 12 years earlier. She was admitted briefly to hospital but at this point in time demonstrates a profound level of neuropsychological compromise with profound level of impairment of working memory and processing speed and a moderately severe level of impairment of perceptual reasoning. In association with this she demonstrates marked compromise of memory functioning currently operating in the extremely severely memory impaired range. Examination of the nature of this pattern of performances reveals that some or all of this performance is attributable to less than genuine effort to perform to the best of her ability, as demonstrated on a number of tests of symptom validity. Her performance on the Test of Memory Malingering reveals a performance consistent with the notion of an active attempt to fake bad.

Summary

The assessment of malingering in neuropsychological assessment is complex. Passing symptom validity testing does not disprove malingering. Conversely, failing symptom validity testing does not necessarily invalidate the examinee's performance on all other tests used in the evaluation (Larrabee, 1992). The final judgment must, in the end, be a clinical one made by a clinician weighing all of the available evidence gathered in the assessment. Nonetheless, it is essential for clinicians to conduct evaluation of dissimulation within the context of their assessments, for as Rogers (1999) has noted, clinicians are crucially dependent upon their clients to be well motivated, cooperative and to exert a maximal level of effort during the examination. Yet again, Sagan's dictum that absence of evidence does not equate to evidence of absence, seems most apposite in this context. If the motivation and cooperation of the examinee are not measured, how then can any tenable opinion be formed as to the nature of these matters?

CHAPTER EIGHT

Reporting Your Findings

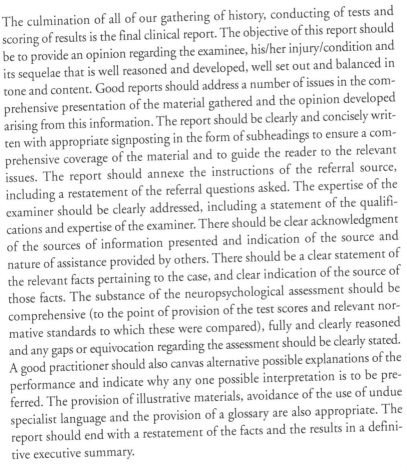

The culmination of all of our gathering of history, conducting of tests and scoring of results is the final clinical report. The objective of this report should be to provide an opinion regarding the examinee, his/her injury/condition and its sequelae that is well reasoned and developed, well set out and balanced in tone and content. Good reports should address a number of issues in the comprehensive presentation of the material gathered and the opinion developed arising from this information. The report should be clearly and concisely written with appropriate signposting in the form of subheadings to ensure a comprehensive coverage of the material and to guide the reader to the relevant issues. The report should annexe the instructions of the referral source, including a restatement of the referral questions asked. The expertise of the examiner should be clearly addressed, including a statement of the qualifications and expertise of the examiner. There should be clear acknowledgment of the sources of information presented and indication of the source and nature of assistance provided by others. There should be a clear statement of the relevant facts pertaining to the case, and clear indication of the source of those facts. The substance of the neuropsychological assessment should be comprehensive (to the point of provision of the test scores and relevant normative standards to which these were compared), fully and clearly reasoned and any gaps or equivocation regarding the assessment should be clearly stated. A good practitioner should also canvas alternative possible explanations of the performance and indicate why any one possible interpretation is to be preferred. The provision of illustrative materials, avoidance of the use of undue specialist language and the provision of a glossary are also appropriate. The report should end with a restatement of the facts and the results in a definitive executive summary.

Structure of the Report

Arthur Shores (2006b) has prepared a set of guidelines for the preparation of medico-legal neuropsychological reports, specifically in relation to mild traumatic brain injury, and these stand as an excellent guide to the sort of material that should be presented in a competent forensic neuropsychological report. He suggests that a comprehensive assessment process should be reported in 13 important areas. These areas are: the source of background information, the description of the injury or event, description of the presentation of the examinee, information obtained from the examinee in relation to the sequelae of the injury, the past medical history of the examinee, the past educational and occupational history of the examinee, details of an interview conducted with a significant other (preferably one who has known the examinee both before and after the injury), the formal neuropsychological examination including a list of the tests administered, test interpretation, a summarising clinical opinion, recommendations for further treatment, a listing of the test results and a curriculum vitae of the examiner.

In a similar vein, Hebben and Milberg (2009, p. 212) recommend the following outline of sections of the assessment report:

- identifying information
- reason for referral
- records reviewed or source of historical information
- relevant history and background information
- behavioural observations
- tests administered
- test results
- summary and impressions
- recommendations
- examiner and report writer, signature(s).

John Mendoza (2001) recommends the following sequence of sections within the report:

(1) referral question
(2) history and background information
(3) behavioural observations
(4) assessment procedures
(5) test results
    (a) orientation
    (b) attention and concentration
    (c) mental flexibility/executive function

(d) primary sensory and perceptual ability

(e) psychomotor functions

(f) speech and language

(g) visual spatial skills

(h) intellectual and academic abilities

(i) learning and memory

(6) personality (psychological) assessment

(7) summary and conclusions

(8) recommendations

(9) diagnostic impressions.

Mendoza notes that these last three sections, should specifically attempt to answer the following questions:

(1) Is there any evidence of behavioural or functional deficits or impairments?

(2) What is the nature, extent, or degree of these deficits or impairment?

(3) Do these deficits or impairments appear to reflect a significant change from the individual's baseline and, if so, over what period of time?

(4) Do these changes appear to be the result of acquired brain dysfunction or impairment?

(5) Does the pattern of deficits suggest any particular syndrome or disease entity?

(6) Are there inconsistencies within the data that need to be addressed?

(7) Are there inconsistencies with the presumptive diagnosis and, if so, what are the alternative hypotheses?

(8) What other possible explanations (e.g., medical, behavioural, demographic, psychological) might account for the findings?

(9) Are there independent psychological (or psychiatric) issues or diagnoses present?

(10) What are the psychological or psychosocial effects of these impairments or this disease (or injury) process on the patient?

(11) How will these impairments or this disease process affect the patient's ability to function on the day-to-day basis?

(12) Are there any specific recommendations for treatment, management, or further diagnostic work-ups?

(13) Are there any positive or negative prognostic indicators? (p. 109)

It is clear in examining the suggestions of Associate Professor Shores, as well as those of Drs Mendoza, Hebben and Milberg, that there is a strong and consistent theme arising from each of the guidelines. I would strongly recommend to you, therefore, that a reporting style including most of these important categories provides for a comprehensive and balanced reporting of your assessment.

What Tests Should I Use and How Many of Them Should There be?

With regard to the specific description of the most important neuropsychological data, particularly for those individuals who have suffered an mTBI, Professor Shores (2006b, p. 15) recommends that:

> The neuropsychological examination should address the following areas:
> * post concussive symptoms within the previous month
> * level of effort
> * estimated pre-morbid ability including the information used to determine this assessment of current intellectual ability including verbal comprehension, perceptual organisation and visuospatial skills
> * level of performance in specific cognitive domains including:
>   memory/learning
>   attention/speed of information processing
>   executive function
>   emotional functioning and its effect on cognition.

The selection of tests and normative data as shown in Table 8.1 are recommended as examples of appropriate measures. These can be supplemented or substituted with other tests at the discretion of the psychologist depending on the circumstances of each specific case. Australian normative data should be used where possible.

Consistent with many of the suggestions made by Associate Professor Shores, with my own assessments I would always include a further set of instruments to those that I have outlined in the clinical cases presented in Chapters 5, 6 and 7. I did not include these in the case formulations as it seemed that it might overwhelm the reader with too much detail. Nonetheless, as a flexible battery/hypothesis testing-based clinician I would administer the following battery of tests (see Table 8.2) in most of the clinical cases that I would undertake (mostly because I test a similar set of hypotheses with each client that I assess, due to the nature of my practice).

In reality, the number of tests that it is necessary to use in an assessment is a function of the number of hypotheses one generates about the client's performance. Thus, if the clinician develops more hypotheses about a set of functions and their relationship to each other or to the condition of focus, this should culminate in the use of more tests.

One other useful clinical rule of thumb to consider regarding test selection is that best practice indicates it is best to have at least two measures of

Table 8.1

Selection of Tests and Normative Data Recommended as Examples of Appropriate Measures by Associate Professor Shores (2006b, p. 15)

Postconcussive symptoms	Post Concussion Syndrome Checklist (Gouvier, Cubic, Jones, Brantley, & Cutlip, 1992), or The Rivermead Post Concussion Symptoms Questionnaire (King, Crawford, Wenden, Moss, & Wade, 1995)
Level of effort	Test of Memory Malingering (Tombaugh, 1996)
Estimated premorbid ability	Wechsler Test of Adult Reading (Corporation, 2001) AUSNART (Lucas, Carstairs, & Shores, 2003)
Current intellectual and memory ability	Wechsler Adult Intelligence Scale — Revised (WAIS-R; Wechsler, 1981) (WAIS-R Ages 18–34; Shores & Carstairs, 2000) and Wechsler Memory Scale — Revised (WMS-R; Wechsler, 1987) (WMS-R Ages 18–34; Shores & Carstairs, 2000) or Wechsler Adult Intelligence Scale — Third Edition (WAIS–III; Wechsler, 1997a) (Dori & Chelune, 2004; D.S. Tulsky, Ivnik, Price, & Wilkins, 2003; Wechsler, 1997a) and Wechsler Memory Scale — Third Edition (WMS–III; Wechsler, 1997) (Dori & Chelune, 2004; D.S. Tulsky et al., 2003; Wechsler, 1997d)
Attention/speed of information processing	WAIS-III Working Memory Index (Dori & Chelune, 2004; D.S. Tulsky et al., 2003; Wechsler, 1997a) WAIS-III Processing Speed Index (Wechsler, 1997) (Dori & Chelune, 2004; D.S. Tulsky et al., 2003; Wechsler, 1997a) Oral and Written Symbol Digit Modalities Test (Smith, 1982)
Executive function	Category Test (R.K. Heaton, Miller, Taylor, & Grant, 2004) FAS–Controlled Oral Word Association Test (R.K. Heaton et al., 2004)
Emotional functioning	Depression Anxiety Stress Scales (Lovibond & Lovibond, 1995) Posttraumatic Stress Diagnostic Scale (Foa, 1995)

any function to achieve a satisfactory level of concurrent validity. Particularly for neuropsychological measures, which tend to be characterised by their relatively high levels of error, a single measure of any function is insufficient to characterise the breadth of the construct, thus the use of two converging measures of the same construct results in the most comprehensive measure of the construct. This is particularly the case in the context of the measurement of less than genuine effort, where I strongly recommend that you use at least two (Larrabee, 2005) and preferably more than two tests of symptom validity. My reason for this suggestion is that the charge of performing with less than optimal level of effort is a serious one, and one you should not make without strong, convergent evidence.

Table 8.2
The Selection of Tests That I Use in Most of the Clinical Cases That I Undertake

Function	Test
Intellectual and academic abilities	WAIS-IV (Wechsler, 2008c)
	Wechsler Individual Achievement Test-II 2nd Ed (WIAT-II) Abbreviated (PsychCorp, 2001)
Premorbid intelligence	Test of Pre-Morbid Function (PsychCorp, 2009)
Orientation	Brief cognitive status examination from the WMS-IV (Wechsler, 2009c)
Attention and concentration	Working Memory Index from the WAIS-IV (Wechsler, 2008c)
	Visual Working Memory Index from the WMS-IV (Wechsler, 2009c)
Mental flexibility/executive function	Phonemic Verbal Fluency (FAS) (Goodglass et al., 2001)
	Semantic Verbal Fluency (Animals) (Goodglass et al., 2001)
	Stroop Color Word Test (Stroop, 1935)
	Trail Making Test Part B (Reitan & Wolfson, 1993b)
	Wisconsin Card Sorting Test 64-Card Version (Kongs et al., 2000)
Primary sensory and perceptual ability	Rey Tangled Lines Test (Rey, 1941, 1964)
	The Grooved Pegboard Test (Kløve, 1963)
Psychomotor functions	Processing Speed Index of the WIAS-IV (Wechsler, 2008c)
	Trail Making Test Parts A and B (Reitan & Wolfson, 1993b)
Speech and language	Boston Naming Test (Goodglass et al., 2001)
	Wechsler Individual Achievement Test-II 2nd Ed (WIAT-II) Abbreviated (PsychCorp, 2001)
	Phonemic Verbal Fluency (FAS) (Goodglass et al., 2001)
	Semantic Verbal Fluency (Animals) (Goodglass et al., 2001)
Visual spatial skills	Perceptual Organization Index of the WAIS-IV (Wechsler, 2008c)
Learning and memory	WMS-IV (Wechsler, 2009c)
	Rey Complex Figure Test (Rey, 1941, 1964)
	RAVLT or CVLT-II (Delis et al., 1999; Rey, 1941, 1964)
Symptom Validity	Rey 15-Item Test (Rey, 1941, 1964)
	Test of Memory Malingering (Tombaugh, 1996)
	Word Choice Test from the Advanced Clinical Solutions for the WAS-IV and WMS-IV (PsychCorp, 2009)
	Reliable Digit Span (PsychCorp, 2009)
	Embedded measures from the recognition components of the WMS-IV; LM-II Recognition; VPA-II recognition; VR-II recognition (Wechsler, 2009c)
Psychological and emotional functioning	DASS (Lovibond & Lovibond, 1995)
	MMPI-RF (Tellegen & Ben-Porath, 2008)
	Illness Behaviour Questionnaire (Pilowsky & Spence, 1994)

Writing Your Report

Hebben and Milberg recommend 13 maxims which they believe are important for report writing:

(1) Be sure you are reporting properly scored tests and accurate data.

(2) Avoid technical words and jargon.

(3) Keep the length of the report appropriate to the anticipated reader of the report.

(4) Include relevant historical data.

(5) Avoid including irrelevant historical data.

(6) Describe physical appearance and behavior.

(7) Name and describe the test procedures.

(8) Include the test scores.

(9) Provide the test scores for all tests, not just the impaired test scores.

(10) Consider all the evidence when interpreting data, not just test scores.

(11) Do not use each test for the lesion localisation.

(12) Provide useful, specific recommendations.

(13) Describe any and all modifications and their potential impact on interpretation. (Hebben & Milberg, 2009, p. 207)

Hebben and Milberg (2009) also caution against the unusually esoteric use of neuropsychological information. Specifically,

> ... reports consisting only of brilliantly justified and exquisitely detailed predictions about lesion localization and offering no usable and specific recommendations, may serve either to hasten the rate of deforestation or increase the profit margins of computer disk drive manufacturers, but they are unlikely to be appreciated by those responsible for taking care of patients. (p. 206)

I can only strongly agree with their sentiments.

Comprehensive assessment involves the systematic collection, description and explanation of relevant information about the individual and his or her situation. Different procedures, however, are indicated for different purposes. The clinical assessment will differ if the aim of the assessment process is to undertake a neuropsychological assessment, which would again be different for behavioural assessment or for determination of eligibility. As a consequence, the nature of the report will be determined by the requirement of the referral question that has prompted the requested assessment in the first place. Thus, an eligibility determination for placement and service access for an intellectually disabled client would be quite different to one in which a medico-legal disputation may ensue regarding subtle diagnostic differentiation.

Once again, it is a matter for of 'horses for courses' and the most appropriate approach should be guided by your referral source and for you to provide a comprehensive answer to the question so posed.

Donders (2001a, 2001b) notes that the mean length of reports provided by clinical neuropsychologists was approximately seven pages, with a few individuals routinely preparing reports of only one page, while a few routinely prepared reports of 30 pages. Clinicians in geriatric facilities and those working in medical settings tended to be more brief, while those who were in private practice, paediatric or medico-legal settings tended to be more wordy. This is a matter of clinical style, as mediated by the need to be sufficiently comprehensive to address those important aspects of the information provided in the report as discussed above.

What Opinions Can be Formed Following a Neuropsychological Assessment?

One of the interesting features of neuropsychological assessment is that the behavioural parameters that they would seek to measure are not generally specific to any given kind of neurological disorder. For example, memory impairment may result from toxic encephalopathy, TBI, alcohol-related brain impairment, epilepsy, hypoxia, major depression, schizophrenia, or a progressive degenerative disorder such as Alzheimer's disease, to name only a few possibilities. Thus, tests of themselves do not indicate brain damage, it is the skilled clinical neuropsychologist's interpretation of the pattern of performance that results in the diagnostic opinion.

> In personal injury cases, the proximate cause of deficits or impairments will be one of the most important conclusions in your report. Proximate cause refers to the direct and immediate cause of injury. For this reason, the choice of words in your report or testimony can be of critical importance. The language should be clear and unambiguous. Avoid the term 'consistent with', as this term implies that the conclusion is not inconsistent with, that is not contradictory. The term cannot be used to imply a causal relationship. For example, a high fever is consistent with encephalitis, but it is also consistent with scarlet fever, pneumonia, measles, and many other diseases. It certainly is not diagnostic of any one of these diseases. (Derby, 2001, p. 219)

This harks back to our discussion in Chapter 1 of the many possible causes of failure on tests of cognitive function, and our confusion between which large animals with four legs we are actually dealing with. It behoves you to try to the best of your ability to clarify, rather than obfuscate the clinical picture, and thus to provide clear and unequivocal answers to the questions that have been posed to you. Nonetheless, if you legitimately do not know, or cannot say, then as in all things, honesty is the best policy.

For the lawyer the most valuable contribution that a cognitive assessment can make include:

1. the history obtained
2. the patient's condition when examined by the clinician
3. the relationship between the patient's injuries and their present condition
4. whether the patient's condition has stabilized
5. the genuineness of the patient's symptomatology
6. the diagnosis and/or the nature of the disability
7. the extent of that disability
8. the prognosis and/or the duration of that disability
9. whether the injuries and the present condition of the client have affected the ability of the client to engage in pre-trauma social, domestic or recreational activities
10. whether the client is fit for work and if so what kind of work
11. if the client is unfit for work, the cause and extent of such incapacity
12. recommendations for further treatment or assessment.

In fact, under the Supreme Court (General Civil Procedure) Rules of 1996 (S.R. No. 19/1996; Rule 44.01) the expert witness is required to agree to abide by the following rules of procedure associated with the production of their opinions.

EXPERT WITNESS CODE OF CONDUCT

(1) A person engaged as an expert witness has an overriding duty to assist the Court impartially on matters relevant to the area of expertise of the witness.

(2) An expert witness is not an advocate for a party.

(3) Every report prepared by an expert witness for the use of the Court shall state the opinion or opinions of the expert and shall state, specify or provide:

(a) the name and address of the expert;

(b) an acknowledgement that the expert has read this code and agrees to be bound by it;

(c) the qualifications of the expert to prepare the report;

(d) the facts, matters and assumption on which each opinion expressed in the report is based (a letter of instructions may be annexed);

(e) (i) the reasons for,
(ii) any literature or other materials utilized in support of,
(iii) a summary of —
each such opinion;

(f) (if applicable) that a particular question, issue or matter falls outside the expert's field of expertise;

(g) any examinations, tests or other investigations on which the expert has relied, identifying the person who carried them out and that person's qualifications;

(h) a declaration that the expert has made all the inquiries which the expert believes are desirable and appropriate, and that no matters of significance which the expert regards as relevant has, to the knowledge of the expert, been withheld from the Court;

(i) any qualifications of an opinion expressed in the report without which the report is or may be incomplete or inaccurate; and

(j) whether any opinion expressed in the report is not a concluded opinion because of insufficient research or insufficient data or for any other reason.

(4) Where an expert witness has provided to a party (or that party's legal representative) a report for the use of the Court, and the expert thereafter changes his or her opinion on a material matter, the expert shall forthwith provide to the party (or that party's legal representative) a supplementary report which shall state, specify or provide the information referred to in paragraphs (a), (d), (e), (g), (h), (i) and (j) of clause 3 of this code and, if applicable, paragraph (f) of that clause.

(5) If directed to do so by the Court, an expert witness shall—

(a) confer with any other expert witness; and

(b) provide the Court with a joint report specifying (as the case requires) matters agreed and matters not agreed and the reasons for the experts not agreeing.

(6) Each expert witness shall exercise his or her independent judgment in relation to every conference in which the expert participates pursuant to a direction of the Court and in relation to each report thereafter provided, and shall not act on any instruction or request to withhold or avoid agreement.

As you can surmise from this code of conduct, the suggestions that I make with regard to the presentation and detail necessary for a satisfactory report arise not just from my own view of how these matters should be conducted, but clearly are those of the courts themselves when they solicit expert opinions.

Issues Surrounding Criminal Matters

The role for neuropsychological assessment in criminal settings has been, to date, much less vigorously pursued than that noted in civil disputation. Sweet (1999) in his comprehensive textbook on forensic neuropsychology, has noted that in the US 'at present there does not appear to be a substantial literature within neuropsychology or a nationally recognised individual whose expertise could be drawn upon to address this subject' (pp. xix). Nonetheless, neuropsychological assessment can provide useful evidence on three particular criminal issues. These are:

1. competency to stand trial, particularly in the evaluation of potential for restoration of fitness to proceed
2. criminal responsibility, diminished capacities and the insanity defence
3. related competencies specific to the criminal process including issues such as automatism.

Competency is the mental ability to make and act upon one's own decisions (Silberfield & Fish, 1994). Competency evaluations may include the assessment of driving ability, competence to stand trial, to care for oneself and property, to make informed decisions about medical care or to manage one's own financial affairs (Searight & Goldberg, 1991). Thus, neuropsychological evidence can be important in the context of issues of guardianship and administration, power of attorney and competence to prepare legally binding wills. We will discuss these issues in considerably more detail in the next chapter.

Obviously, not all disputed cases require neuropsychological evidence. Neuropsychological evaluations are more time-consuming and, as a result, more expensive than traditional psychological assessments. There are, however, a number of issues noted in the disputation process for which neuropsychological investigation is strongly indicated. These include:

1. if there has been loss of consciousness or disorientation, even if this did not culminate in hospitalisation. These might come about as a result of motor vehicle accidents, assaults, physical abuse or combat injuries
2. if there is a significant history of alcohol or substance abuse over several years
3. if the examinee has been exposed to toxins in their environment
4. if the examinee is showing compromise of cognitive functioning as a result of dementia of the Alzheimer's type, dementia of the frontal type, Parkinson's disease, Huntington's disease, stroke, seizure or psychiatric disorder
5. if there is a presence of a development injury (i.e., perinatal or in childhood) to the central nervous system
6. if a particular pattern of behaviour is completely out of character for the examinee
7. if there is a pattern of problems with impulse control, memory dysfunction or violent behaviour.

In the context of the individual case, two separate issues pertain to neuropsychological evidence. The first of these is whether the fault of the defendant or defender led directly to the damage suffered by the plaintiff or pursuer. The consequent issue is then to determine what are the damages for the defendant? Kemp (1975) contends that damages fall into two principal categories: (1) nonpecuniary loss and (2) pecuniary loss.

Nonpecuniary loss includes pain and suffering and loss of amenity. Relevant items under the latter category include reduction in or loss of the prospects of marriage for young persons, loss or impairment of any of the five senses, interference with the plaintiff or pursuer's sex life, loss of the pleasure and pride a craft person takes in his or her work, the loss of enjoyment of a holiday, or particularly the loss of a favourite or regular hobby (Furnell, 1996).

Pecuniary loss includes the adverse economic effects of an adult individual returning in the postaccident state to the care of relatives or friends; the loss of employment or pension; modification of the housing of the injured person; alteration in the individual's ability to drive and the requirement for alternative means of transport; and the need to furnish other aids and equipment such as computers, communication devices, intercoms, alarms and alteration to infrequent activities such as holidaying (Furnell, 1996).

The emotional after-effects of the injury including depression, anxiety and posttraumatic stress disorder (PTSD) may also be a notable aspect of the claim (Crowe, 2008). The differential diagnosis of posttraumatic stress disorder from minor traumatic brain injury, for example, has been a hotly debated issue in the context of the postinjury state, recovery and long-term sequelae (Crowe, 2008).

Psychologists are not entitled to make determinations under the *American Medical Association Guidelines to the Evaluation of Permanent Impairment* (2nd and 4th editions, 1984 and 1995 respectively as stipulated in the various workers compensation acts and now in its 6th Edition (2008), as psychologists are not medical practitioners. Nonetheless, many of the issues canvassed in neuropsychological assessment impinge upon issues addressed in the guides including impairment related to aphasia or dysphasia; mental status impairments including intelligence, attention and concentration, memory function, planning and judgement; as well as emotional or behavioural impairments.

Conclusion

Writing reports is like any other form of communication, something that improves with practice and something that takes a lot of work and focus to get right. One of my favourite pieces of advice to my students at every stage of their studies is that there is no such thing as good writing, there is only good rewriting. The time invested in drafting and redrafting your reports is time well spent and, as you become yet more skilled, it will result in more concise and precise presentation of your views. In this chapter I have provided you with some of the most important aspects of what I believe it takes to write competent reports for the variety of referral sources who will seek your opinion. One of the most important points to keep in mind is that it is communication, so keeping at the front of your mind what the person who has requested the report might find useful is a high priority. I also identified some of the things that I think need to be incorporated into a useful clinical report, and applying these guidelines will improve the quality of your reports if you adhere to them. In the final analysis as an expert you are a 'friend of the court' and, as such, production of a clear, concise, scientifically well-founded and comprehensive report is what will best serve the folk who have requested your report in the first place and result in your being asked to do more work as you satisfy yet another customer.

CHAPTER NINE

SIX NOT-SO-EASY
CLINICAL DILEMMAS

In this chapter we will address a number of clinical issues and dilemmas that arise in the context of cognitive assessment. This list of issues is most certainly not exhaustive and the issues addressed are ones that I think many clinicians face and deal with in their regular practice. The list includes differentiation of the full neuropsychological examination from the screening examination and the appropriate indications for each, what to do if your client has problems communicating or responding, suggestions with regard to the selection of norms, determining whether the neuropsychological assessment can be usefully used to make diagnostic categorisations, ascertaining whether reliable change has occurred in repeated assessment, and finally the implication of neuropsychological assessment to prediction of behaviour in the real world.

What is the Difference Between a Full Examination and a Screening Examination and When Should I Use These?

The use of neuropsychological screening in clinical practice raises many issues with regard to the validity, reliability and defensibility of this approach. Neuropsychological screening tests are administered to obtain preliminary information regarding a patient's cognitive status. While not intended as formal (stand-alone) clinical assessment, screening tests can be useful in evaluating patients with mild cognitive impairments and patients thought to be at risk of having or developing cognitive impairment, or in the presence of cognitive concerns in the context of other diagnoses.

In practice the distinction between a screening examination and a comprehensive examination can be quite difficult and the length of the procedures involved may vary. A screening procedure can range from a single, very short task such as the mini-mental status examination (MMSE) (Folstein, Folstein, & McHugh, 1975), an abbreviated intelligence scale such as the Wechsler Abbreviated Scale of Intelligence (WASI; Wechsler, 1999) or the Kaufman Brief Intelligence Test-II (KBIT-II; Kaufman & Kaufman, 2004), a brief neuropsychological battery such as the Repeatable Battery for the Assessment of Neuropsychological Status (RBANS; Randolph, 1998) through to three or more hours of testing. The crucial distinction between the application of a screening procedure versus a full assessment is principally dependent upon the problem that the clinical examiner is hoping to solve.

Thus, if the aim is to screen for the presence or absence of a potential problem or change, performance above or below a certain threshold on a task such as the MMSE (in the case of the potential diagnosis of dementia, for example) may be of use. Screening data, however in and of itself is typically not used for making the diagnosis and should not be used in treatment planning.

In some situations it may also be useful to identify persons at risk for a particular diagnosis. For example, in the United States national depression screening days occur, and the aim of these events is to attempt to identify as many people as possible at risk for the diagnosis of depression. The aim of this exercise is principally to heighten awareness of the problem, to promote understanding and identification of the problem in the general public and, ultimately, to identify those folk who need treatment and to hopefully direct them to it. The purpose of the exercise then is not to provide a definitive diagnosis for each individual involved in the screening program, the assumption being that those who are screened positively will be more appropriately referred on for definitive evaluation (Armengol & Jamieson, 2001).

Ultimately, the quality of screening procedures will be dependent upon their ability to be able to usefully identify the incidence of the clinical phenomenon of note. Thus, the important test operating characteristics of the screening instrument are based on its sensitivity (the clinical diagnosis is there and the instrument identifies it) and specificity (the clinical diagnosis is not there and the instrument identifies that it is not). The determination of sensitivity and specificity for a given instrument or battery culminates in two parameters of interest for a screening instrument: positive predictive power (the test says that the diagnosis is there and it is there) and negative predictive power (the test says that the diagnosis is not there and it is not). Clearly, in opting to use a screening instrument, what we hope to achieve is the maximal hit rate (we identify the problem when it is there) with a minimum of false alarms (we identify that the problem is there when it is not there). The balance between these competing factors, usually as mediated by the applied cutting score that either rules the diagnosis in or out, are crucially important in ensuring that the diagnostic usefulness of the instrument is sufficiently high to identify the clinically relevant variable, but that this does not come at the cost of inappropriately consigning a diagnosis to those individuals who do not have it. This latter concern, as you would guess, is one of the principal issues that has moved me to write this book.

Armengol and Jamieson (2001) propose the following guidelines for reporting the results in those situations in which screening evaluations are appropriate.

1. Specify the scope and purpose of the screening, which may range from the detection of specific deficits through to a standardised protocol specific to a particular neurological condition.

2. Describe the procedures used.

3. Specify how the cut-off scores were determined.

4. If possible, go beyond the cut-off scores, providing observations and qualitative analysis of the performance.

5. When concluding, any limitations inherent in the procedures employed should be stipulated.

On balance, it would be my advice not to employ a screening procedure unless there are very strong and compelling reasons for doing so. A typical neuropsychological battery may consist of a dozen or more tests and provides quantifiable diagnostic information on cognition that is highly detailed and specific. It is neither possible nor desirable that a screening examination could substitute for such a procedure. As Armengol and Jamieson note:

> The main point is that an adequate assessment of neuropsychological functions is not amenable to easy shortcuts. It is sometimes worth reminding consumers that the brain is infinitely more complex and sophisticated than the most advanced computer. Yet, although we do not hesitate to leave a computer in the shop for a day to be repaired, and the car for even longer, some consumers appear to balk at the notion that one should spend even an hour examining the human mind. (p. 70)

What Do I Do If My Client Has a Problem Communicating?

Much of our current discussion has assumed that the client examined is of sufficiently sound functioning to be capable of performing the assessment without significant modification of the administration procedures. Unfortunately, in the real world the frequency at which this situation occurs is somewhat less than 100%. As a result, the clinician is forced to his/her mettle to attempt to provide useful clinical insights in the less than optimal situation of the client who has difficulty communicating or in determining the level of response of the client. These deficits can occur either as a result of sensory deficits, including visual and auditory impairment, cultural and linguistic diversity (CALD)-related effects or due to motor outflow effects that would undermine performance measures of various types.

Unfortunately, the only solution to these problems, if we are not to walk away tearing our hair out and complaining that the sky is falling, is to attempt to undertake assessment in as fair and consistent a manner as it is possible to do (see Appendix D, Wechsler, 2008a). When the only alternative is no assessment at all, then an assessment that is less than optimal but nonetheless balanced and fair is still of value. At this point, a healthy caution needs to be injected, that assessment undertaken under these circumstances *must always* be viewed with greater caution, and the diagnostic implications of assessments undertaken under these conditions must be viewed with greater reservation than would an assessment undertaken in a more optimal testing circumstance.

Yvonne Stolk (2009) in her editorial for the special issue of the *Australian Psychologist* on the effects of culture and language on cognitive assessment published in 2009, notes that:

> … in 2006, 14% of Australia's population (or more than 2.8 million people) was born in a country where English was not the first language (Australian Bureau of Statistics [ABS], 2006a). In some areas, such as Dandenong, in Melbourne's south-eastern suburbs, as much is 47% of the population had been born in a non-English-speaking country (ABS, 2006b). Australia's population has come from more than 270 different countries, and more than 400 different languages, including indigenous languages, are spoken at home by 16% of the population (ABS, 2006a, c). (p. 2)

Despite the ethnic and linguistic diversity of Australia, the alteration of instrumentation for the purposes of conducting cognitive testing with these groups has been less than optimal. This is clearly illustrated by the observations of Walker, Batchelor and Shores (2009) in their systematic review on this topic. Walker and colleagues note that:

> … despite recognition of the impact of culture, normative data for most tests are based largely on white, monolingual English-speaking individuals within the United States. Moreover, African-American, Hispanic and 'other' cultural groups represented in the standardisation samples of tests developed in the United States do not match cultures outside North America. In Australia there are increased levels of migration of people from Asian, African and Middle Eastern cultures (ABS, 2007), and the application of predominantly white normative data to groups of such diverse cultural backgrounds has been questioned. (Harris, Tulsky, & Schulteis, 2003). (p. 217)

In addition to the effects associated with language and cultural context, there are also significant effects associated with the issues of the level of education, as well is issues associated with background. Education is significantly correlated with performance on most indices and subtests of the WAIS-III and the WMS-III in the standardisation sample (Heaton, Taylor, & Manly, 2003). A similar effect was noted in the extensive Macquarie University Neuropsychological Normative Study (MUNNS; Shores & Carstairs, 2000) with significant correlations of education with the WAIS-R measures, but less correlation for those from the WMS-R.

Individuals from CALD backgrounds performed more poorly on performance aspects of the WAIS-R including performance IQ and the Picture Completion subtest in comparison to individuals from English-speaking backgrounds (Carstairs, Myors, Shores, & Fogarty, 2006); and Maori subjects from New Zealand performed at a level lower than white New Zealanders on the WAIS-R vocabulary subtest, the WMS-R Logical Memory I and II, but not on the WAIS-R digit span or digit symbol substitution tests (Ogden, Cooper, & Dudley, 2003). Walker, Batchelor, Shores and Jones (2010) noted a similar effect with TBI patients from CALD backgrounds.

Walker and colleagues (Walker et al., 2009) noted a number of important insights arising from their review. Despite the relationship between level of education and the Wechsler Intelligence scales, the limited available research with regard to demographic correction did not demonstrate a significant improvement in classification accuracy as a result of this demographic correction, indicating that this relatively painless approach to solving the problem may not necessarily result in a reliable solution. They further noted that cultural effects are more likely to be significant the more divergent the culture is from western culture and from the English language (Ardila & Moreno, 2001) and, as a result, the neuropsychological test performances of CALD individuals should be cautiously interpreted, particularly with regard to diagnosing cognitive impairment.

Walker and colleagues (Walker et al., 2009) went on to make a number of useful suggestions with regard to assessment in the context of educational and cultural background. These included: (1) encouraging a family member to accompany the individual during testing to alleviate test anxiety; (2) providing a clear rationale for the use of the testing and the positive implications of the assessment to rehabilitation goals; (3) when interpreters are, if necessary, used they should be familiarised with the materials beforehand and any doubts or concerns should be raised with the examiner after the assessment (once again these cautions are comprehensively stated in Appendix D of the *Technical and Interpretive Manual of the WAIS-IV*, Wechsler, 2008a); (4) the final report should clearly indicate that an interpreter has been used, the nature of the normative comparison employed and the limitations associated with this approach; (5) diagnoses and decisions regarding incapacity should not rely solely on test scores and in this context should be supplemented with direct observation and collateral information about adaptive behaviour (Heilbronner, 2007).

Which Norms Should I Use?

Mitrushina, Boone and D'Elia (Mitrushina, Boone, & D'Elia, 1999; Mitrushina, Boone, Razani, & D'Elia, 2005) have noted that,

> because normative data are used for comparison purposes, the clinician or researcher must locate available norms that most closely match the characteristics of the patient or subject under study as well as match the administration/scoring procedures of the test utilized. It is well known that performance on most neuropsychological test is highly related to the subject's age, intellectual level, education, and for a few tests, sex. The influence of these factors is even more apparent for neurologically normal individuals than for those who have cerebral dysfunction. (Heaton, Grant, & Matthews, 1986, cited in Mitrushina et al., 1999, p. 25)

They further note:

> In order to choose the best set of norms for comparison purposes, it is therefore essential to know the subject characteristics and test administration procedures for the normative sample. *Subject characteristics* are specific identifiers regarding the subjects under study, such as their age, education, IQ, and gender. *Procedural variables* represent details of test administration such as whether a 30-minute versus a one-hour delay was followed. In general, it is advised that selection of the normative data be based on careful review of the subject and procedural variables employed by the normative study, since the population to which the reported findings apply may be either restricted or ambiguous. (Mitrushina et al., 1999, p. 25)[1]

For these authors, the important subject variables include: age, sample size, education/IQ, gender and handedness, if appropriate. They note that the important procedural variables include the method of administration and scoring of the test; the mean, standard deviation and range of the scores; and the testing history, including the order of testing (Mitrushina et al., 1999; 2005). As we noted in Chapter 4, administration of these instruments should always be undertaken in the manner identical to that described in the manual for the test, to ensure that the procedural variables do not vary with regard to the administration of the tests and thereby invalidate the normative implication of the results.

Thus, in choosing the normative basis on which we will compare the currently examined client with the normative sample, precise focus must be placed on the similarity between the client and the nature of the normative group to which they are being compared in terms of as many comparable demographic variables as it is possible to include. After all, what we are attempting to do, is to compare the client with the condition, to the best available estimate of the same individual without it. This problem is particularly important in the context of our ageing population, as an increasing proportion of the community now live longer, thus we have more elderly within the client pool. To date in Australia there are 2.5 million people aged over 65. Appropriate instrumentation capable of reliably assessing the elderly client is thus crucially important. With regard to the Wechsler scales, the age increased from WAIS-R age of 74 to age of 89 with the WAIS-III, and the age increased again to the age of 90 with the WAIS-IV.

Perhaps the most vexing issue with regard to the choice of normative standard for the tests employed pertains to the degree to which the test has been standardised in the population of interest. In short, do we require an Australian standardisation of the Wechsler scales and other neuropsychological instruments? While the answer to this is of course an unqualified 'yes' for all the reasons outlined in the previous paragraphs in this section (more and better data are always welcome), issues associated with prudent business practice and the bottom line for test developers do not always make what is ideal the reality. It is most certainly heartening to note that Pearson Corporation has conducted Australian standardisations of the WISC-IV and the WPPSI-IV, but it seems that the best that we can hope for with regard to the WAIS-IV and the WMS-IV at this stage are Australian and New Zealand adaptations of these instruments (i.e., amendments for various cultural and linguistic idiosyncrasies but not full normative studies).

Insights into how much of a problem the lack of an Australian standardisation of the WAIS-IV and the WMS-IV might pose can be gained from our experience with regard to the WAIS-III. In the original standardisation of the WAIS-III, the Psychological Corporation (currently NCS Pearson Inc.) collected 297 cases of performance on the WAIS-III in Australia and New Zealand (Holdnack, Lissner, Bowden, & McCarthy, 2004). The results of the study indicated that the Australian samples performed better than the U.S., Canadian and U.K. samples, with a mean FSIQ of 111 (using the U.S. norms). While I am sure that our national chests puff out at such a finding, the degree to which this actually reflects the clinical and sociocultural reality needed to be more fully investigated. Further analysis of the data revealed that the examined participants were not fully representative of the broader Australian population in so far as 79% of the sample were sourced through universities (the study was conducted by asking the clinics and training programs in psychology to undertake the data collection). Generally, it is the case in my experience that when a master's student is asked to do such a thing, they tend to source their participants from their network of friends and colleagues, most of whom would, due to selection bias, be university-educated themselves.

Diagnostic analysis of these data indicated that the Australian sample responded to the subtests in a way similar to U.S. sample. As a result Holdnack and colleagues (2004), investigated the differences between the U.S. and the Australian samples to determine whether, once the demographic differences between the samples had been compensated for, they proved to be essentially the same. Using various statistical techniques, specific discussion of which is beyond the scope of this guide (see Bowden, Cook, Bardenhagen, Shores, & Carstairs, 2004; Bowden, Lissner, McCarthy, Weiss, & Holdnack, 2007; Bowden, Weiss, Holdnack, & Lloyd, 2006; Holdnack et al., 2004), it was possible for the investigators to make a finding of 'strong' metric invariance between the Australian sample and the U.S. standardisation data (Holdnack et al., 2004) that indicates that the two samples display equivalent latent variable scores when demographic variables were taken into account. In a subsequent study, Bowden and colleagues (2004) compared the latent structure of the WAIS-III in an Australian sample of mixed neuropsychological disorders to the US standardisation sample where, once again, strict metric invariance was supported.

These data provide strong support for the notion that the WAIS-III has the same characteristics in normal and clinical populations, both in the Australian and U.S. contexts. As Dr Bowden and colleagues note (2007): 'These results provide important evidence for the equivalence of measurement of core cognitive abilities with the WAIS-III and suggest that latent cognitive abilities in the US and Australia do not differ' (p. 768). Clearly, this does not apply to the more recently standardised WAIS-IV, which should be equally subjected to the same type of analysis, but it certainly goes some way to reassuring clinicians that, where they have been examined, similar results arise from Australian samples in comparison to U.S. samples as measured by the US norms.

One final point in terms of the selection of the normative basis of choice is to ascertain that the most recent and most up-to-date standardisation of the instrument is the one that we use. James Robert Flynn (1984, 1987, 1994, 1999), in his extensive body of work, has noted that norms for IQ tests in the United States become outdated at a rate of 3 points per decade (i.e., ⅓ to ½ of an IQ point per year). Thus, if we are to administer an intelligence test, the most appropriate one to administer to achieve the greatest accuracy of score is the one that has been most recently standardised. If we take the example of the use of the WAIS-R published in 1981, and applied it to a client examined in 2008 (i.e., a period of 27 years), we would find that the level of inflation of the client's score would be in the range from 9.0 to 13.5 IQ points (i.e., 0.6–0.9 standard deviations) above the same client assessed in 2008 when the most recent standardisation of the WAIS (Wechsler, 2008c). This level of discrepancy, of itself, is sufficient to cause significant concern that a false–negative diagnosis of brain impairment may be made, and is to be avoided.

Various hypotheses have been proposed with regard to the reason for the inflation of scores as a function of time, and these possibilities have included improvement in: education, nutrition, health and speeded performance. Irrespective of the reason for the inflation of the score, it is always best to use the most accurate estimate of intellectual functioning and, as a result, the most recently normed test will provide the most accurate figure.

In Tables 9.1 and 9.2 below, we see the mean incremental improvement in scores across all of the IQ and index score estimates from the WAIS-R to the WAIS-III (Table 9.1) and from the WAIS-III to the WAIS-IV (Table 9.2), clearly indicating the effects observed by Flynn in each case.

Table 9.1

Incremental Improvement in IQ scores From the WAIS-R to the WAIS-III

Scale	WAIS-R (1981)	WAIS-III (1997)	WAIS-R minus WAIS-III (16 yrs)	WAIS-R to WAIS-III correlation
VIQ	103.4	102.2	+1.2	.94
PIQ	108.3	103.5	+4.8	.86
FSIQ	105.8	102.9	+2.9	.93

Table 9.2

Incremental Improvement in IQ and Index Scores From the WAIS-III to the WAIS-IV

Scale	WAIS-IV (2008)	WAIS-III (1997)	WAIS-III minus WAIS-IV (11 yrs)	r
VCI-VCI	100.1	104.4	+4.3	.91
PRI-POI	100.3	103.7	+3.4	.85
WMI-WMI	99.3	100.0	+0.7	.86
PS I-PSI	100.1	100.8	−0.7	.86
VCI-VIQ	100.1	102.8	+2.7	.89
PRI-PIQ	100.3	102.5	+2.2	.84
FSIQ-FS IQ	100.0	102.9	+2.9	.94

Overall, the clinician is best served by employing the normative standard that, as closely as possible, approximates the client under investigation. Numerous issues impinge on this choice, including demographic and procedural factors as well as the recency with which the normative basis of the test has been revalidated. Appropriate attention to the choice of norms is an important clinical concern for all clinicians to ensure that neither false-positive nor false-negative diagnoses of neuropsychological deficit are made.

Does Any Brain Impairing Condition Have a Distinct Neuropsychological Signature or Are They All Equally Sensitive but Not Specific?

In neuropsychology a great deal of emphasis is placed on the identification and incidence of pathognomonic indicators. The term 'pathognomonic' (pronounced patho-no-monic) comes from the Greek *pathognomonikos* meaning 'skilled in judging diseases'. A pathognomonic sign of a particular neuropsychological condition is defined as a sign or symptom noted with the diagnosis that is so characteristic of that diagnosis that in and of itself it makes the diagnosis (Net.com, 2010). While neuropsychologists spend a lot of time looking for pathognomonic signs and they place a great of emphasis upon them when they do find them (perhaps even undue emphasis), the frequency with which such signs have been described in the neuropsychological literature is very rare indeed. Today, with more than 25 years of experience as a neuropsychologist under my belt, I find it hard to even think of any neuropsychological indicator that is so characteristic of any one diagnosis that it could be considered to be pathognomonic of that condition.

This is not to suggest that particular signs do not very often co-occur with particular diagnoses — for example, the substitution of body parts for objects in ideomotor apraxia, visuo-spatial neglect in right parietal stroke, material-specific amnesia in large temporal lobe lesions or disinhibition in lesions of the base of the frontal lobe — but to move beyond the observation of correlation to pathognomonic indicator (i.e., so characteristic that it occurs in this condition only) is, I believe, as elusive as world peace.

Is it possible for us then to make any suggestion with regard to any neuropsychological sign that is consistently noted with a particular diagnosis? As we noted in Chapter 3, the Wechsler scales are the most commonly used instruments in the conduct of neuropsychological assessment, perhaps then it is possible that performance on the scales will yield specific symptom clusters that only occur with particular diagnoses.

In the figures below, which are drawn from the clinical sample studies published in the *Technical and Interpretive Manuals* from the WAIS-IV and the WMS-IV (Wechsler, 2008a, 2009b) I present the mean scores on the various index scores for a variety of clinical groups (i.e., gifted, TBI, Borderline, mild and moderate intellectual disability, reading disorder, mathematics disorder, ADHD, Autism, Asperger's syndrome, depression, mild cognitive impairment and Alzheimer's disease, as well as memory data for right- and left-sided temporal lobe epilepsy [TLE], schizophrenia and anxiety). I do not contend that these are definitive clinical studies of the phenomena and as the *Technical and Interpretive Manual* notes:

> It is important to note the limitations of these studies. Samples were not randomly selected but were selected based on availability. Therefore, the studies may not be representative of the diagnostic category as a whole. Because data for each special group sample were collected in a variety of clinical settings, the diagnoses of individuals within the same special group might have been made on the basis of different criteria and procedures. In addition, the sample sizes for some of the studies are small and cover only a portion of the WAIS-IV age range. Finally, only group performance is reported. For these reasons, the data from the samples are presented as examples and are not intended to be fully representative of the diagnostic groups. The purpose of the studies is to provide evidence that the WAIS-IV can provide valid estimate of intellectual ability for individual in these special groups. Scores on the WAIS-IV should never be used as the sole criteria for diagnostic or classification purposes. (Wechsler, 2008a, p. 98)

Commenting on this data, David Loring and Russell Bauer (2010) have further noted that:

> Prior to market introduction, drug or device manufacturers must rigorously demonstrate the efficacy and safety of their products for the intended clinical application. Psychological test publishers are not required to adhere to a similar principle. The absence of clinical data to guide interpretation is readily acknowledged in the manual; 'the data from the samples are presented as examples and are not intended to be fully representative of the diagnostic groups'. (Wechsler, 2008a, p. 105)

> Indeed, the clinical samples are surprisingly small. For example, only 8 patients who had undergone left anterior temporal lobectomy were included in the clinical samples, and no preoperative epilepsy surgery candidates were present, precisely the group in whom diagnostic sensitivity and specificity would be most helpful. (p. 688)

With each of these cautions in mind, it does at least seem worthwhile to ask, do the most commonly used clinical instruments (i.e., the WAIS-IV and the WMS-IV) discriminate between diagnostic entities?

Taken as a whole and as based on an eyeball view of the data only, rather than on any detailed analysis of the performance of the various groups, it

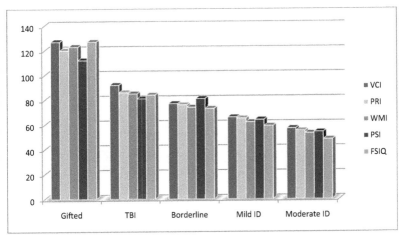

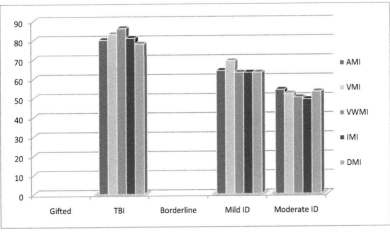

Figure 9.1

Mean performance of the gifted, TBI, borderline, mild intellectual disability, and moderate intellectual disability special groups on the index scores of the WAIS-IV (top panel) and the WMS-IV (lower panel); (Wechsler, 2008a, 2009b).

would certainly appear that there are differences between levels of performance on the WAIS-IV performance presented in Figure 9.1. Clearly, there is a stepwise decrease in the performance level from gifted to TBI, to borderline to mild to moderate intellectual disability. These levels are also noted with the WMS-IV data for these groups where they were available.

The other notable exception is the difference between the right versus left TLE groups presented in Figure 9.4, with the TLE-R group demonstrating a higher level of performance on the AMI index than did the TLE-L. However,

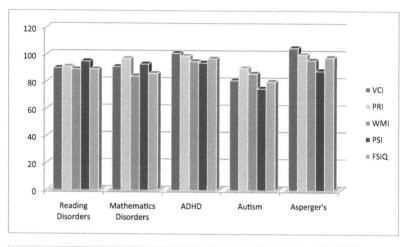

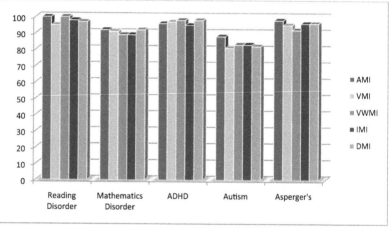

Figure 9.2

Mean performance of the reading disorder, mathematics disorder, ADHD, autism, and Asperger's disorder special groups on the index scores of the WAIS-IV (top panel) and the WMS-IV (lower panel); (Wechsler, 2008a, 2009b).

other than these relatively obvious effects it would not appear, at least at a gross level, that there are other clear differences between the variety of other diagnostic entities. Clearly, as Loring and Bauer (2010) note, this is exactly the sort of data that would usefully support the claim that these tasks are better than their predecessors and hopefully they and other research clinicians will gather this data as the experience with the new instruments ensues. For our purposes, however, what we can say at best is that these instruments certainly are responsive to the various clinical conditions but are not clearly diagnostic of

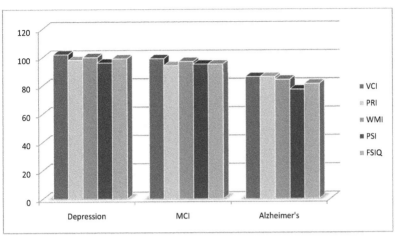

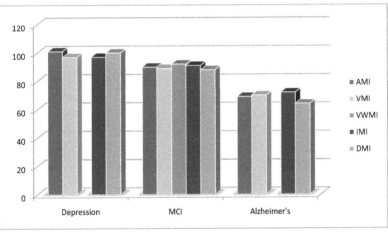

Figure 9.3
Mean performance of the depression, mild cognitive impairment (MCI) and Alzheimer's disease special groups on the index scores of the WAIS-IV (top panel) and the WMS-IV (lower panel) (These groups were assessed using the Older Adult Battery of the WMS-IV); (Wechsler, 2008a, 2009b).

them. In effect, the instruments are sensitive to the various clinical conditions (i.e., people with the diagnosis do worse than those without), but they are not specific to any particular diagnosis. For example, in the case of the comparison of the MCI versus the depressed participants, at a gross level the index scores do not appear to be very different from each other, thus this crucial clinical distinction would need to be made on the basis of more extensive information gathering than of the administration of these instruments alone.

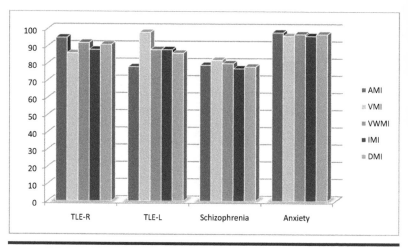

Figure 9.4

Mean performance of the right temporal lobe epilepsy (TLE-R), left TLE (TLE-L), schizophrenia and anxiety special groups on the index scores of the WMS-IV (lower panel); (Wechsler, 2009b).

The clinical caution to be heeded here is that these tests are sensitive, but largely not specific to the various conditions that you will encounter in your clinical travels and, as a result, the wise clinician would prudently reserve diagnostic formulation to information derived from other sources in concert with the formalised testing, or preferably in my view, speak only in terms of the strengths and weaknesses of the client on the basis of the types of analysis I have advocated in Chapters 4 to 8.

How Much Change in Performance is Sufficient to Signal Reliable Improvement or Deterioration?

It has now become increasingly the case that retesting is more common in neuropsychological assessment. This trend addresses three clinical assessment scenarios, the first in which an injured individual is in the process of recovery or rehabilitation and we want to see whether they are improving; the second in which they have a diagnosis of some degenerative condition and we want to ascertain whether they have reliably deteriorated; and the third situation is in the medico-legal context in which we want to ascertain whether the client has changed in some way from an earlier point in the evolution of the condition in comparison to the present. The operative constraint in each of these cases is the degree to which the client has *reliably* improved or deteriorated (Temkin, Heaton, Grant, & Dikmen, 1999).

The second assessment is a fundamentally different situation from the initial assessment as many parameters associated with the assessment process have changed. At the second assessment the client has had previous exposure to the instruments, hence practice effects are most likely at work. Other unexpected and difficult to measure effects that could affect the final score include the intrinsic reliability of the instruments themselves, fluctuation in the attitude of the client in the first versus the second testing situation and the interaction between the individual presentation of the client and the nature of the test(s) on the day on which the assessment occurs. Each of these can have a unique and interactive impact culminating in bias and error in repeated evaluation (Lineweaver & Chelune, 2003). To successfully ascertain reliable change we must take into account how much change should normally be expected and then attempt to ascertain the impact the observed changes actually have. Lineweaver and Chelune (2003) note that repeat assessment scores have their own metric and it is the job of the clinician to determine whether true change has actually occurred.

Five potentially important effects on the change score must be considered (Temkin et al., 1999): (1) baseline performance issues including initial performance level; (2) participant variables (age, history of neuropsychological risk, level of competence at baseline); (3) features of the test itself (test–retest reliability, practice effects, floor and ceiling effects); (4) duration of the test–retest interval and (5) indicators of the client's functioning at the time of the testings (mood, cooperation, medication effects).

In their comparison of various methods of determining reliable change, Temkin and colleagues (Temkin et al., 1999) evaluated four possible models of change. These were: (1) the method originally developed by Jacobson and Truax (1991) that bases the significant change on the difference between the initial and retest scores for the normative subject sample; (2) Method 2, which uses the Jacobsen and Truax approach but attempts to improve upon this by adjusting for practice effect; (3) the third method uses linear regression of the retest scores in the normative sample to generate a formula to predict the follow-up score from the baseline score and (4) Method 4 uses a stepwise linear regression technique for the prediction of retest scores on the basis of the multiple factors considered to be important (e.g., baseline score, test–retest interval, demographics and competence level at baseline).

In their comparison of the four methods using 384 neurologically stable adults they noted that the simple model (i.e., Method 1) performed least well and that the multiple regression models (i.e., Methods 2, 3 and 4) performed with the smallest prediction confidence intervals (i.e., were the most accurate). Indeed, they noted that Model 2 (i.e., Reliable Change Index (RCI) adjusting for practice effects) did not perform much differently from the more sophisticated models 3 and 4.

Clearly this is an important issue for clinicians, particularly in the context of the increasingly common situation in which assessment and reassessment are becoming more commonplace. It is heartening to note that the Advanced Clinical Solutions Package (PsychCorp, 2009) includes a module that allows for the determination of reliable change indices using the WAIS-IV and the WMS-IV, which will be most useful when the reassessments with these instruments are required. At this point, the clinician needs to be aware that these parameters are available and that the determination of these issues will be expected. It will not be sufficient in the not-too-distant future for the clinician to stare lovingly into the eyes of the data and opine that improvement or deterioration has occurred. Appropriate evidence to support these conclusions will soon be required as a matter of course.

Does Test Performance Tell Us Anything About the Ability of the Client to Function in the 'Real' World?

The last two decades have seen increasing pressure on clinicians to provide ecologically valid information about our clients. This has contributed to considerable self-examination on the part of the discipline in the attempt to reliably predict real-life performance (Sbordone, 2001; Sbordone & Guilmette, 1999; Sbordone & Long, 1996). This issue is particularly important in the area of competency evaluations. Competency is defined as the ability of the individual to make and act upon his or her own decisions (Silberfield & Fish, 1994). Competency assessments usually require the clinician to make judgments regarding the need for intervention in an individual's financial, legal, medical or domestic affairs, once ethical and legal principles have been taken into consideration. It thus represents an issue of profound impact on quality of life for the individual in question, and a responsibility on the part of clinicians that they must not take lightly.

The practice of clinical neuropsychology has evolved considerably since the early focus of these techniques to attempt to detect cerebral lesions. With the development and increased acceptance of sophisticated neuroimaging techniques during the 1980s and 1990s, the focus of clinical neuropsychology shifted away from attempting to diagnose cerebral lesions towards an emphasis on identifying the patients' cognitive strengths and weaknesses, and the implication of the cognitive profile to adaptive behavioural functioning in the world.

More recently, there has been a further shift in neuropsychology, partially driven by the need from referral sources for neuropsychologists to comment on the functional consequences of an individual's acquired brain injury (Wilson, 2006). Referral sources commonly request long-term predictions of patients' functional skills, treatment options and assessment of rehabilitation potential. No longer satisfied with general, descriptive statements about abstract cognitive abilities, referrers are now confronting neuropsychologists with questions that their tests were not specifically designed to answer (Farmer & Eakman, 1995), and indeed may not even be capable of answering. Unless we have extensive normative data on how people perform on a wide variety of ecological measures (e.g., decision-making, money management, driving, testamentary capacity) and how these measures relate to the performance on standardised measures of cognitive functioning, we are simply hypothesising about how the person might perform based on test results and associated clinical judgment (or worse still, guessing).

In this context, it is worthwhile to make the distinction between the implications of brain impairment to the issues of impairment, disability and handicap. The International Classification of Impairments, Disabilities, and Handicaps (ICIDH: World Health Organization [WHO], 1980), presents a conceptual model for the relationship of impairment, such as might be noted in the performance of a cognitive assessment, and the disabilities and handicaps that may arise as a consequence of this impairment in everyday life. Impairment is any loss or abnormality of psychological, physiological or anatomical structure or function. Disability, in contrast, is defined as the restriction or inability to perform an activity in the manner within the range considered normal for a human being, as a consequence of the impairment. Disability is measured by self-report or by measures or observations of activities of daily living, including such things as eating, toileting, walking, dressing or bathing (Williams, 1996). Instrumental activities of daily living refer to more complex activities of the brain-injured individual including such things as shopping, driving, and managing money. Handicap is defined as the societal disadvantage to the brain-injured individual that results from the impairment or disability and that limits or prevents the fulfilment of a normal social role for that individual (Unstun et al., 1995). Thus for example, aphasia (the impairment) results in inability to use the telephone (the disability) preventing work as a receptionist (the handicap).

The limitation of cognitive assessment is that it only measures the deficit at the level of impairment. Most cognitive tests have not been empirically validated to predict the impact of impairment on activities of daily living or instrumental activities (Heinrichs, 1990). This has resulted in a considerable move within neuropsychology for increased ecological validity, and the focus on real-world performance (Chaytor, Schmitter-Edgecombe, & Burr, 2006; Sbordone, 2001; Sbordone & Long, 1996), in its procedures and practices.

One example of this change has been the substitution of traditional neuropsychological tests with tasks that are thought to more accurately mirror the demands of 'real-life' activities (Chaytor et al., 2006; Ponsford, Sloan, & Snow, 1995). However, this approach has been criticised, both for lacking experimental control and for lacking a true ecological validity, resulting in a situation in which 'the cognitive task had merely been embellished with the surface features of real-life situations' (Goldberg & Podell, 2000, p. 60).

The evolution of these dichotomous theoretical positions increases the challenge for neuropsychologists to develop techniques that simultaneously satisfy the external demand for applications of an ecological science and the demands of scientific experimental control (Braver & Smith, 1996). The quest for ecological validity, however, is not an easily achievable goal as real-life phenomena are complex and difficult to measure within a controlled, hypothesis-driven framework. Even some of the most elementary human activities involve numerous abilities, acting and interacting in different combinations and at varying levels of complexity (Acker, 1990; Chelune & Moehle, 1986; Naugle & Chelune, 1990; Tupper & Cicerone, 1990).

To date, research into the ecological validity of neuropsychological tests has characteristically used existing standardised clinical instruments, primarily because evaluating their potential validity eliminates the need to create new tools. Relevant literature indicates that complex tests (e.g., the Halstead Category Test) appear to be better predictors of functional abilities than are tests of elementary perceptual and motor skills (Long & Collins, 1997; Sbordone & Guilmette, 1999).

Despite the reported improved prediction when using complex tests, the literature continues to demonstrate that when standardised test data is correlated with 'real-life' competency, its predictive capacity is modest with an upper limit of about 40% of explained variance, although many of these studies are hindered by methodological limitations (Long & Collins, 1997; Sbordone & Long, 1996).

In a study investigating the ecological validity of tests of executive function, Burgess, Alderman, Evans, Emslie and Wilson (1998) tested 92 neurological patients of mixed aetiology and control participants on a range of neuropsychological tests, including 10 neuropsychological measures of executive function derived from 6 different tests. In addition, relatives or carers of the patient completed a questionnaire about the patient's dysexecutive problems in everyday life. All tests were significantly predictive of at least some of the behavioural and cognitive deficits reports by carers. However, factor analysis of the patients' dysexecutive syndrome suggested a fractionation of the dysexecutive syndrome, with neuropsychological tests loading differentially on three underlying cognitive factors (inhibition, intentionality and executive memory), supporting the conclusion that different tests measure different cognitive processes, and that there may be limits to the fractionation of the executive system.

Overall, these results indicate that cognitive tests developed with ecological validity in mind such as the Rivermead Behavioural Memory Test (RBMT; Wilson, Cockburn, & Baddeley, 1985; Wilson et al., 2008), the Test of Everyday Attention (TEA; Robertson, Ward, Ridgeway, & Nimmo-Smith, 1996) and the Behavioural Assessment of Dysexecutive Syndromes (BADS; Norris & Tate, 2000) may well be better predictors of functional disability than either questionnaires or specific neuropsychological tests. For example, one study that investigated memory and attention in a multiple sclerosis population found a 67% prediction to functional disability using the RBMT and TEA compared to 38% using standard clinical measures of memory and attention (Higginson, Arnett, & Voss, 2000).

These investigations also provide evidence that global indices deduced from the 'ecologically valid' tests and tradition tests did not correlate significantly, suggesting that the tests developed with ecological validity in mind may be measuring something different to that measured by the standard clinical instruments.

Acquired brain injury (ABI) is a condition for which there is a clear need for establishing improved ecological validity. Because ABI is often sustained relatively early in an individual's life span, patients typically experience many years of functional disability. Literature in this area shows that factors associated with greater functional disability in ABI are: longer duration of condition; greater level of physical disability; fewer years of education, greater depression and greater cognitive dysfunction. However, the possible relationship between ABI, functional disability and the above factors is variable and interactive and not a simple, univariate association. Disability may precede, develop as a consequence, exacerbate, be linked with, not be related to or originate from any of the above factors.

Money management is a complex instrumental activity of daily living that is crucial to independent functioning in our society (Marson, 2001). However, it is an area that has been largely neglected in rehabilitation research (Marson, 2001; Marson et al., 2000). According to the model proposed by Olson and Beard (1985), money management involves planning according to individual resources and values, carrying out the plans, avoiding actions in contradiction of these plans and monitoring and modifying plans in response to changing circumstances.

Money management presents a challenge to growing numbers of people in the general population. Total credit card debt in Australia, for example, reached over $16 billion in November 2000, and has been rising by 30% annually (Colebatch, 1999; S. Walker, 2001), a trend that has been attributed to various sociocultural, psychological and economic factors (Livingstone & Lunt, 1992; Lunt & Livingstone, 1991).

In so far as money management is a complex cognitively demanding activity, people with ABI would be expected to have more problems with money management than would individuals in the general population. A small number of studies have indicated that approximately 30% of people with ABI, including those who are institutionalised, demonstrate money management problems (Dawson & Chipman, 1995; Ponsford, Olver, & Curran, 1995). However, there is little research describing the difficulties people with ABD typically have with money management.

One notable exception is an informative report presenting four case studies of transition to independent living after ABI (McColl et al., 1999). The first individual was a 24-year-old man who had purchased a top of the range stereo that prevented him from paying his rent. He stated his financial difficulties were due to the fact that he did not understand the 'implications of being poor' (p. 317). Similarly, clinicians report that some people with ABI are unable to cope with changes to their circumstances, such as a change to the day on which their rent is due, an unexpected bill or a decrease in income.

The second man in McColl and colleagues' study expressed the goal to budget and control his spending, but this intention did not translate into action. Instead he spent any cash in his pocket on impulsive purchases such as lottery tickets and alcohol and did not put money aside for rent.

The third man accrued debts that he was unable to finance. The fourth individual did not have any problems noted with money management of his pension, but was about to receive the financial settlement of his lawsuit that may have introduced the need for more complex decision-making regarding spending and investment (Heaton & Pendleton, 1981; McColl et al., 1999).

Different and additional complications in money management can occur for people with Alcohol-Related Brain Injury (ARBI, brain dysfunction as a direct result of chronic heavy alcohol use). Some people with ARBI continue to spend excessive amounts on alcohol, without leaving money for their basic needs for shelter, food, clothing and medical care (Spittle, 1992). People with ABI also report difficulties with access to their money, in that they require assistance with transport (Ponsford, Olver, & Curran, 1995), and they have difficulty or avoid using new technologies such as automatic teller machines and automated telephone responding devices (Crowe, Mahony, & Jackson, 2004; Crowe, Mahony, O'Brien, & Jackson, 2003).

Problems with access to money can be overcome to some degree through compensatory strategies, such as additional support with transport and bank transactions (Heaton & Pendleton, 1981; Todd & Lipton, 1995). However, it is more difficult to compensate for problems with the actual budgeting and regulation of impulse buying, because the main consequence of these problems is overspending of money that cannot be reclaimed. Moreover, these problems have serious implications for the person's wellbeing, including threatening their access to essential goods and services.

Competence to manage money is a legal concept determined by courts and tribunals. Competence involves the ability to make considered decisions regarding financial matters, as well as the instrumental abilities needed to execute those decisions (Carney & Tait, 1997; Moye, 1999).

Neuropsychologists are frequently asked for opinions on capacity to manage money to assist in determinations of competence (Mullaly et al., 2007; Todd & Lipton, 1995). The neuropsychological approach to capacity to manage money typically involves a clinical interview and assessment of cognitive and behavioural strengths and weaknesses across a range of neuropsychological tests (Mullaly et al., 2007; Todd & Lipton, 1995). As we have already discussed, information gathered from collateral sources is also commonly used. The neuropsychologist then forms an opinion of capacity based on the abilities purported to be related to money management (Marson, 2001; Todd & Lipton, 1995).

There is, however, little evidence to support or negate the contribution a neuropsychological assessment can make in predicting capacity. Few studies have addressed the relationship between strengths and weaknesses on neuropsychological assessment and everyday money management in an ABI population (Webber, Reeve, Kershaw, & Charlton, 2002). At present, neuropsychologists must rely on clinical judgment regarding the abilities salient to money management and the tests sensitive to these abilities (Mullaly et al., 2007). Given the serious implications of capacity assessments, this is an area that demands further empirical evidence on which to base neuropsychological opinion.

Several studies illustrate the relatively weak association that cognitive tests often demonstrate in relation to ecological criteria. In a study of chronic obstructive airways disease, McSweeney, Grant, Heaton, Prigatano and Adams (1985) noted a relatively modest series of correlations (0.16 to 0.43) between testing and everyday functioning. In stroke patients a 0.35 correlation was found between HRB and a measure of quality of life (Baird, Adams, Ausman, & Diaz, 1985), no relationship was found between cognitive tests and quality of driving in a head-injured sample (Van Zomeren, Brouwer, Rothenager, & Snoek, 1988), and cognitive tests were found to be moderately predictive of functional daily living skills in geriatric patients (Dunn, Searight, Grisso, Margolis, & Gibbons, 1990).

One area that has received some research input has been in predicting return to driving following brain impairment. Sivak, Olson, Kewman, Won and Henson (1981) used a battery of tests including the Wechsler scales and visuo-spatial tests, and found a modest predictive power to on-road driving ability using the Picture Completion and Picture Arrangement subtests of the WAIS. Gouvier, Maxfield, Schweitzer, Horton, Shipp, Seaman and Hale (1988) correlated cognitive test results in small-scale vehicles on a closed track and noted that 70% of the variance in driving performance was explained by the Digit Symbol Modalities Test.

To date, only one study has examined the relationship between cognitive test performance and the competence to stand trial (Nestor, Daggett, Haycock, & Price, 1999). Nestor et al. proposed that competence to stand trial involves three important skills: episodic memory, semantic knowledge and social judgment. The participants were 181 male defendants charged primarily with serious felonies and who had previously undergone competence to stand trial evaluations. They administered a battery of tests including the WAIS-R, the WMS-R, the WRAT-R, the WCST and the TMT. They then selected a number of the tests to measure each of their variables: Logical memory from the WMS-R to measure episodic memory, WAIS-R Vocabulary, Information and Similarities to measure semantic memory, and WAIS-R Comprehension and Picture Arrangement to measure social judgment. The participants were divided into two groups: those deemed competent to stand trial and those deemed incompetent. Both groups of participants had limited education and performed in the low average range on tests of educational achievement, intelligence and memory. Defendants recommended as competent to stand trial scored significantly higher than noncompetent individuals on measures of intelligence, memory (especially verbal memory), attention and concentration. There were no significant differences between the groups in the areas of academic ability or executive function. The investigators concluded that episodic memory and social judgment were powerful discriminators, while semantic knowledge was not.

With regard to employment following brain injury Butler, Anderson, Furst, Namerow and Satz (1989) found significant correlations between the WCST and the visual reproduction subtest of the WMS and work-related behaviours in 20 brain-injured subjects and this level of association improved when a structured behavioural assessment was added to the test performance.

Prediction of more complex and nonroutine everyday abilities, such as decision-making capacity, competence to stand trial and the ability to use automated teller machines, has also met with greater success than prediction of basic or routine tasks such as self-care and mobility (Bassett, 1999; Crowe et al., 2004; Crowe et al., 2003; Marson, 2001; Marson et al., 2000; McCue, 1997; Nestor et al., 1999). Overall, previous research has found only modest associations between neuropsychological test performance and performance in everyday life, but there is growing evidence that neuropsychological assessment can be used to predict performance of cognitively demanding everyday tasks.

On the basis of this evidence is seems fair to suggest that cognitive examination has moderately good success at predicting academic achievement and work skill, but falls down considerably on other quality of life type issues. As much as possible, a detailed description of what the client's job involves can allow some insight into what the requirements will be on return to work and whether the deficits as observed will create significant complications on the return to work. Ideally, the approach of replicating the work environment in the consulting room is our best hope, but I fear this may be unduly optimistic. In this regard it is interesting that Shallice and Burgess (1991) note that their frontal lobe lesioned subjects who performed in exemplary fashion on most tests of 'frontal' function were severely impaired on their multiple subgoal tasks. As Dr Graeme Senior (personal communication, July 3, 1999) has proposed, the most appropriate way to assess how someone functions in the real world after an injury is to move in with them for a month and watch how they cope in their daily lives, but how many clinicians have the time, patience or interest to undertake such an assessment?

In sum, the clinical neuropsychologist is in an excellent position to provide a detailed description of the examinee's present cognitive functioning, but to make the leap of faith from deficit to disability may well be unnecessary and unwarranted on the basis of the available evidence, and any such leap must be made with appropriate qualification.

Conclusion

Clearly, numerous issues are developing in the clinical literature surrounding cognitive assessment that are resulting in improvements in reliability, validity and clinical precision. These developments are to be welcomed and it is clear that the clinician has no choice but to keep abreast of the many complex and developing issues in our discipline to ensure the highest standards of clinical expertise. This chapter has addressed only a few of these issues, but I would like to impress upon all clinicians the necessity to ensure that they keep abreast of these types of developing issues both by continuing education efforts as well as by keeping well informed of the clinical literature. We owe it to the clients we serve to ensure that we provide the most up-to-date and scientifically well-founded opinions regarding their cognitive functioning that it is possible for us to provide.

Endnotes

1   Italics added in the original.

CHAPTER TEN

Summary

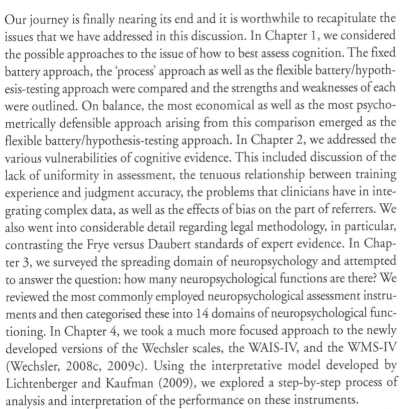

Our journey is finally nearing its end and it is worthwhile to recapitulate the issues that we have addressed in this discussion. In Chapter 1, we considered the possible approaches to the issue of how to best assess cognition. The fixed battery approach, the 'process' approach as well as the flexible battery/hypothesis-testing approach were compared and the strengths and weaknesses of each were outlined. On balance, the most economical as well as the most psychometrically defensible approach arising from this comparison emerged as the flexible battery/hypothesis-testing approach. In Chapter 2, we addressed the various vulnerabilities of cognitive evidence. This included discussion of the lack of uniformity in assessment, the tenuous relationship between training experience and judgment accuracy, the problems that clinicians have in integrating complex data, as well as the effects of bias on the part of referrers. We also went into considerable detail regarding legal methodology, in particular, contrasting the Frye versus Daubert standards of expert evidence. In Chapter 3, we surveyed the spreading domain of neuropsychology and attempted to answer the question: how many neuropsychological functions are there? We reviewed the most commonly employed neuropsychological assessment instruments and then categorised these into 14 domains of neuropsychological functioning. In Chapter 4, we took a much more focused approach to the newly developed versions of the Wechsler scales, the WAIS-IV, and the WMS-IV (Wechsler, 2008c, 2009c). Using the interpretative model developed by Lichtenberger and Kaufman (2009), we explored a step-by-step process of analysis and interpretation of the performance on these instruments.

The approach outlined in Chapter 4 was then applied to three commonly encountered clinical presentations in Chapters 5, 6 and 7. The clinical presentations included: using cognitive measures as one component of the process of making the diagnosis of intellectual disability, characterising the range of cognitive deficits noted with the presentation of traumatic brain injury and finally, in Chapter 7, examining the patterns of performance noted on the Wechsler scales and other instruments in individuals with less than genuine effort.

In Chapter 8, we presented some guidelines for reporting the findings arising from cognitive assessment, and finally, in Chapter 9 we focused on six commonly encountered clinical dilemmas including the difference between a full examination and a screening examination, what to do if your client has a problem communicating, deciding what matters are important in the selection of the normative basis for your assessment, determining whether any brain-impairing condition has a distinctive neuropsychological signature, discussion of the issue of Reliable Change Indices and culminating in a discussion of whether test performance tells us anything about the ability of the client to function in the 'real' world.

The principal focus of this book and the one that I hope that you will carry into your day-to-day practice as you move forward along your psychological path, is the importance of providing clear and, as much as possible, unequivocal clinical decision-making. I am firmly of the view that the best clinical assessors are those that do not feel any personal slight or offence in the fact that they are naturally predisposed to be biased. The principal focus of this discussion is to make you aware of your intrinsic biases and hopefully to allow you to move beyond them.

It is my advice that you should not make *any* clinical decision, unless you absolutely have to. The method that I have presented to you in this discussion is based upon relieving you of as much of the final decision-making obligation regarding the assessment as is possible. To state the obvious, if two scores are not significantly different from each other, then they are the same. This holds true in the analysis of any research study, as it does in the analysis of any cognitive dataset. If the scores are not different from each other, then they do not constitute impairment, and any technique that recommends that you should treat these as representing a diagnostic clinical reality, is one that must be very carefully evaluated. In essence, don't make any decisions if you don't have to! There is plenty of opportunity for you to become involved in interpreting what the data might mean after the important work of establishing whether differences actually do exist has been undertaken.

As we discussed in the introduction to this book, *absence of evidence does not constitute evidence of absence.* I hope that the profound repercussions of this clinical truism resonate in your mind, as it does in mine. It is a moral and ethical obligation of every assessor not to condemn a client to an unjust diagnosis of brain impairment. Hopefully, this book has gone some way to sensitising you to the important issues that will prevent this travesty from occurring.

References

Acker, M.B. (1990). Review of ecological validity of neuropsychological tests. In D.E. Tupper & K.D. Cicerone (Eds.), *The neuropsychology of everyday life: Assessment and basic competencies* (pp. 19–55). Boston, MA: Kluwer Academic Publishers.

Allen, L.M., Conder, R.L., Green, P., & Cox, D.R. (1997). *CARB'97 Manual for the computerized assessment of response bias.* Durham, NC: CogniSyst.

Anastasi, A., & Urbina, S. (1997). *Psychological testing* (7th ed.). Upper Saddle River, NJ: Prentice-Hall.

Anderson, S.D. (1995). Postconcussional disorder: Common result of head injury. *Canadian Journal of Diagnostics, 12*(4), 77–86.

Arbisi, P.A., & Ben-Porath, Y.S. (1995). An MMPI-2 infrequent response scale for use with psychopathological populations: The F(p) Scale. *Psychological Assessment, 7*, 424–431.

Ardila, A., & Moreno, S. (2001). Neuropsychological test performance on Aruaco Indians: An exploratory study. *Journal of the International Neuropsychological Society, 7*, 510–515.

Armengol, C.G., & Jamieson, W. (2001). Screening versus comprehensive neuropsychological examinations. In C.G. Armengol, E. Kaplan & E.J. Moes (Eds.), *The consumer-oriented neuropsychological report* (pp. 61–81). Lutz, FL: Psychological Assessment Resources Inc.

Armitage, S. G., (1946). An analysis of certain psychological tests used in the evaluation of brain injury. *Psychological Monographs, 60*, 1–48.

Army Individual Test Battery. (1944). *Manual of Directions and Scoring.* Washington, DC: War Department, Adjutant General's Office.

American Psychiatric Association. (2000). D*iagnostic and statistical manual of mental disorders (4th ed., text rev.).* Washington, DC: Author.

Australian Bureau of Statistics (ABS). (1996). *Disability, ageing and carers: Brain injury and stroke, Australia 1993.* (Vol. 4437.0). Canberra, ACT: Commonwealth of Australia.

Australian Bureau of Statistics. (2006a). *Country of birth of person (full classification list) by sex* (Cat. No. 2068.0 — 2006 Census Tables). Retrieved 14 May 14, 2008, from http://www.abs.gov.au/websitedbs/D3310114.nsf/home/Census+data

Australian Bureau of Statistics (ABS). (2006b.) *Greater Dandenong (C) (Local Government Area) —Vic. Country of birth of person (full classification list) by sex.* (Cat. No. 2068.0 — 2006 Census Tables). Retrieved May 14, 2008, from http://www.abs.gov.au/websitedbs/D3310114.nsf/home/Census+data

Australian Bureau of Statistics (ABS). (2006c). *Language spoken at home (full classification list) by sex.* (Cat. No. 2068.0 — 2006 Census Tables) Retrieved May 14, 2008, from http://www.abs.gov.au/websitedbs/D3310114.nsf/home/Census+data

Australian Bureau of Statistics (ABS.) (2007) *Year book Australia 2007 ABS*. Canberra, Australia: Author.

Baade, L.E., & Schoenberg, M.R. (2004). A proposed method to estimate premorbid intelligence utilizing group achievement measures from school records. *Archives of Clinical Neuropsychology, 19*(2), 227–243.

Bach, P.J. (1993). Demonstrating relationships between natural history, assessment results and functional loss in civil proceedings. In H.V. Hall & R.J. Sbordone (Eds.), *Disorders of executive functions: Civil and criminal law applications* (pp. 135–159). Delray Beach, FL: St. Lucie Press.

Baddeley, A.D. (2000). The episodic buffer: A new component of working memory? Trends *in Cognitive Sciences, 4*(11), 417–423.

Baddeley, A.D., & Hitch, G.J. (1974). Working memory. In G.A. Bower (Ed.), *The psychology of learning and motivation* (pp. 47–89). New York, NY: Academic Press.

Baird, A.D., Adams, K.M., Ausman, J.I., & Diaz, F.G. (1985). Medical, neuropsychological, and quality-of-life correlates of cerebrovascular disease. *Rehabilitation Psychology, 30*(3), 145–155.

Bassett, S.S. (1999). Attention: Neuropsychological predictor of competency in Alzheimer's Disease. *Journal of Geriatric Psychiatry and Neurology, 12*, 200–205.

Bayless, J.D., Varney, N.R., & Roberts, R.J. (1989). Tinker Toy Test performance and vocational outcome in patients with closed-head injuries. *Journal of Clinical and Experimental Neuropsychology, 11*(6), 913–917.

Beck, A.T., Steer, R.A., & Brown, G.K. (1996). *Beck Depression Inventory: Second Edition (BDI-II)*. San Antonio, TX: Psychological Corporation.

Ben-Porath, Y.S., & Tellegen, A. (2008). *Minnesota Multiphasic Personality Inventory-2 Restructured Form (MMPI-2 RF)*. San Antonio, TX: NCS Pearson Inc.

Bender, L. (1938). *A visual motor gestalt test and its clinical use* (Research Monograph No. 3). New York: American Orthopsychiatric Association

Benton, A.L. (1968). Differential behavioural effects in frontal lobe disease. *Neuropsychologia, 6*, 53–60.

Benton, A.L. (1974). *The Revised Visual Retention Test* (4th ed.). New York: Psychological Corporation.

Benton, A.L. (1994). Neuropsychological assessment. *Annual Review of Psychology, 45*(1), 1–23.

Benton, A.L., Hamsher, K.D., & Sivan, A.B. (1994). *Multilingual aphasia examination: Manual of instruction*. Iowa City, IA: AJA Associates.

Bernard, L.C., McGrath, M.J., & Houston, W. (1996). The differential effects of simulating malingering, closed head injury, and other CNS pathology on the Wisconsin Card Sorting Test: support for the 'pattern of performance' hypothesis. *Archives of Clinical Neuropsychology, 11*(3), 231–245.

Berry, D., Wetter, M., Baer, R., Youngjohn, J., Gass, C., Lamb, D., et al. (1995). Overreporting of closed head injury symptoms on the MMPI-2. *Psychological Assessment, 7*, 517–523.

Berry, D.T., Baer, R.A., & Harris, M.J. (1991). Detection of malingering on the MMPI: A meta-analysis. *Clinical Psychology Review, 11*, 585–598.

Bigler, E.D. (2001). The lesion(s) in traumatic brain injury: Implications for clinical neuropsychology. *Archives of Clinical Neuropsychology, 16*(2), 95–131.

Binder, L.M. (1993). Assessment of malingering after mild head trauma with the Portland Digit Recognition Test. *Journal of Clinical and Experimental Neuropsychology, 15*(2), 170–182.

Binder, L.M. (2005). Forensic assessment of medically unexplained illness. In G.J. Larrabee (Ed.), *Forensic neuropsychology: A scientific approach* (pp. 298–333). New York: Oxford University Press.

Binder, L.M., & Campbell, K.A. (2004). Medically unexplained symptoms and neuropsychological assessment. *Journal of Clinical and Experimental Neuropsychology, 26*, 369–392.

Binder, L.M., & Kelly, M.P. (1996). Portland Digit Recognition Test performance by brain dysfunction patients without financial incentives. *Assessment, 3,* 403–409.

Binder, L. M., Villanueva, M.R., Howieson, D., & Moore, R.T. (1993). The Rey AVLT recognition memory task measures motivational impairment after mild head trauma. *Archives of Clinical Neuropsychology, 8*(2), 137–147.

Binder, L.M., & Willis, S.C. (1991). Assessment of motivation after financially compensable minor head trauma. *Psychological Assessment, 3,* 175–181.

Bittner, R., & Crowe, S.F. (2006). The relationship between naming difficulty and FAS performance following traumatic brain injury. *Brain Injury, 20*(9), 971–980.

Bittner, R., & Crowe, S.F. (2007). The relationship between working memory, processing speed and verbal comprehension and FAS performance following traumatic brain injury. *Brain Injury, 21*(7), 709–719.

Boffeli, T.J., & Guze, S.B. (1992). The simulation of neurological disease. *Psychiatric Clinics of North America, 15,* 301–310.

Boll, T.J. (1981). The Halstead-Reitan Neuropsychological Battery. In S.B. Filskov & T.J. Boll (Eds.), *Handbook of clinical neuropsychology* (Vol. 1, pp. 577–607). New York: Wiley.

Bowden, S.C. (1995). Hypothesis testing in Australian neuropsychology. *Australian Psychologist, 30*(1), 35–38.

Bowden, S.C., Cook, M.J., Bardenhagen, F.J., Shores, E.A., & Carstairs, J.R. (2004). Measurement invariance of core cognitive abilities in heterogenous neurological and community samples. *Intelligence, 33,* 363–389.

Bowden, S.C., Lissner, D., McCarthy, K.A.L., Weiss, L.G., & Holdnack, J.A. (2007). Metric and structural equivalence of core cognitive abilities measured with the Wechsler Adult Intelligence Scale-III in the United States and Australia. *Journal of Clinical and Experimental Neuropsychology, 29*(7), 768–780.

Bowden, S.C., Weiss, L.G., Holdnack, J.A., & Lloyd, D. (2006). Age-related invariance of abilities measured with the Wechsler Adult Intelligence Scale-III. *Psychological Assessment, 18,* 334–339.

Bradley Burton, D., Ryan, J.J., Axelrod, B.N., Schellenberger, T., & Richards, H.M. (2002). A confirmatory factor analysis of the WMS-III in a clinical sample with cross validation in the standardization sample. *Archives of Clinical Neuropsychology, 18,* 629–641.

Braver, S.L., & Smith, M.C. (1996). Maximizing both external and internal validity in longitudinal true experiments with voluntary treatments: The 'combined modified' design. *Evaluation and Program Planning, 19,* 287–300.

Bridges, K.W., & Goldberg, D.P. (1984). Psychiatric illness in inpatients with neurological disorders: patients' views on discussion of emotional problems with neurologists. *British Medical Journal, 289,* 656–658.

Brooks, N. (1984). *Closed head injury: Psychological, social and family consequences.* Oxford: Oxford University Press.

Brophy, L., Jackson, M., & Crowe, S.F. (2009). Interference effects on commonly used memory tasks. *Archives of Clinical Neuropsychology, 24,* 105–112.

Brown, R.G. (1989). Models of cognitive dysfunction in Parkinson's disease. In N.P. Quinn & P.G. Jenner (Eds.), *Disorders of movement* (pp. 73–84). London: Academic Press.

Brussel, J.A., & Hitch, K.S. (1943). The military malingerer. *The Military Surgeon, 93,* 33–44.

Burges, C., & McMillan, T.M. (2001). The ability of naive participants to report symptoms of post-traumatic stress disorder. *British Journal of Clinical Psychology, 40*(2), 209–214.

Burgess, P.W., Alderman, N., Evans, J., Emslie, H., & Wilson, B.A. (1998). The ecological validity of tests of executive function. *Journal of the International Neuropsychological Society, 4,* 547–558.

Burgess, P.W., & Shallice, T. (1997). *The Hayling and Brixton Tests.* Thurston, Suffolk: Thames Valley Test Company.

Butcher, J.N., Dahlstrom, W.G., Graham, J.R., Tellegen, A., & Kaemmer, B. (1989). *The Minnesota Multiphasic Personality Inventory-2 (MMPI-2): Manual for administration and scoring*. Minneapolis, MN: University of Minnesota Press.

Butler, R.W., Anderson, L., Furst, C.J., Namerow, N.S., & Satz, P. (1989). Behavioural assessment in neuropsychological rehabilitation: A method for measuring vocational-related skills. *The Clinical Neuropsychologist, 3*(3), 235–243.

Camara, W.J., Nathan, J.S., & Puente, A.E. (2000). Psychological test usage: Implications in professional psychology. *Professional Psychology: Research and Practice, 31*, 141–154.

Carney, T., & Tait, D. (1997). *The Adult Guardianship Experiment*. Sydney, Australia: Federation Press.

Carroll, J.B. (1993). *Human cognitive abilities: A survey of factor analytic studies*. New York: Cambridge University Press.

Carroll, J.B. (1997). The three-stratum theory of cognitive abilities. In J.L. Genschaft & P.L. Harrison (Eds.), *Beyond traditional intellectual assessment: Theories, tests and issues* (pp. 122–130). New York: Guilford Press.

Carson, A.J., Ringbauer, B., & Stone, J. (2000). Do medically unexplained symptoms matter? A prospective cohort study of 300 new referrals to neurology outpatient clinic. *Journal of Neurology, Neurosurgery and Psychiatry, 68*, 207–210.

Carstairs, J.R., Myors, B., Shores, E.A., & Fogarty, G. (2006). Influence of language background on tests of cognitive abilities: Australian data. *Australian Psychologist, 41*(1), 48–54.

Catell, R.B., & Scheier, I.H. (1963). *Handbook for the IPAT Anxiety Scale Questionnaire*. Champaign, ID: Institute for Personality and Ability Testing.

Chaytor, N., Schmitter-Edgecombe, M., & Burr, R. (2006). Improving the ecological validity of executive functioning assessment. *Archives of Clinical Neuropsychology, 21*, 217–227.

Chelune, G., & Moehle, K. (1986). Neuropsychological assessment and everyday functioning. In D. Wedding, A.M. Horton & J. Webster (Eds.), *The neuropsychology handbook: Behavioural and clinical perspectives* (pp. 15–28). New York: Springer.

Christensen, A.L. (1975). *Luria's neuropsychological investigation*. New York: Spectrum.

Christensen, A.L. (1984). The Luria method of examination of the brain-impaired patient. In P.E. Logue & J.M. Schear (Eds.), *Clinical neuropsychology: A multidisciplinary approach* (pp. 5–28). Springfield, IL: C.C. Thomas.

Colebatch, T. (1999, November 19). Credit card debt soars to $12 billion. *The Age*. p. 5.

Conder, R., Allen, L., & Cox, D.R. (1992). *Manual for the computerized assessment of response bias*. Durham, NC: CogniSyst, Inc.

Corporation, T.P. (1997). *WAIS-III WMS-III technical manual*. San Antonio, TX: Harcourt Brace & Co.

Corporation, T.P. (2001). *Wechsler Individual Achievement Test* (2nd ed.) (WIAT-II). San Antonio, TX: Harcourt Assessment Company.

Crawford, J.R., Besson, J.A.O., Bremner, M., Ebmeier, K.P., Cochrane, R.H.B., & Kirkwood, K. (1992). Estimation of premorbid intelligence in schizophrenia. *British Journal of Psychiatry, 161*, 69–74.

Crawford, J.R., Stewart, L.E., Parker, D.M., Besson, J.A.O., & Cochrane, R.H.B. (1989). Estimation of premorbid intelligence: Combining psychometric and demographic approaches improves predictive accuracy. *Personality and Individual Differences, 10*(7), 793–796.

Crowe, S.F. (1992). Dissociation of two frontal lobe syndromes by a test of verbal fluency. *Journal of Clinical and Experimental Neuropsychology, 14*, 327–339.

Crowe, S.F. (1996a). The performance of schizophrenic and depressed subjects on tests of fluency: Support for a compromise in dorso-lateral pre-frontal functioning. *Australian Psychologist, 31*, 204–209.

Crowe, S.F. (1996b). Traumatic anosmia coincides with an organic disinhibition syndrome as assessed by performance on a test of verbal fluency. *Psychiatry, Psychology and Law, 3,* 39–45.

Crowe, S.F. (1997). Deterioration in the production of verbal and non-verbal material as a function of time is contingent upon the meaningfulness of the items. *Archives of Clinical Neuropsychology, 12,* 661–666.

Crowe, S.F. (1998a). Decrease in performance on the verbal fluency tests as a function of time: An evaluation in a young, healthy sample. *Journal of Clinical and Experimental Neuropsychology, 20,* 391–401.

Crowe, S.F. (1998b). The differential contribution of mental tracking, cognitive flexibility, visual search and motor speed to performance on Parts A and B of the Trail Making Test. *Journal of Clinical Psychology, 54,* 585–591.

Crowe, S.F. (2000). Traumatic brain injury without loss of consciousness: A case study. *Brain Impairment, 1*(2), 105–110.

Crowe, S.F. (2008). *The behavioural and emotional complications of traumatic brain injury.* New York: Psychology Press.

Crowe, S.F., Barclay, L., Brennan, S., Farkas, L., Gould, E., Katchmarsky, S., et al. (1999). The cognitive determinants of performance on the Austin maze. *Journal of the International Neuropsychological Society, 5,* 1–9.

Crowe, S.F., Benedict, T., Enrico, J., Mancuso, N., Matthews, C., & Wallace, J. (1999). Cognitive determinants of performance on the Digit Symbol-Coding Test and the Symbol Search test of the WAIS III and the Symbol Digit Modalities Test: An analysis in a healthy sample. *Australian Psychologist, 34,* 204–210.

Crowe, S.F., & Bittner, R.M. (2001). The effect of word-finding difficulty on a test of verbal fluency in traumatically brain injured participants. *Brain and Cognition, 47*(1–2), 323–326.

Crowe, S.F., Dingjan, P., & Helme, R. (1997). The neurocognitive basis of word finding difficulty in Alzheimer's disease. *Australian Psychologist, 32,* 114–119.

Crowe, S.F., & Hoogenraad, K. (2000). Differentiation of dementia of the Alzheimer's type from depression with cognitive impairment on the basis of a cortical versus subcortical pattern of cognitive deficit. *Archives of Clinical Neuropsychology, 15,* 9–19.

Crowe, S.F., Mahony, K., & Jackson, M. (2004). Predicting competency in automated machine use in an acquired brain injury population using neuropsychological measures. *Archives of Clinical Neuropsychology, 19,* 673–691.

Crowe, S.F., Mahony, K., O'Brien, A., & Jackson, M. (2003). An evaluation of usage patterns and competence in dealing with automated delivery of services in an acquired brain injury population. *Neuropsychological Rehabilitation, 13*(5), 497–515.

Crowe, S.F., & Ponsford, J. (1999). The role of imagery in sexual arousal disturbances in the male traumatically brain injured individual. *Brain Injury, 13,* 347–354.

Cullum, C.M., Heaton, R.K., & Grant, I. (1991). Psychogenic factors influencing neuropsychological performance: Somatoform disorders, factitious disorders and malingering. In H.O. Doerr & A.S. Carlin (Eds.), *Forensic neuropsychology: Legal and scientific basis* (pp. 141–174). New York: Guilford Press.

Cunnien, A. (1997). Psychiatric and medical syndromes associated with deception. In R. Rogers (Ed.), *Clinical assessment of malingering and deception* (2nd ed.; pp. 23–46). New York: Guilford.

D'Elia, L.F., Satz, P., Uchiyama, C.L., & White, T. (1996). *Color Trails Test. Professional manual.* Odessa, FL: Psychological Assessment Resources.

Darby, D., & Walsh, K.W. (2005). *Walsh's neuropsychology: A clinical approach.* New York: Elsevier.

Dawson, D., & Chipman, M. (1995). The disablement experienced by traumatically brain-injured adults living in the community. *Brain Injury, 9*(4), 339–353.

De Renzi, E., & Vignolo, L. (1962). The Token Test: A sensitive test to detect receptive disturbances in aphasics. *Brain, 85*, 665–678.

Deary, I.J. (2001). *Intelligence: A very short introduction.* Oxford: Oxford University Press.

Delis, D., Kaplan, E., & Kramer, J. (2001). *Delis-Kaplan Executive Function System.* San Antonio, TX: The Psychological Corporation.

Delis, D.C., Kramer, J., Kaplan, E., & Ober, B. (1999). *California Verbal Learning Test-Second Edition (CVLT-II).* San Antonio: TX: The Psychological Corporation.

Delis, D.C., Kramer, J.H., Kaplan, E., & Ober, B.A. (1987). *The California Verbal Learning Test.* San Antonio, TX: Psychological Corporation.

Delmonico, R.L., Hanley-Peterson, P., & Englander, J. (1998). Group psychotherapy for persons with traumatic brain injury: management of frustration and substance abuse. *Journal of Head Trauma Rehabilitation, 13*(6), 10–22.

Derby, W.M. (2001). Writing the forensic neuropsychological report. In C.G. Armengol, E. Kaplan & E.J. Moes (Eds.), *The consumer-oriented neuropsychological report* (pp. 203–224). Lutz, FL: Psychological Assessment Resources, Inc.

Derogatis, L.R. (1983). *SCL-90-R: Administration, scoring and procedures manual.* Towson, MD: Clinical Psychometric Research.

DiCarlo, M.A., Gfeller, J.D., & Oliveri, M.V. (2000). Effects of coaching on detecting feigned cognitive impairment with the Category test. *Archives of Clinical Neuropsychology, 15*(5), 399–413.

Dikmen, S., Bombadier, C.H., Machamer, J.E., Fann, J.E., & Temkin, N.R. (2004). Natural history of depression in traumatic brain injury. *Archives of Physical Medicine and Rehabilitation, 85*, 1457–1464.

Donders, J. (2001a). A survey of report writing by neuropsychologists: I. General characteristics and content. *The Clinical Neuropsychologist, 15*, 137–149.

Donders, J. (2001b). A survey of report writing by neuropsychologists: II. Test data, report format, and document at length. *The Clinical Neuropsychologist, 15*, 150–161.

Dori, G.A., & Chelune, G.J. (2004). Education-stratified base-rate information on discrepancy scores within and between the Wechsler Adult Intelligence Scale-Third Edition and the Wechsler Memory Scale-Third Edition. *Psychological Assessment, 16*(2), 146–154.

Dunn, E.J., Searight, H.R., Grisso, T., Margolis, R.B., & Gibbons, J. (1990). The relation of the Halstead-Reitan Neuropsychological Battery to functional daily living skills in geriatric patients. *Archives of Clinical Neuropsychology, 5*(2), 103–117.

Escobar, J., & Canino, G. (1989). Unexplained physical complaints: psychopathology and epidemiological correlates. British Journal of Psychiatry, 154(Suppl 4), 24-27.

Fink, P., Hansen, M. S., & Sondergaard, L. (2003). Mental illness in new neurology patients. *Journal of Neurology, Neurosurgery and Psychiatry, 74*, 817–819.

Etcoff, L.M., & Kampfer, K.M. (1996). Practical guidelines in the use of symptom validity and other psychological tests to measure malingering and symptom exaggeration in traumatic brain injury cases. *Neuropsychology Review, 6*(4), 171–201.

Exner, J.E.J. (1993). *The Rorschach: A comprehensive system, Vol. 1: Basic foundations* (3rd ed.). New York: John Wiley and Sons.

Fann, J. (1997). Traumatic brain injury and psychiatry. *Journal of Psychosomatic Research, 43*, 335–343.

Fann, J.R., Burington, B., Leonetti, A., Jaffe, K., Katon, W.J., & Thompson, R.S. (2004). Psychiatric illness following Traumatic Brain Injury in an adult health maintenance organization population. *Archives of General Psychiatry, 61*, 53–61.

Farmer, J.E., & Eakman, A.M. (1995). The relationship between neuropsychological functioning and instrumental activities of daily living following acquired brain injury. *Applied Neuropsychology, 2*(3), 107–115.

Faust, D. (1986). Research on human judgement and its implications to clinical practice. *Professional Psychology: Research and Practice, 17*, 420–430.

Faust, D. (1991). Forensic neuropsychology: The art of practicing a science that does not yet exist. *Neuropsychology Review, 2*(3), 205–231.

Faust, D., Hart, K., & Guilmette, T.J. (1988). Pediatric malingering: The capacity of children to fake believable deficits on neuropsychological testing. *Journal of Consulting and Clinical Psychology, 56*(4), 244–247.

Faust, D., & Ziskin, J. (1995). *Coping with psychiatric and psychological testimony.* New York: Law & Psychology Press.

Faust, D., Ziskin, J., & Hiers, J.B. (1991). *Brain damage claims: Coping with neuropsychological evidence* (Vols. 1 & 2). Los Angeles, CA: Law and Psychology Press.

Flanagan, D.P., McGrew, K.S., & Ortiz, S.O. (2000). *The Wechsler Intelligence scales and the Gf-Gc theory.* Boston: Allyn & Bacon.

Flynn, J.R. (1984). The mean IQ of Americans: Massive gains 1932 to 1978. *Psychological Bulletin, 95*, 29–51.

Flynn, J.R. (1987). Massive IQ gains in 14 nations: What IQ tests really measure. *Psychological Bulletin, 101*, 171–191.

Flynn, J.R. (1994). IQ gains over time. In R.J. Sternberg (Ed.), *Encyclopedia of human intelligence* (pp. 617–623). New York: Macmillan.

Flynn, J. R. (1999). Searching for justice: The discovery of IQ gains over time. American Psychologist, 54, 5–20.

Foa, E.B. (1995). *Posttraumatic Stress Diagnostic Scale Manual.* Minneapolis, MN: National Computer Systems, Inc.

Folstein, M.F., Folstein, S.E., & McHugh, P.R. (1975). Mini-mental state. *Journal of Psychiatric Research, 12*, 189–198.

Freckelton, I., & Selby, H. (1989). *Expert evidence.* Sydney, Australia: Thomson Legal and Regulatory Group.

Furnell, J. (1996). Legal Issues. In L. Harding & J.R. Beech (Eds.), *Assessment in neuropsychology* (pp. 155–164). London: Routledge.

Garb, H.N. (1999). Call for a moratorium on the use of the Rorschach Inkblot in clinical and forensic settings. *Assessment, 6*, 313–315.

Geffen, G. (1995). Approaches to neuropsychological assessment: a comment. *Australian Psychologist, 30*(1), 45–46.

Gervais, R.O., Rohling, M.L., Green, P., & Ford, W. (2004). A comparison of WMT, CARB, and TOMM failure rates in non-head injury disability claimants. *Archives of Clinical Neuropsychology, 19*(4), 475–487.

Goldberg, E., & Podell, K. (2000). Adaptive decision making, ecological validity and the frontal lobes. *Journal of Clinical and Experimental Neuropsychology, 22*, 56–68.

Golden, C.J., Freshwater, S.W., & Vayalakkara, J. (2000). The Luria-Nebraska Neuropsychological Battery. In G. Groth-Marnat (Ed.), *Neuropsychological assessment in clinical practice: A guide to test interpretation and integration* (pp. 263–289). New York: John Wiley and Sons.

Golden, C.J., & Maruish, M. (1986). The Luria-Nebraska Neuropsychological Battery. In D. Wedding, A.M. Morton & J. Webster (Eds.), *The neuropsychology handbook: Behavioral and clinical perspectives* (pp. 161–193). New York: Springer Publishing Co.

Golden, C.J., Purisch, A.D., & Hammeke, T.A. (1985). *Luria-Nebraska Neuropsychological Battery: Forms I and II.* Los Angeles, CA: Western Psychological Services.

Goldstein, K.H., & Sheerer, M. (1941). Abstract and concrete behaviour: An experimental study with special tests. *Psychological Monographs, 53*(2), Whole No. 239.

Goodglass, H., Kaplan, E., & Barresi, B. (2001). *The assessment of aphasia and related disorders* (3rd ed.). Philadelphia: Lippincott Williams & Wilkins.

Gouvier, W.D. (1999). Base rates and clinical decision-making in neuropsychology. In J.J. Sweet (Ed.), *Forensic neuropsychology: Fundamentals and practice* (pp. 27–37). Lisse, Netherlands: Swets and Zeitlinger.

Gouvier, W.D., Cubic, B., Jones, G., Brantley, P., & Cutlip, Q. (1992). Postconcussion symptoms and daily stress in normal and head-injured college populations. *Archives of Clinical Neuropsychology, 7,* 193–211.

Gouvier, W.D., Maxfield, M.W., Schweitzer, J.R., Horton, C.R., Shipp, M., Seaman, R.L., et al. (1988). A systems approach to assessing driving skills among TBI and other severely disabled individuals. *Rehabilitation Education, 2,* 197–204.

Grant, D.A., & Berg, E.A. (1948). A behavioral analysis of the degree of reinforcement and ease of shifting to new responses in a Weigl-type card sorting problem. *Journal of Experimental Psychology, 38,* 404–411.

Green, P., Allen, L.M., & Astner, K. (1996). *Manual for the Computerized Word Memory Test.* Durham, NC: Cognisyst.

Green, P., Rohling, M.L., Lees-Haley, P.R., & Allen, L.M., III. (2001). Effort has a greater effect on test scores than severe brain injury in compensation claimants. *Brain Injury, 15*(12), 1045–1060.

Greene, R.L. (2000). *The MMPI-2: An interpretive manual* (2nd ed.). Boston: Allyn and Bacon.

Greiffenstein, M.F., Baker, W.J., & Gola, T. (1994). Validation of malingered amnesia measures with a large clinical sample. *Psychological Assessment, 6,* 218–224.

Greiffenstein, M.F., Baker, W.J., & Gola, T. (1994). Validation of malingered amnesia measures with a large clinical sample. *Psychological Assessment, A Journal of Consulting and Clinical Psychology, 6,* 218–224.

Greiffenstein, M.F., Baker, W.J., & Gola, T. (1996). Motor dysfunction profiles in traumatic brain injury and postconcussion syndrome. *Journal of the International Neuropsychological Society, 2*(6), 477–485.

Greiffenstein, M.F., & Cohen, L. (2005). Neuropsychology and the law: principles of productive attorney-neuropsychologist relations. In G.J. Larrabee (Ed.), *Forensic neuropsychology: a scientific approach* (pp. 29–91). New York: Oxford University Press.

Greve, K.W., Bianchini, K.J., Mathias, C.W., Houston, R.J., & Crouch, J.A. (2003). Detecting malingered performance on the Wechsler Adult Intelligence Scale. Validation of Mittenberg's approach in traumatic brain injury. *Archives of Clinical Neuropsychology, 18*(3), 245–260.

Grober, E., & Sliwinski, M. (1991). Development and validation of a model for estimating premorbid verbal intelligence in the elderly. *Journal of Clinical and Experimental Neuropsychology, 13*(6), 933–949.

Groher, M. (1977). Language and memory disorders following closed head trauma. *Journal of Speech and Hearing Research, 20,* 212–223.

Gronwall, D.M.A. (1977). Paced Auditory Serial Addition Task: A measure of recovery from concussion. *Perceptual and Motor Skills, 44,* 367–373.

Guilmette, T., & Giuliano, A. (1991). Taking the stand: Issues and strategies in forensic neuropsychology. *The Clinical Neuropsychologist, 5,* 197–219.

Guilmette, T.J., & Faust, D. (1991). Characteristics of neuropsychologists who prefer the Halstead-Reitan or the Luria-Nebraska Neuropsychological Battery. *Professional Psychology: Research and Practice, 22*(1), 80–83.

Guilmette, T.J., Faust, D., Hart, K., & Arkes, H.R. (1990). A national survey of psychologists who offer neuropsychological services. *Archives of Clinical Neuropsychology, 5,* 373–392.

Guilmette, T.J., Hart, K., Giuliano, A.J., & Leininger, B.E. (1994). Detecting simulated memory impairment: Comparison of the Rey Fifteen-Item Test and the Hiscock Forced-Choice Procedure. *Clinical Neuropsychologist, 8*(3), 283–294.

Hannay, H.J., Bieliauskas, L., Crosson, B.A., Hammeke, T.A., deS. Hamsher, K., & Koffler, S. (1998). Proceedings of the Houston conference on specialty training in clinical neuropsychology, September 3–7, 1997. *Archives of Clinical Neuropsychology, 13*, 157–249.

Harris, J.G., Tulsky, D.S., & Schulteis, M.T. (2003). Assessment of the non-native English speaker: Assimilating history and research findings to guide clinical practice. In D.S. Tulsky, D.H. Saklofske, G.J. Chelune, R.J. Heaton & R.J. Ivnik (Eds.), *Clinical interpretation of the WAIS-III and WMS-III* (pp. 183–219). San Diego, CA: Academic Press.

Harrison, P.L., Kaufman, A.S., Hickman, J.A., & Kaufman, N.L. (1988). A survey of tests used for adult assessment. *Journal of Psychoeducational Assessment, 6*, 188–198.

Heaton, R., & Pendleton, M. (1981). Use of neuropsychological tests to predict adult patients' everyday functioning. *Journal of Consulting and Clinical Psychology, 49*(6), 807–821.

Heaton, R.K., Taylor, M.J., & Manly, J. (2003). Demographic effects and use of demographically correct its norms with the WAIS-III and WMS-III. In D.S. Tulsky, D.H. Saklofske, G.J. Chelune, R.J. Heaton & R.J. Ivnik (Eds.), *Clinical interpretation of the WAIS-III and WMS-III* (pp. 183–219). San Diego, CA: Academic Press.

Heaton, R.K. (1981). *Wisconsin Card Sorting Test: Manual.*Odessa, FL: Psychological Assessment Resources.

Heaton, R.K., Grant, I., & Matthews, C.G. (1986). Differences in neuropsychological test performance associated with age, education, and sex. In I. Grant & K.M. Adams (Eds.), *Neuropsychological assessment of neuropsychiatric disorders*. New York: Oxford University Press.

Heaton, R.K., Miller, S.W., Taylor, M.J., & Grant, I. (2004). *Revised comprehensive norms for an expanded Halstead-Reitan Battery: Demographically adjusted neuropsychological norms for African American and Caucasian adults*. Odessa, FL: Psychological Assessment Resources.

Heaton, R.K., Smith, H.H.J., Lehman, R.A., & Vogt, A.T. (1978). Prospects for faking believable deficits on neuropsychological testing. *Journal of Consulting and Clinical Psychology, 46*(5), 892–900.

Hebben, N. (2009). Review of special group studies and utility of process approach with the WISC-IV. In D.P. Flanagan & A.S. Kaufman (Eds.), *Essentials of WISC-IV assessment* (2nd ed.; pp. 216–242). Hoboken, NJ: John Wiley and Sons, Inc.

Hebben, N., & Milberg, W. (2009). *Essentials of neuropsychological assessment* (2nd ed.). New York: John Wiley & Sons.

Heilbronner, R.L. (2007). American Academy of Clinical Neuropsychology (AACN) practice guidelines for neuropsychological assessment and consultation. *The Clinical Neuropsychologist, 21*, 209–231.

Heinrichs, R.W. (1990). Current and emergent applications of neuropsychological assessment: Problems of validity and utility. *Professional Psychology: Research and Practice, 12*(3), 171–176.

Higginson, C.I., Arnett, P.A., & Voss, W.D. (2000). The ecological validity of clinical tests of memory and attention in multiple sclerosis. *Archives of Clinical Neuropsychology, 15*, 185–204.

Holdnack, J.A., Lissner, D., Bowden, S.C., & McCarthy, K.A.L. (2004). Utilizing the WAIS-III/WMS-III in clinical practice: Update of research and issues relevant to Australian normative research. *Australian Psychologist, 39*, 220–227.

Hooper, H.E. (1958). *The Hooper Visual Organization Test Manual*. Beverly Hills, CA: Western Psychological Services.

Horn, J.L. (1989). Cognitive diversity: A framework of learning. In P.L. Ackerman, R.J. Sternberg & R. Glaser (Eds.), *Learning and individual differences* (pp. 61–116). New York: Freeman.

Incagnoli, T., Goldstein, G., & Golden, C.J. (1986). *Clinical application of neuropsychological test batteries*. New York: Plenum Press.

Inman, T.H., & Berry, D.T. (2002). Cross-validation of indicators of malingering: a comparison of nine neuropsychological tests, four tests of malingering, and behavioral observations. *Archives of Clinical Neuropsychology, 17*(1), 1–23.

Iverson, G.L. (2005). Outcome from mild traumatic brain injury. *Current Opinion in Psychiatry, 18*, 301–317.

Iverson, G.L., & Tulsky, D.S. (2003). Detecting malingering on the WAIS-III. Unusual Digit Span performance patterns in the normal population and in clinical groups. *Archives of Clinical Neuropsychology, 18*(1), 1–9.

Jacobson, N.S., & Truax, P. (1991). Clinical significance: A statistical approach to defining meaningful change in psychotherapy research. *Journal of Consulting and Clinical Psychology, 59*, 12–19.

Jennett, B. (1990). Scale and scope of the problem. In M. Rosenthal, M.R. Bond, E.R. Griffiths & J.D. Miller (Eds.), *Rehabilitation of the adult and child with traumatic brain injury* (2nd ed., pp. 89–93). Philadelphia, PA: F.A. Davis.

Jorge, R.E. (2005). Neuropsychiatric consequences of traumatic brain injury: a review of recent findings. *Current Opinion in Psychiatry, 18*(3), 289–299.

Kaplan, E. (1988a). The process approach to neuropsychological assessment. *Aphasiology, 2*(3), 309–311.

Kaplan, E. (1988b). A process approach to neuropsychological assessment. In T.J. Boll & B. Bryant (Eds.), *Clinical neuropsychology and brain function: Research, measurement and practice* (pp. 143–156). Washington, DC: American Psychological Association.

Kaplan, E. (1990). The process approach to neuropsychological assessment of psychiatric patients. *Journal of Neuropsychiatry and Clinical Neurosciences, 2* (1), 72–87.

Kaplan, E., Fein, D., Morris, R., & Delis, D. (1991). *WAIS-R as a neuropsychological instrument.* San Antonio, TX: The Psychological Corporation.

Kaplan, E., Goodglass, H., & Weintraub, S. (1976). *Boston Naming Test* [experimental edition]. Boston, MS: Aphasia Research Center, Boston University.

Kaufman, A.S. (1979). *Intelligent testing with the WISC-R.* New York: John Wiley & Sons.

Kaufman, A.S. (1990). Assessing adolescent and adult intelligence. Boston, MA: Allyn and Bacon.

Kaufman, A.S., & Kaufman, N.L. (1993). *Kaufman Adolescent and Adult Intelligence Test.* Circle Pines, MN: American Guidance Service.

Kaufman, A.S., & Kaufman, N.L. (2004). *Kaufman Brief Intelligence Test,* (2nd ed.) (KBIT-2). San Antonio, TX: NCS Pearson Inc.

Kaufman, A.S., & Lichtenberger, E.O. (1999). *Essentials of WAIS-III assessment.* New York: John Wiley and Sons.

Kaufman, A.S., & Lichtenberger, E O. (2006). *Assessing adolescent and adult intelligence* (3rd ed.). New York: John Wiley and Sons, Inc.

Kemp, D.A.M. (1975). *The quantum of damages in personal injury and accident claims.* London: Sweet and Maxwell.

Killgore, W.D., & DellaPietra, L. (2000). Using the WMS-III to detect malingering: empirical validation of the rarely missed index (RMI). *Journal of Clinical and Experimental Neuropsychology, 22*(6), 761–771.

King, N.S., Crawford, S., Wenden, F.J., Moss, N.E.G., & Wade, D.T. (1995). The Rivermead Post Concussion Symptoms Questionnaire: A measure of symptoms commonly experienced after head injury and its reliability. *Journal of Neurology, 242*, 587–592.

Kinsella, G.J. (1998). Assessment of attention following traumatic brain injury: A review. *Neuropsychological Rehabilitation, 8*(3), 351–375.

Kløve, H. (1963). Clinical neuropsychology. In F.M. Forster (Ed.) (Ed.), *The medical clinics of North America* (pp. 1647–1658). New York: Saunders.

Kongs, S.K., Thompson, L.L., Iverson, G.L., & Heaton, R.K. (2000). *Wisconsin Card Sorting Tests-64 Card version: Professional manual.* Odessa, FL: Psychological Assessment Resources, Inc.

Kroenke, K., & Price, R. K. (1993). Symptoms in the community: prevalence, classification, and psychiatric comorbidity. Archives of Internal Medicine, 153, 2474-2480.

Krug, S.E., & Laughlin, J.E. (1976). *Handbook for the IPAT Depression Scale.* Champaign, IL: Institute of Personality and Ability Testing.

Larrabee, G.J. (1992). On modifying recognition memory tests for detection of malingering. *Neuropsychology Review, 6*(1), 23–27.

Larrabee, G.J. (1998). Somatic malingering on the MMPI and MMPI-2 in personal injury litigants. *The Clinical Neuropsychologist, 12*(2), 179–188.

Larrabee, G.J. (2000). Association between IQ and neuropsychological test performance: commentary on Tremont, Hoffman, Scott, and Adams (1998). *The Clinical Neuropsychologist, 14*(1), 139–145.

Larrabee, G.J. (2001, November). *Assessment of malingering.* Paper presented at the National Academy of Neuropsychology Conference, San Francisco, CA.

Larrabee, G.J. (2005). *Forensic neuropsychology: A scientific approach.* New York: Oxford University Press.

Lees-Haley, P.R. (1992). Neuropsychological complaint base rates of personal injury claimants. *Forensic-Reports, 5*(4), 385–391.

Lees-Haley, P.R., & Dunn, J.T. (1994). The ability of naive subjects to report symptoms of mild brain injury, post-traumatic stress disorder, major depression, and generalized anxiety disorder. *Journal of Clinical Psychology, 50*(2), 252–256.

Lees-Haley, P.R., Smith, H.H., Williams, C.W., & Dunn, J.T. (1996). Forensic neuropsychological test usage: An empirical survey. *Archives of Clinical Neuropsychology, 11*(1), 45–51.

Lees-Haley, P.R., Williams, C.W., Zasler, N.D., Marguilies, S., English, L.E., & Stevens, K.B. (1997). Response bias in plaintiffs' histories. *Brain Injury, 11*(11), 791–799.

Levin, H.S., Grossman, R.G., Rose, J.E., & Teasdale, G. (1979). Long-term neuropsychological outcome of closed head injury. *Journal of Neurosurgery, 50*(April), 412–422.

Lewinsohn, P.M. (1973). *Psychological assessment of patients with brain injury.* Unpublished manuscript, University of Oregon, OR.

Lezak, M.D. (1983). *Neuropsychological assessment* (2nd ed.). New York: Oxford University Press.

Lezak, M.D. (1988). IQ: RIP. *Journal of Clinical and Experimental Neuropsychology, 10,* 351–361.

Lezak, M.D. (1995). *Neuropsychological assessment* (3rd ed.). New York: Oxford University Press.

Lezak, M.D. Howieson, D.B., & Loring, D. (2004). *Neuropsychological assessment* (4th ed.). Oxford: Oxford University Press.

Lichtenberger, E.O., & Kaufman, A.S. (2009). *Essentials of WAIS-IV assessment.* New York: John Wiley and Sons Inc.

Lichtenberger, E.O., Kaufman, A.S., & Lai, Z.C. (2002). *Essentials of WMS-III assessment.* New York, NY: John Wiley & Sons, Inc.

Lichter, D.G., & Cummings, J.L. (2001). *Frontal-subcortical circuits in psychiatric and neurological disorders.* New York: Guilford Press.

Lilienfeld, A., & Graham, S. (1958). Validity of determining circumcision status by questionnaire as related to epidemiological studies of cancer of the cervix. *Journal of the National Cancer Institute, 21,* 713–770.

Lineweaver, T.T., & Chelune, G.J. (2003). Use of the WAIS-III and the WMS-III in the context of serial assessments: Interpreting reliable and meaningful change. In D.S. Tulsky, D.H. Saklofske, G.J. Chelune, R.K. Heaton, R.J. Ivnik, R. Bornstein, A. Prifitera & M.F. Ledbetter (Eds.), *Clinical interpretation of the WAIS-III and WMS-III* (pp. 303–337). San Diego, CA: Academic Press.

Lishman, W.A. (1997). *Organic psychiatry: The psychological consequences of cerebral disorder* (3rd ed.). Oxford: Blackwell Scientific.

Livingstone, S.M., & Lunt, P.K. (1992). Predicting personal debt and debt repayment: Psychological, social and economic determinants. *Journal of Economic Psychology, 13*, 111–134.

Long, C.J., & Collins, L.F. (1997). Ecological validity and forensic neuropsychological assessment. In R.J. McCaffrey (Ed.), *The practice of forensic neuropsychology: Meeting challenges in the courtroom* (pp. 24–41). New York: Plenum.

Loring, D.W., & Bauer, R.M. (2010). Testing the limits: Cautions and concerns regarding the new Wechsler IQ and Memory scales. *Neurology, 74*, 685–690.

Lovibond, S.H., & Lovibond, P.F. (1995). *Manual for the Depression Anxiety Stress Scales* (2nd ed.). Sydney, Australia: Psychological Foundation.

Lucas, S.K., Carstairs, J.R., & Shores, E.A. (2003). A comparison of methods to estimate premorbid intelligence in an Australian sample: Data from the Macquarie University Neuropsychological Normative Study (MUNNS). *Australian Psychologist, 38*, 227–237.

Lunt, P.K., & Livingstone, S.M. (1991). Psychological, social and economic determinants of saving: Comparing recurrent and total savings. *Journal of Economic Psychology, 12*, 621–641.

Luria, A.R. (1966). *Higher cortical functions in man*. New York: Basic Books.

Luria, A.R. (1973). *The working brain*. New York: Basic Books.

Luria, A.. (1990). *The neuropsychological analysis of problem-solving*. Orlando, FL: Paul M. Deutsch Press.

Malec, J.F., Ivnik, R.., & Hinkeldey, N.S. (1991). Visual Spatial Learning Test. *Psychological Assessment, 3*, 82–88.

Malhotra, N.K. (1982). Information load and consumer decision making. *The Journal of Consumer Research, 8*(4), 419–430.

Marson, D.C. (2001). Loss of financial competency in dementia: Conceptual and empirical approaches. *Aging, Neuropsychology and Cognition, 8*(3), 164–181.

Marson, D.C., Sawrie, S., Snyder, S., McIntruff, B., Stalvey, T., & Boothe, A. (2000). Assessing financial capacity in patients with Alzheimer's Disease: A conceptual model and prototype instrument. *Archives of Neurology, 57*, 877–884.

Martell, D.A. (1992). Forensic neuropsychology and the criminal law. *Law and Human Behavior, 16*(3), 313–336.

Matarazzo, J. D. (1990). Psychological assessment vs. psychological testing. Validation from Binet to school, clinic and courtroom. *American Psychologist, 45*, 999–1017.

Matarazzo, J.D., & Herman, D.O. (1985). Clinical uses of the WAIS-R: Base rates of differences between the VIQ and PIQ in the WAIS-R standardization sample. In B.B. Wolman (Ed.), H*andbook of intelligence: Theories, measurements and applications* (pp. 899–932). New York: Wiley.

Mathias, J.L., Bowden, S.C., & Barrett-Woodbridge, M. (2007). Accuracy of the Wechsler Test of Adult Reading (WTAR) and National Adult Reading Test (NART) when estimating IQ in a healthy Australian sample. *Australian Psychologist, 42*(1), 49–56.

McColl, M.A., Davies, D., Carlson, P., Johnston, J., Harrick, L., & Minnes, P. (1999). Transitions to independent living after ABI. *Brain Injury, 13*(5), 331–340.

McCue, M. (1997). The relationship between neuropsychology and functional assessment in the elderly. In P.D. Nussbaum (Ed.), *Handbook of neuropsychology and aging* (pp. 394–408). New York: Plenum Press.

McGuire, B.E. (1999). The assessment of malingering in traumatic stress claimants. *Psychiatry, Psychology and Law, 6*(2), 163–173.

McSweeney, A.J., Grant, I., Heaton, R.K., Prigatano, G., & Adams, K.M. (1985). Relationship of neuropsychological status to everyday functioning in healthy and chronically ill persons. *Journal of Clinical and Experimental Neuropsychology, 7*, 281–291.

MedicineNet.com. (2010). Definition of pathognomonic. Retrieved April 3, 2010 from http://www.medicinenet.com/script/main/hp.asp

Meehl, P.E. (1954). *Clinical versus statistical prediction: A theoretical analysis and a review of the evidence*. Minneapolis, MN: University of Minnesota Press.

Meehl, P.E. (1965). Seer over sign: The first good example. *Journal of Experimental Research in Personality, 1*, 27–32.

Meehl, P.E. (1984). Foreword. In D. Faust (Ed.), *The limits of scientific reasoning* (pp. xi–xxiv). Minneapolis, MN: University of Minnesota Press.

Meehl, P.E. (1986). Causes and effects of my disturbing little book. *Journal of Personality Assessment, 50*, 370–375.

Mendoza, J. (2001). Reporting the results of a neuropsychological evaluation. In C.G. Armengol, E. Kaplan & E.J. Moes (Eds.), *The consumer-oriented neuropsychological report* (pp. 95–122). Lutz, FA: Psychological Assessment Resources, Inc.

Meyer, G.J., Finn, S.E., Eyde, L.D., Kay, G.G., Moreland, K.L., Dies, R.R., et al. (2001). Psychological testing and psychological assessment: A review of evidence and issues. *American Psychologist, 56*(2), 128–165.

Meyers, J.E., & Meyers, K.R. (1995). *Rey Complex Figure Test and Recognition Trial: Professional Manual*. Odessa: FL: Psychological Assessment Resources, Inc.

Miceli, G., Caltagirone, C., Gainotti, G., Masullo, C., & Silveri, M.C. (1981). Neuropsychological correlates of localized cerebral lesions in nonaphasic brain-damaged patients. *Journal of Clinical Neuropsychology, 3*(1), 53–63.

Miller, E. (1983). A note on the interpretation of data derived from neuropsychological tests. *Cortex, 19*, 131–132.

Miller, L. (2001). Not just malingering: Syndrome diagnosis in traumatic brain injury litigation. *NeuroRehabilitation, 16*, 109–122.

Millis, S.R. (1992). The Recognition Memory Test in the detection of malingered and exaggerated memory deficits. *The Clinical Neuropsychologist, 6*, 406–414.

Millis, S.R., & Kler, S. (1995). Limitations of the Rey Fifteen-Item Test in the detection of malingering. *The Clinical Neuropsychologist, 9*, 241–244.

Millis, S.R., Malina, A.C., Bowers, D.A., & Ricker, J.H. (1999). Confirmatory factor analysis of the Wechsler Memory Scale–III. *Journal of Clinical and Experimental Neuropsychology, 21*, 87–93.

Millis, S.R., Ross, S.R., & Ricker, J.H. (1998). Detection of incomplete effort on the Wechsler Adult Intelligence Scale-Revised: A cross-validation. *Journal of Clinical and Experimental Neuropsychology, 20*, 167–173.

Millon, T. (1994). Personality disorders: Conceptual distinctions and classification issues. In P.T.J. Costa & T.A. Widiger (Eds.), *Personality disorders and the five-factor model of personality* (pp. 279–301). Washington, DC: American Psychological Association.

Milner, B. (1971). Interhemispheric differences in the localization of psychological processes in man. *British Medical Bulletin, 27*(3), 272–277.

Mitrushina, M.N., Boone, K.B., & D'Elia, L.F. (1999). *Handbook of normative data for neuropsychological assessment*. New York, NY: Oxford University Press.

Mitrushina, M.N., Boone, K.B., Razani, J., & D'Elia, L.F. (2005). Handbook of normative data for neuropsychological assessment (2nd ed.). New York: Oxford University Press.

Mittenberg, W., Azrin, R., Millsaps, C., & Heilbronner, R. (1993). Identification of malingered head injury on the Wechsler Memory Scale-Revised. *Psychological Assessment, 5*, 34–40.

Mittenberg, W., Patton, C., Canyock, E.M., & Condit, D.C. (2002). Base rates of malingering and symptom exaggeration. *Journal of Clinical and Experimental Neuropsychology, 24*(8), 1094–1102.

Mittenberg, W., Rotholc, A., Russell, E., & Heilbronner, R.L. (1996). Identification of malingered head injury on the Halstead-Reitan battery. *Archives of Clinical Neuropsychology, 11*(4), 271–281.

Mittenberg, W., Theroux-Fichera, S., Zielinski, R., & Heilbronner, R.L. (1995). Identification of malingered head injury on the Wechsler Adult Intelligence Scale-Revised. *Professional Psychology: Research and Practice, 26*, 491–498.

Mooney, G., & Speed, J. (2001). The association between mild traumatic brain injury and psychiatric conditions. *Brain Injury, 15*(10), 865–877.

Morse, P.A., & Montgomery, C.E. (1992). Neuropsychological evaluation of traumatic brain injury. In R.F. White (Ed.), *Clinical syndromes in adult neuropsychology: The practitioner's handbook* (pp. 85–176). New York: Elsevier Science Publishers B.V.

Moye, J. (1999). Assessment of competency and decision making capacity. In C. Lichtenberg (Ed.), *Handbook of assessment in clinical gerontology* (pp. 488–528). New York: Wiley.

Mullaly, E., Kinsella, G., Berberovic, N., Cohen, Y., Dedda, K., Froud, B., et al. (2007). Assessment of decision-making capacity: Exploration of common practices among neuropsychologists. *Australian Psychologist, 42*(3), 178–186.

Murray, H.A. (1943). *Thematic Apperception Test manual.* Cambridge, MA: Harvard University Press.

National Academy of Neuropsychology. (2001). National Academy of Neuropsychology (NAN) definition of a clinical neuropsychologist: Official Position of the National Academy of Neuropsychology Approved by the Board of Directors 05/05/2001. Available at www.nanonline.org

Naugle, R.I., Chelune, G.J., Cheek, R., Luders, H., & Awad, I.A. (1993). Detection of changes in material-specific memory following temporal lobectomy using the Wechsler Memory Scale-Revised. *Archives of Clinical Neuropsychology, 8*(5), 381–395.

Naugle, R.J., & Chelune, G.J. (1990). Integrating neuropsychological and 'real-life' data: A neuropsychological model for assessing everyday functioning. In D.E. Tupper & K.D. Cicerone (Eds.), *The neuropsychology of everyday life: Assessment and basic competencies* (pp. 57–73). Boston: Kluwer Academic Publishers.

Nelson, H.E., & Willison, J. (1991). *National Adult Reading Test (NART)* (2nd ed.). Windsor: UK: NFER/Nelson.

Nelson, N.W., Hoelzle, J.B., Sweet, J.J., Arbisi, P.A., & Demakis, G.J. (2010). Updated meta-analysis of the MMPI-2 symptom validity scale (FBS): Verified utility in forensic practice. *Clinical Neuropsychologist, 24*(4), 701–726.

Nelson, N.W., Parsons, T.D., Grote, C.L., Smith, C.A., & Sisung, J.R. (2006). The MMPI-2 Fake Bad Scale: Concordance and specificity of true and estimated scores. *Journal of Clinical and Experimental Neuropsychology, 28*(1), 1–12.

Nelson, N.W., Sweet, J.J., & Demakis, G.J. (2006). Meta-Analysis of the MMPI-2 Fake Bad Scale: Utility in forensic practice. *The Clinical Neuropsychologist, 20*(1), 39–58.

Nestor, P., Daggett, D., Haycock, J., & Price, M. (1999). Competence to stand trial: A neuropsychological inquiry. *Law and Human Behavior, 23*(4), 397–412.

Nies, K.J., & Sweet, J.J. (1994). Neuropsychological assessment and malingering: a critical review of past and present strategies. *Archives of Clinical Neuropsychology, 9*(6), 501–552.

Norris, G., & Tate, R.L. (2000). The behavioural assessment of the dysexecutive syndrome: Ecological, concurrent and construct validity. *Neuropsychological Rehabilitation, 10*(1), 33–45.

NSW Health Department. (1996). *Review of the Psychologists Act 1989 — Issues Paper, December 1996.* Sydney, Australia: Author.

Ogden, J.A., Cooper, E., & Dudley, M. (2003). Adapting neuropsychological assessment for minority groups: A study comparing white and Maori New Zealanders. *Brain Impairment, 4*, 122–134.

Olson, G.I., & Beard, D.M. (1985). Assessing managerial behavior. In S.Y. Nickols (Ed.), *Thinking globally, acting locally* (pp. 138–148). Washington, DC: American Home Economics Association.

Oskamp, S. (1965). Overconfidence in case study judgements. *Journal of Consulting Psychology, 29*, 261–265.

Osterreith, P. A. (1944). Le test de copie d'une figure complexe: Contribution a l'etude de la perception et de la memoire. *Archives de Psychologie, 30*, 286–356.

Owen, A.M., McMillan, K.M., Laird, A.R., & Bullmore, E. (2005). N-back working memory paradigm: A meta-analysis of normative functional neuroimaging studies. *Human Brain Mapping, 25*, 46–59.

Panayiotou, A., Jackson, M., & Crowe, S.F. (2010). A meta-analytic review of the emotional symptoms associated with mild traumatic brain injury. *Journal of Clinical and Experimental Neuropsychology, 32*(5), 463–473.

Paniak, C., Reynolds, S., Phillips, K., Toller-Lobe, G., Melnyk, A., & Nagy, J. (2002). Patient complaints within 1 month of mild traumatic brain injury: A controlled study. *Archives of Clinical Neuropsychology, 17*, 319–334.

Pankratz, L. (1979). Symptom validity testing and symptom retraining: Procedures for the assessment and treatment of functional sensory deficits. *Journal of Consulting and Clinical Psychology, 47*, 409–410.

Pankratz, L., Fausti, S.A., & Peed, S. (1975). A forced-choice technique to evaluate deafness in the hysterical or malingering patient. *Journal of Consulting & Clinical Psychology, 43*(3), 421–422.

Perret, E. (1974). The left frontal lobe of man and the suppression of habitual responses in verbal categorical behaviour. *Neuropsychologia, 12*, 323–330.

Petersen, L.R., & Petersen, M.J. (1959). Short-term retention of individual verbal items. *Journal of Experimental Psychology, 58*, 193–198.

Pieniadz, J., & Kelland, D.Z. (2001). Reporting scores in neuropsychological assessments: ethicality, validity, practicality and more. In C.G. Amengol, E. Kaplan & E.J. Moes (Eds.), *The consumer-oriented neuropsychological report* (pp. 123–140). Lutz, FL: Psychological Assessment Resources, Inc.

Pillon, B., Bazin, B., Deweer, B., Ehrlé, N., Baulac, M., & Dubois, B. (1999). Specificity of memory deficits after right or left temporal lobectomy. *Cortex, 35*(4), 561–571.

Pilowsky, I., & Spence, N. (1994). *Manual for the Illness behaviour Questionnaire* (3rd ed.). Adelaide, South Australia: University of Adelaide.

Pollens, R.D., McBrantie, B.P., & Burton, P.L. (1988). Beyond cognition: Executive functions in closed head injury. *Cognitive Rehabilitation, September/October*, 26–30.

Ponsford, J., Olver, J.H., & Curran, C. (1995). A profile of outcome two years following traumatic brain injury. *Brain Injury, 9*, 1–10.

Ponsford, J., Sloan, S., & Snow, P. (1995). *Traumatic brain injury: Rehabilitation for everyday adaptive living.* East Sussex, UK: Lawrence Erlbaum Associates.

Porteus, S.D. (1965). *Porteus Maze Test: 50 years application.* New York: Psychological Corporation.

Price, J.R., & Stevens, K.B. (1997). Psycholegal implications of malingered head trauma. *Applied Neuropsychology, 4*(1), 75–83.

Price, L.R., Tulsky, D., Millis, S., & Weiss, L. (2002). Redefining the factor structure of the Wechsler Memory Scale—III: Confirmatory factor analysis with cross-validation. *Journal of Clinical and Experimental Neuropsychology, 24*, 574–585.

Proctor, A., Wilson, B., Sanchez, C., & Wesley, E. (2000). Executive function and verbal working memory in adolescents with closed head injury (CHI). *Brain Injury, 14*(7), 633–647.

Psychological Corporation. (1992). *Wechsler Individual Achievement Test manual.* San Antonio, TX: Author.

PsychCorp. (2001). *Wechsler Test of Adult Reading Manual.* San Antonio, TX: The Psychological Corporation.

PsychCorp. (2009). *Advanced clinical solutions for WAIS-IV and WMS-IV: Administration and scoring manual.* San Antonio, TX: Pearson NCS.

Randolph, C. (1998). *RBANS: Manual-Repeatable Battery for the Assessment of Neuropsychological Status.* San Antonio, TX: Psychological Corporation.

Rao, V., & Lyketsos, C. (2000). Neuropsychiatric sequelae of traumatic brain injury. *Psychosomatics, 41,* 95–103.

Rapport, L.J., Farchione, T.J., Coleman, R.D., & Axelrod, B.N. (1998). Effects of coaching on malingered motor function profiles. *Journal of Clinical and Experimental Neuropsychology, 20*(1), 89–97.

Raven, J.C., Court, J.H., & Raven, J. (1995). *Raven manual: Coloured progressive matrices.* Oxford, England: Oxford Psychologists Press.

Raven, J., Raven, J.C., & Court, J.H. (1998). *Raven manual: Standard progressive matrices.* Oxford, UK: Oxford Psychologists Press.

Rawling, P., & Brooks, N. (1990). Simulation Index: A method for detecting factitious errors on the WAIS-R and WMS. [Special Section: Forensic-legal medical issues of neuropsychology]. *Neuropsychology Review, 4,* 223–238.

Reed, J.E. (1996). Fixed vs. flexible neuropsychological test batteries under the Daubert standard for the admissibility of scientific evidence. *Behavioral Sciences and the Law, 14*(3), 315–322.

Reitan, R.M. (1986). Theoretical and methodological bases of the Halstead-Reitan Neuropsychological Battery. In G. Grant & K.M. Adams (Eds.), *Neuropsychological assessment of neuropsychiatric disorders* (pp. 3–29). New York: Oxford University Press.

Reitan, R.M., & Wolfson, D. (1986). The Halstead-Reitan Neuropsychological Test Battery. In D. Wedding & J.A.M. Horton (Eds.), *The neuropsychology handbook: Behavioral and clinical perspectives* (pp. 134–160). New York: Springer Publishing Co, Inc.

Reitan, R.M., & Wolfson, D. (1993a). *The Halstead-Reitan Neuropsychological Test Battery: Theory and clinical interpretation.* Tucson, AZ: Neuropsychology Press.

Reitan, R.M., & Wolfson, D. (1993b). *The Halstead-Reitan Neuropsychological test battery: Theory and clinical interpretation* (2nd ed.). Tucson, AZ: Neuropsychology Press.

Reschly, D.J., Myers, T.G., & Hartel, C.R. (Eds.). (2002). *Mental retardation: Determining eligibility for Social Security benefits* (Committee on Disability Determination for Mental Retardation). Washington, DC: National Academy Press.

Rey, A. (1941). Psychological examination of traumatic encephalopathy. *Archives de Psychologic, 28,* 286–340.

Rey, A. (1964). *L'examen clinique en psychologie.* Paris: Presses Universitaires de France.

Robertson, I.H., Ward, T., Ridgeway, V., & Nimmo-Smith, I. (1994). *The Test of Everyday Attention.* Bury St. Edmunds, UK: Thames Valley Test Company.

Robertson, I.H., Ward, T., Ridgeway, V., & Nimmo-Smith, I. (1996). The structure of normal human attention: The Test of Everyday Attention. *Journal of the International Neuropsychological Society, 2*(6), 525–534.

Rogers, R. (1988). *Clinical assessment of malingering and deception.* New York: Guilford Press.

Rogers, R. (1999). *Clinical assessment of malingering and deception* (2nd ed.). New York: Guilford.

Rogers, R., Sewell, K.W., & Salekin, R.J. (1994). A meta-analysis of malingering on the MMPI-2. *Assessment, 1,* 227–237.

Rogers, R., Sewell, K.W., & Ustad, K.L. (1995). Feigning among chronic outpatients on the MMPI-2: A systematic examination of Fake-Bad indicators. *Assessment, 2,* 81–89.

Ross, L., Lepper, M.R., & Hubbard, M. (1975). Perseverance in self-perception and social perception: Biased attributional process in the debriefing paradigm. *Journal of Personality and Social Psychology, 32,* 880–892.

Ross, L., Lepper, M.R., Strach, F., & Steinmetz, J. (1977). Social explanations and social expectations. Effects of real and hypothetical explanations on subjective likelihood. *Journal of Personality and Social Psychology, 35,* 817–829.

Russell, E.W. (1990). *Twenty ways of diagnosing brain damage when there is none.* St. Petersburg Beach, FL: Florida Psychological Association.

Sackett, D.L., Straus, S.E., Richardson, W.S., Rosenberg, W., & Haynes, R.B. (2000). *Evidence-based medicine: how to practice and teach EBM.* Edinburgh, UK: Churchill Livingstone.

Saling, M.M. (1995). Neuropsychology in the clinic: A comment on Caine (1995) and Bowden (1995). *Australian Psychologist, 30*(1), 42–44.

Salthouse, T.A. (2000). Aging and measures of processing speed. *Biological Psychology, 54*(1–3), 35–54.

Salthouse, T.A., & Babcock, R.L. (1991). Decomposing adult age differences in working memory. *Developmental Psychology, 27*(5), 763–776.

Salvador-Carulla, L., & Bertelli, M. (2008). Mental retardation' or 'intellectual disability': Time for a conceptual change. *Psychopathology, 41,* 10–16.

Sattler, J.M. (2008). *Assessment of children: Cognitive foundations* (5th ed.). San Diego, CA: Author.

Sbordone, R.J. (2001). Limitations of neuropsychological testing to predict the cognitive and behavioral functioning of persons with brain injury in real-world settings. *NeuroRehabilitation, 16*(4), 199–201

Sbordone, R.J., & Guilmette, T.J. (1999). Ecological validity: Prediction of everyday and vocational functioning from neuropsychological test data. In J.J. Sweet (Ed.), *Forensic neuropsychology: Fundamentals and practice.* (pp. 227–254). Lisse, The Netherlands: Swets & Zeitlinger.

Sbordone, R.J., & Long, C.J. (Eds.). (1996). *Ecological validity of neuropsychological testing.* Delray Beach, FL: Gr Press/St Lucie Press, Inc.

Schretlen, D., Brandt, J., Krafft, L., & Van Gorp, W. (1991). Some caveats in using the Rey 15-Item memory test to detect malingered amnesia. *Psychological Assessment, 3,* 667–672.

Schretlen, D., & Shapiro, A.M. (2003). A quantitative review of the effects of traumatic brain injury on cognitive functioning. *International Review of Psychiatry, 15,* 341–349.

Searight, H.R., & Goldberg, M.A. (1991). The Community Competence Scale as a measure of functional daily living skills. Special Section: Level of functioning. *Journal of Mental Health Administration, 18*(2), 128–134.

Seretny, M.L., Dean, R.S., Gray, J.W., & Hartlage, L.C. (1986). The practice of clinical neuropsychology in the United States. *Archives of Clinical Neuropsychology, 1,* 5–12.

Shallice, T. (1982). Specific impairments of planning. Philosophical Transcripts of the Royal Society of London, *Behavioral Sciences and the Law, 298,* 199–209.

Shallice, T., & Burgess, P.W. (1991). Deficits in strategy application following frontal lobe damage in man. *Brain, 114,* 727–741.

Shallice, T., & Warrington, E.K. (1970). Independent functioning of verbal memory store: A neuropsychological study. *Quarterly Journal of Experimental Psychology, 2* (2), 261–273.

Shapiro, M. (1970). Intensive assessment of the single case: An inductive-deductive approach. In P. Mittler (Ed.), *The psychological assessment of mental and physical handicaps* (pp. 645–666). London: Methuen.

Shearer, E., & Apps, R. (1975). A restandardization of the Burt-Vernon and Schonell Graded Word Reading Tests. *Educational Research, 18*(1), 67–73.

Shores, E.A. (2006a). *Appendices to guidelines for conducting neuropsychological assessment in New South Wales CTP scheme* (pp. 1–11): Sydney, Australia: Motor Accidents Authority of New South Wales.

Shores, E.A. (2006b). *Neuropsychological assessment of adults with mild traumatic brain injury: Guidelines for the NSW CTP Scheme.* Sydney, Australia: Motor Accidents Board, NSW.

Shores, E.A., & Carstairs, J.R. (2000). The Macquarie University Neuropsychological Normative Study (MUNNS): Australian Norms for the WAIS-R and WMS-R. *Australian Psychologist, 35*, 36–40.

Shores, E.A., & Carstairs, J.R. (2000). The Macquarie University Neuropsychology Normative Study (MUNNS): Norms for the WAIS-R and WMS-R. *Australian Psychologist, 35*, 41–59.

Shum, D.H.K., McFarland, K.A., & Bain, J.D. (1990). Construct validity of eight tests of attention: Comparison of normal and closed head injured samples. *The Clinical Neuropsychologist, 4*, 151–162.

Silberfield, M., & Fish, A. (1994). *When the mind fails: A guide to dealing with incompetency.* Toronto, Canada: University of Toronto.

Sivak, M., Olson, P.L., Kewman, D.G., Won, H., & Henson, D.L. (1981). Driving and perceptual/cognitive skills: Behavioural consequences of brain damage. *Archives of Physical Medicine Rehabilitation, 62*, 476–483.

Slattery, J.P. (1990). *Report of Royal Commission into Deep Sleep Therapy.* Sydney, Australia: Government Printing Service.

Slick, D., Hopp, G., Strauss, E., Hunter, M., & Pinch, D. (1994). Detecting dissimulation: profiles of simulated malingerers, traumatic brain-injury patients, and normal controls on a revised version of Hiscock and Hiscock's Forced-Choice Memory Test. *Journal of Clinical and Experimental Neuropsychology, 16*(3), 472–481.

Slick, D.J., Sherman, E.M., & Iverson, G.L. (1999). Diagnostic criteria for malingered neurocognitive dysfunction: proposed standards for clinical practice and research. *Clinical Neuropsychology, 13*(4), 545–561.

Slick, D.J., Tan, J.E., Strauss, E.H., & Hultsch, D.F. (2004). Detecting malingering: a survey of experts' practices. *Archives of Clinical Neuropsychology, 19*(4), 465–473.

Smith, A. (1982). *Symbol Digit Modalities Test.* Los Angeles, CA: Western Psychological Services.

Sparrow, S.S., Cicchetti, D.V., & Balla, D.A. (2005). *Vineland Adaptive Behavior Scales* (2nd ed.) *(Vineland-II), Survey Interview Form/Caregiver Rating Form.* Livonia, MN: Pearson Assessments.

Spittle, B. (1992). Paternalistic interventions with the gravely disabled. *Australian and New Zealand Journal of Psychiatry, 26*(1), 107–110.

Spreen, O., & Benton, A.L. (1965). Comparative studies of some psychological tests for cerebral damage. *Journal of Nervous and Mental Disease, 140*, 323–333.

Spreen, O., & Strauss, E. (1998). *A compendium of neuropsychological tests: Administration, norms and commentary* (2nd ed.). New York: Oxford University Press.

Squire, L.R. (1987). *Memory and brain.* New York: Oxford University Press.

Squire, L.R., & Kandel, E.R. (1999). *Memory: From mind and molecules.* New York: Scientific American Library/Scientific American Books.

Stanley, R.J. (1989). The psychiatrist as expert witness. *Australian Forensic Psychiatry Bulletin, 9*, 2–7.

Stolk, Y. (2009). Approaches to the influence of culture and language on cognitive assessment instrument: the Australian context will stop. *Australian Psychologist, 44*(1), 1–5.

Strauss, E., Sherman, E.M.S., & Spreen, O. (2006). *A compendium of neuropsychological tests* (3rd ed.). New York: Oxford University Press.

Strauss, E., & Spreen, O. (1990). A comparison of the Rey and Taylor Figures. *Archives of Clinical Neuropsychology, 5*, 417–420.

Stroop, J.R. (1935). Studies of interference in serial verbal reactions. *Journal of Experimental Psychology, 18*, 643–662.

Suhr, J.A., & Boyer, D. (1999). Use of the Wisconsin Card Sorting Test in the detection of malingering in student simulator and patient samples. *Journal of Clinical and Experimental Neuropsychology, 21*(5), 701–708.

Sullivan, K., & Bowden, S.C. (1997). Which tests do neuropsychologists use? *Journal of Clinical Psychology, 53*(7), 657–661.

Sundberg, N.D., & Tyler, L.E. (1962). *Clinical psychology: An introduction to research and practice.* New York: Appleton-Century-Crofts.

Sweet, J.J. (1999). *Forensic neuropsychology: Fundamentals and practice.* Lisse, Netherlands: Swets and Zeitlinger.

Sweet, J.J., Wolfe, P., Sattlberger, E., Numan, B., Rosenfeld, J.P., Clingerman, S., et al. (2000). Further investigation of traumatic brain injury versus insufficient effort with the California Verbal Learning Test. *Archives of Clinical Neuropsychology, 15*, 105–113.

Tarter, R.E., & Edwards, K.L. (1986). Multifactorial etiology of neuropsychological impairment in alcoholics. *Alcoholism: Clinical and Experimental Research, 10*(2), 128–135.

Tate, R.L. (1987). Issues in the management of behaviour disturbance as a consequence of severe head injury. *Scandinavian Journal of Rehabilitation Medicine, 19*(1), 13–18.

Taylor, L.B. (1969). Localization of cerebral lesions by psychological testing. *Clinical Neurosurgery, 16*, 269–281.

Taylor, L.B. (1979). Psychological assessment of neurosurgical patients. In T.T. Rasmussen & R. Marino (Eds.), *Functional neurosurgery* (pp. 165–180). New York: Raven Press.

Tellegen, A., & Ben-Porath, Y.S. (2008). *MMPI-2-RF Technical Manual.* Minneapolis, MN: University of Minnesota Press.

Temkin, M.R., Heaton, R.K., Grant, I., & Dikmen, S.S. (1999). Detecting significant change in neuropsychological test performance: A comparison of four models. *Journal of the International Neuropsychological Society, 5*, 357–369.

Tenhula, W.N., & Sweet, J.J. (1996). Double cross-validation of the Booklet Category Test in detecting malingered traumatic brain injury. *The Clinical Neuropsychologist, 10*, 104–116.

Teuber, H.L. (1969). Neglected aspects of the post-traumatic syndrome. In A.E. Walker, W.F. Caveness & M. Critchley (Eds.), *The late effects of head injury* (pp. 13–34). Springfield, IL: Charles C. Thomas.

Thomassen, R., van Hemert, A.M., Huyse, F.J., van der Mast, R.C., & Hengeveld, M.W. (2003). Somatoform disorders in consultation-liaison psychiatry: A comparison with other mental disorders. *General and Hospital Psychiatry, 25*, 8–13.

Thorndike, R.L., Hagen, E.P., & Sattler, J.M. (1986). *Stanford-Binet Intelligence Scale* (4th ed.). Chicago, IL: Riverside.

Todd, J.A., & Lipton, J.D. (1995). Financial management of the elderly: Legal issues and the role of neuropsychological assessment. *Psychiatry, Psychology and Law, 3*(1), 25–38.

Tombaugh, T.N. (1996). *Test of memory malingering (TOMM).* North Tonawanda, NY: Multi-Health Systems.

Tombaugh, T.N. (2006). A comprehensive review of the Paced Auditory Serial Addition Test (PASAT). *Archives of Clinical Neuropsychology, 21*(1), 53–76.

Trennery, M.R., Crosson, B., DeBoe, J., & Leber, W.R. (1989). *The Stroop Neuropsychological Screening Test.* Odessa, FL: Psychological Assessment Resources.

Tsushima, W.T., & Tsushima, V G. (2001). Comparison of the Fake Bad Scale and other MMPI-2 validity scales with personal injury litigants. *Assessment, 8*(2), 205–212.

Tulsky, D.S., Ivnik, R.J., Price, L.R., & Wilkins, C. (2003). Assessment of cognitive functioning with the WAIS-III and WMS-III: Development of a six-factor model. In S. Tulsky, D.H. Saklofske, G.J. Chelune, R.K. Heaton, R.J. Ivnik, R. Bornstein, A. Prifitera & M.F. Ledbetter (Eds.), *Clinical interpretation of the WAIS-III and WMS-III* (pp. 147–179). San Diego, CA: Academic Press.

Tulsky, S., Chiaravalloti, N.D., Palmer, B.W., & Chelune, G.J. (2003). The Wechsler Memory Scale, Third Edition: A new perspective. In S. Tulsky, D.H. Saklofske, G.J. Chelune, R.K. Heaton, R.J. Ivnik, R. Bornstein, A. Prifitera & M.F. Ledbetter (Eds.), *Clinical interpretation of the WAIS-III and the WMS-III* (pp. 93–139). San Diego, CA: Academic Press.

Tulving, E. (1972). Episodic and semantic memory. In E. Tulving & W. Donaldson (Eds.), *Organization of memory* (pp. 381–403). New York: Academic Press.

Tupper, D.E., & Cicerone, K.D. (1990). *The neuropsychology of everyday life: Assessment and basic competencies*. Boston: Kluwer Academic Publishers.

Unstun, T., Cooper, J., Van Duuren, K.S., Kennedy, C., Hendershot, G., & Sartorius, N. (1995). Revision of the ICIDH: Mental health aspects. *Disability and Rehabilitation, 17*(3/4), 202–209.

Vallabhajosula, B., & Van Gorp, W.G. (2001). Post-Daubert admissibility of scientific evidence on malingering of cognitive deficits. *Journal of the American Academy of Psychiatry and Law, 29*(2), 207–215.

Van Gorp, W.G., & McMullen, W.J. (1997). Potential sources of bias in forensic neuropsychological evaluations. *The Clinical Neuropsychologist, 11*(2), 180–187.

Van Zomeren, A.H., Brouwer, W.H., Rothenager, J.A., & Snoek, J.W. (1988). Fitness to drive a car after recovery from severe head injury. *Archives of Psychical Medicine and Rehabilitation, 69*(90–96).

Walker, A.J., Batchelor, J., & Shores, E.A. (2009). Effect of education and cultural background on performance on WAIS-III, WMS-III, WAIS-R and WMS-R measures: Systematic review. *Australian Psychologist, 44*(4), 216–223.

Walker, A.J., Batchelor, J., Shores, E.A., & Jones, M. (2010). Effects of cultural background on WAIS-III and WMS-III performances after moderate–severe traumatic brain injury. *Australian Psychologist, 45*(2), 112–122.

Walker, S. (2001). Swiping the buck. *Personal Investor, 19*(2), 48–53.

Walsh, K.W. (1991). *Understanding brain damage: A primer of neuropsychological examination* (2nd ed.). Edinburgh: Churchill Livingstone.

Walsh, K., & Darby, D. (1999). *Neuropsychology: A clinical approach* (4th ed.). Edinburgh: Churchill Livingstone.

Warrington, E.K. (1984). *Recognition Memory Test*. Windsor, UK: NFER-Nelson.

Waterfall, M.L., & Crowe, S.F. (1995). Meta-analytic comparison of the components of visual cognition in Parkinson's disease. *Journal of Clinical and Experimental Neuropsychology, 17*(5), 759–772.

Webber, L.S., Reeve, R.A., Kershaw, M.A., & Charlton, J.L. (2002). Assessing financial competence. *Psychiatry, Psychology and Law, 9*(2), 248–256.

Wechsler, D. (1975). Intelligence defined and undefined: A relativistic appraisal. *American Psychologist, 30,* 135–139.

Wechsler, D. (1944). *The measurement of adult intelligence* (3rd ed.). Baltimore, MD: Williams & Wilkins.

Wechsler, D. (1945). A standardized memory scale for clinical use. *Journal of Psychology, 19,* 87–95.

Wechsler, D. (1958). *Measurement and appraisal of adult intelligence* (4th ed.). Baltimore, MD: Williams and Wilkins.

Wechsler, D. (1981). *Wechsler Adult Intelligence Scale-Revised*. San Antonio, TX: The Psychological Corporation.

Wechsler, D. (1987). *The Wechsler Memory Scale-Revised manual*. San Antonio, TX: The Psychological Corporation.

Wechsler, D. (1997). *The Wechsler Adult Intelligence Scale* (3rd ed.). San Antonio, TX: The Psychological Corporation.

Wechsler, D. (1997c). *Wechsler Memory Scale* (3rd ed.). San Antonio, TX: The Psychological Corporation.

Wechsler, D. (1999). *Manual for the Wechsler Abbreviated Scale of Intelligence*. San Antonio, TX: Harcourt Brace.

Wechsler, D. (2002). *WAIS-III/WMS-III technical manual,* updated. San Antonio, TX: The Psychological Corporation.

Wechsler, D. (2008a). *Wechsler Adult Intelligence Scale* (4th ed.): *Technical and Interpretive Manual*. San Antonio, TX: NCS Pearson Inc.

Wechsler, D. (2008b). *Wechsler Adult Intelligence Scale* (4th ed.): *Administration and Scoring Manual*. San Antonio, TX: NCS Pearson, Inc.

Wechsler, D. (2008c). *Wechsler Adult Intelligence Scale Version* (4th ed.). San Antonio, Texas: NCS Pearson.

Wechsler, D. (2009a). *Wechsler Memory Scale* (4th ed.): *Administration and Scoring Manual*. San Antonio, TX: NCS Pearson Inc.

Wechsler, D. (2009b). *Wechsler Memory Scale* (4th ed.): *Technical and Interpretive Manual*. San Antonio, TX: NCS Pearson Inc.

Wechsler, D. (2009c). *Wechsler Memory Scale* (4th ed.). San Antonio, Texas: NCS Pearson.

Wedding, D. (1983). Clinical and statistical prediction in neuropsychology. *The Clinical Neuropsychologist, 5*, 49–55.

Wedding, D. (1991). Clinical judgement in forensic neuropsychology: A comment on the risks of claiming more than can be delivered. *Neuropsychology Review, 2*(3), 233–239.

Wedding, D., & Faust, D. (1989). Clinical judgment and decision making in neuropsychology. *Archives of Clinical Neuropsychology, 4*(3), 233–265.

Weinstein, J.B., & Dewsbury, I. (2006). Comment on the meaning of 'proof beyond a reasonable doubt'. *Law, Probability and Risk, 5*, 167–173.

Weinstein, S. (1978). Functional cerebral hemispheric asymmetry. In M. Kinsbourne (Ed.), *Asymmetrical function of the brain* (pp. 17–48). New York: Cambridge University Press.

Weiss, L.G., Saklofske, D.H., Schwartz, D.M., Prifitera, A., & Courville, T. (2006). Advanced clinical interpretation of WISC-IV index scores. In L.G. Weiss, D.H. Saklofske, A. Prifitera & J.A. Holdnack (Eds.), *WISC-IV advanced clinical interpretation* (pp. 99–138). San Diego, CA: Elsevier, Inc.

Werner, H. (1937). Process and achievement. A basic problem of education and developmental psychology. *Harvard Education Review, 7*, 353–368.

Wetter, M.W., Baer, R.A., Berry, D.T.R., Smith, G.T., & Larsen, L.H. (1992). Sensitivity of MMPI-2 validity scales to random responding and malingering. *Psychological Assessment: A Journal of Consulting and Clinical Psychology, 4*, 369–374.

Wilde, E.A., Bigler, E.D., Gandhi, P.V., Lowry, C.M., Blatter, D.D., Brooks, J., et al. (2004). Alcohol abuse and traumatic brain injury: Quantitative magnetic resonance imaging and neuropsychological outcome. *Journal of Neurotrauma, 21*(2), 137–147.

Wilkinson, G.S., & Robertson, G.J. (2006). *Wide Range Achievement Test 4 (WRAT4) professional manual*. Lutz, FL: Psychological Assessment Resources.

Williams, J.M. (1996). A practical model of everyday assessment. In R.J. Sbordone & C.J. Long (Eds.), *Ecological validity of neuropsychological testing* (pp. 129–145). Delray Beach, FL: GR/St. Lucie.

Wilson, B.A. (2006). Current challenges for neuropsychological rehabilitation. *Brain Impairment, 7*(2), 151–165.

Wilson, B.A., Cockburn, J., & Baddeley, A.D. (1985). *Rivermead Behavioural Memory Test*. Flempton, Bury St. Edmunds, UK: Thames Valley Test Company.

Wilson, B.A., Greenfield, E., Clare, L., Baddeley, A., Cockburn, J., Watson, P., et al. (2008). Rivermead Behavioural Memory Test (3rd ed.) (RBMT-3). San Antonio, TX: Pearson.

Wood, R.L. (1990). Towards a model of cognitive rehabilitation. In R.L. Wood & I. Fussey (Eds.), *Cognitive rehabilitation in perspective* (pp. 3–25). Hove, UK: Lawrence Erlbaum Associates.

Woodcock, R.W., McGrew, K.S., & Mather, N. (2000). *Woodcock-Johnson Psycho-Educational Battery* (3rd ed.). Chicago: Riverside.

World Health Organization. (1980). *International classification of impairment, disabilities and handicap: A manual of classification relating to consequences of disease*. Geneva, Switzerland: Author.